KU-296-157

The Landscape

of Memory

The Landscape of Memory

A Study of Wordsworth's Poetry

CHRISTOPHER SALVESEN

London
EDWARD ARNOLD (PUBLISHERS) LTD

© C. Salvesen 1965

First Published 1965

HERTFORDSHIRE
COUNTY LIBRARY

821/WOR

3871089

PRINTED IN GREAT BRITAIN
BY BILLING AND SONS LIMITED, GUILDFORD AND LONDON

Preface

In this study I have tried to suggest that the workings of memory provide a useful and illuminating 'way-in' to much of Wordsworth's best poetry; and that memory – in literature a comparatively new mode of experience – is closely involved in Wordsworth's originality, in his poetic development, in his historical position, and in his own feelings (and those of his age) about time, landscape, and autobiography, the evocation of the personal past.

I would like to thank Mr John Jones for his valuable advice and encouragement during much of the writing of this book.

Abbreviations

PW = *The Poetical Works* (ed. de Selincourt and Darbishire),
    5 vols., Oxford, 1940–49 (revised 1952–).

Prel = *The Prelude, or Growth of a Poet's Mind* (ed. de Selincourt
    and Darbishire), Oxford, 1959 (rev. edn.).

(All references to the *Prelude* are, unless otherwise stated, to the 1805
 text.)

EL = *The Early Letters of William and Dorothy Wordsworth*
    (1787–1805) (ed. de Selincourt), Oxford, 1935.

O.E.D. = *The Oxford English Dictionary.*

C.H.E.L. = *The Cambridge History of English Literature.*

For other short references used in notes, see List of Books.

Contents

Introduction

(i) Personal Time

THE workings of memory make their first fully subjective appearance in English literature in the poetry of Wordsworth. Much of his best poetry is essentially retrospective; his deepest emotions were stirred by memories of his own past, and some of his deepest thinking went both to evoke and to consider such memories. The force of memory is often evident where the expression is strongest, and there are a number of more or less explicit statements to show that Wordsworth was fully aware of its power, both generally ('. . . each man is a memory to himself')[1] and personally:

> The thought of our past years in me doth breed
> Perpetual benediction.[2]

In fact, his most famous statement about the nature of poetry describes the working and suggests the importance of memory very accurately; the point is not merely that poetry 'takes its origin from emotion recollected in tranquillity': the recollection is consciously sustained, there is a deliberate use of memory to evoke, to create again a past feeling:

> the emotion is contemplated till, by a species of re-action, the tranquillity gradually disappears, and an emotion, kindred to that which was before the subject of contemplation, is gradually produced, and does itself actually exist in the mind.[3]

One of the most obvious things about Wordsworth is that he used past personal experience to create poetry: it might seem over-obvious to do more than draw attention, in general and in a few specific instances, to the importance of memory in his work. Nonetheless, to

---

[1] *Prel* III, 189. [2] 'Immortality' *Ode*, ll. 134–5.
[3] *Preface* (1800), *PW* 2, pp. 400–1.

I

examine as a whole the poetry when he is remembering intensely, or when he is strongly aware of time, proves to be one of the best ways of bringing out Wordsworth's great variety, of explaining his development (and his decline), and of demonstrating his originality – as well as of doing the primary job of illuminating particular poems. Nowadays, it can sometimes be casually assumed that a subjective involvement with time, an awareness of duration, is a condition not only under which life is experienced and work is done, but which most literature embodies. A moment's reflection, of course, shows this to be anything but the case. But such a notion is partly a tribute to our own ways of thinking about time which Wordsworth was one of the first to put into action naturally and in detail. Attitudes to time which are also indications of identity, expressions of self, are rare until the Eighteenth century. Before this, autobiography of any sort is a marginal literary mode; and although people had in various ways been ready to give some account of themselves, these had been usually factual or didactic, without unfolding any inner sense of time, or even suggesting that the passage of time is automatically but interestingly involved. Margery Kempe, say, or Hoccleve, or Lord Herbert of Cherbury present themselves very much 'on their own merits', without benefit of introspection or studied retrospection; and while it is true that even today the average autobiography is still written in a purely anecdotal or documentary spirit, we tend to think of its highest form as writing which responds to a sense of time *within* the person concerned. This kind of autobiography is a Romantic phenomenon, involving the conscious relation of past with present. Time is felt to be a condition of one's *whole* existence; a condition universally recognized, but essentially private, slightly different for each person – remembered experience turned to poetry is the Wordsworthian medium for responding to time.

Time, of course, is a permanent philosophical problem; though it has not always affected literature, nor has it necessarily been referred to memory except in purely impersonal terms. One of the great autobiographers, St Augustine, demanding 'Quid est tempus?' brings to the question (in the context of his whole book) an exceptional union of qualities – personal, introspective, no less than philosophical and theological. 'Quid est ergo tempus? Si nemo ex me quaerat, scio; si quaerenti explicare velim, nescio.' ('What is time then? If nobody asks me,

I know: but if I were desirous to explain it to one that should ask me, plainly I know not.')[1] This common-sense approach is perhaps the one most valid in studying literature. The awareness of time brings enough mystery without its further becoming a problem for explanation; and although Augustine here goes on to formulate systematically his thinking about time, and although this comes in the evidently philosophical section of the *Confessions*, for most readers part of the vividness of his book springs from his own interest in the whole activity of recording a life in time and of living in time – from how he expresses a full delight 'in mente hominis atque memoria et sensibus et vegetante vita', 'in the mind and memory, in the senses and lively soul of man'.[2]

But the individual life as an expressive medium for time is an alien concept throughout medieval thought. Even with the gradual forming of new (Renaissance) ways of viewing both history and the individual, a subjective time-consciousness only finds its way into literature very much later. As Georges Poulet observes in his *Studies in Human Time*,[3] 'The great discovery of the eighteenth century is the phenomenon of memory.' There, a genuinely new sense of being grows up. 'To exist . . . is to be one's present, and also to be one's past and one's recollections.' This consciousness grows, becomes more complicated; in English literature its highest development is shown in Wordsworth, Hazlitt, and de Quincey. And although this awareness of time and identity by way of memory is still growing, is still very much with us, the quality of Wordsworth's and Hazlitt's and de Quincey's experience remains both distinctive and unsurpassed. Their particular kind of self-awareness represents – each in its very different way – a peculiarly Romantic achievement, historically speaking: some of the forms taken by it (and how it is adumbrated and embodied by Rousseau) are touched on in our concluding chapter. Wordsworth's meditations and active memories, Hazlitt's 'Rousseauesques', these express a characteristic Romantic awareness of time; there is an assurance about them which is no longer available. To define this quality, one might say that both the poet and the essayist have a completely unself-conscious self-consciousness – to put it clumsily, if also to indicate a slight, significant shift in what we now think of as the state of being alert – over-alert – to one's own existence: for Wordsworth, it was enough to be aware of his

---

[1] *Confessions*, XI, 14 (Watts translation). [2] ibid., II, 6.
[3] Baltimore, 1956. v. pp. 23–4.

being; for us, to be self-conscious presents too many possibilities also to be natural – there is bound to be an artificial element. Rousseau, Wordsworth, Hazlitt, each brings to the personal or subjective sense of time an intensity of treatment and a clarity of pitch that permanently alters thinking and feeling about time. Subsequent treatments of this theme, of the self in time, will be different, less spontaneous, perhaps more sophisticated; it could be suggested that, after the first half of the Nineteenth century, time as a mode of experience is likely to be treated with a new explicitness, to become more associated with technical problems, and to be more readily objectified: the potentialities of memory continue to be exploited, but now in all directions.

The self in time involves both memory and a sense of relation to one's contemporaries. But there is an obvious contrast between, say, Hazlitt's confident personal involvement in the whole business of writing, and the way in which much of the most important Twentieth-century writing (e.g. Proust or Joyce, Eliot or Pound) relies equally, or far more, on 'personal' matter and allusion. In our own age, however much personality and memories are involved, they are nearly always objectified, not presented 'straight'. And yet, quite often, the writer is nonetheless assuming some interest in himself, is assuming a place for *himself* in his work. This subjective impersonality is perhaps the result, quite simply, of being aware of literary history – that comparatively new (in its more intense form, very recent) mode of experiencing time: a mode not to be confused with earlier conventional appeals to Fame. At the end of *Axel's Castle*, Edmund Wilson says of the writers he deals with 'that they have tended to overemphasize the importance of the individual, that they have been preoccupied with introspection sometimes almost to the point of insanity . . .'; this, even in 1931, is overstating things a little, but it is essentially the case. Though these writers have achieved a measure of impersonality, it is by way of a highly subjective approach. And if they have learnt to 'objectify their egocentricity', it is something they owe in the first place to the literature of the self in time. Wilson observes that they have 'an intellectual mastery of their materials, rare among their Romantic predecessors . . .': they have certainly mastered themselves in a way that perhaps defeated Hazlitt, and in a sense that perhaps eluded Wordsworth. The Hazlitt essay is a magnificent achievement; but it would be hard to say how far it is a conscious formal one. The *Prelude* is fully planned, complete

4

in itself: but, for Wordsworth, it was only part of a larger work. The expression of the Romantic self is something primarily intuitive, a form dependent on a sureness of touch in turn depending on that sureness of emotion which can only come from the immediate fusion of personality and memory, the unadulterated present flowing back into the past.

Some response to time in any given work or author or period is perhaps available for analysis; but such investigation, in critical, explanatory terms, is most usefully reserved for works which show obvious signs of time-consciousness to begin with: it is more appropriate to Wordsworth than, say, to Dickens – though illuminating things about the childhood experience of time could be discovered in *Oliver Twist* and *David Copperfield*. It is certainly appropriate in historical terms to Wordsworth: with whom, and with whose early career, whatever reservations are made, one can quite clearly say 'our way of thinking' begins. But time is a problem which spreads out very rapidly into philosophy, psychology, physics, biology, history, and soon reduces abstract thinking to near helplessness. (A main philosophical problem still seems to be whether or not time can be said to exist at all, whether it has any reality; it puzzles the physicist and the logical positivist equally.) Today, history seems the nearest, most relevant field, in which the literary problem of time takes further shape. This study does not attempt any systematic paraphrase or précis of time in Wordsworth's poetry. It tries simply to accept Wordsworth's sense of time: to consider it as straightforwardly as possible is the main object – but the subject is still Wordsworth's poetry. By way of introduction, and to proceed by way of selective examples, rather than theory, it may be worth noting a few instances where time is experienced 'as literature' or is vividly active in one form or another; if only to create a context in which to consider Wordsworth's poetry and to suggest that a turning of the personal past to full account is an essentially Wordsworthian achievement, something which particularly deserves to be identified with Wordsworth.

> But, Lord Crist! whan that it remembreth me
> Upon my yowthe, and on my jolitee,
> It tikleth me aboute myn herte roote.
> Unto this day it dooth myn herte boote   [good

The Landscape of Memory

That I have had my world as in my tyme.[1]

When the Wife of Bath looks back, we are struck not only by her general vitality but also by the vitality of her emotion, by her consciousness of accumulated experience and her feeling that while life continues she can still draw on reserves of her past. She feels the value of her past in the present – these two conditions of her existence are inseparable: if, as she says, the 'flour' has gone, the 'bran' is still there, the organic residue of it. This feeling strikes a rare note in Chaucer's world: we are surprised to find time being expressed, however briefly, in terms of memory and a continuous personality. Chaucer understands time as a powerful force; but he equates it most nearly with Fortune, including the fortunes of love – the story of *Troilus and Criseyde* is controlled, if not dominated, by a cyclic movement alike of the heavens and human behaviour. Time is impersonal, admonitory, not geared to individual consciousness: the interest lies in how it affects fate rather than feeling.

Time becomes a major Renaissance symbol; and, as a personification, Father Time, it assimilates many medieval characteristics;[2] and it becomes too a complex philosophical and imaginative force. But it remains an external power, not something which could be explored personally, from within, not something which could be incorporated subjectively. 'Devouring time' (as in Shakespeare's Sonnet 19) is the typically Elizabethan kind, certainly the most obvious; and the *Sonnets*, for all their remarkable 'personal' feeling, use Time basically as a figure, a character from Petrarch's *Trionfi*, the final destructive stage in the dialectic towards eternity. Shakespeare battles with time mainly in his character as poet, not as a man submitting to emotion: art is a weapon against time, a tool of eternity – he will write (he says in Sonnet 18) 'eternal lines to time' (i.e. Sonnet 19) and in this way perpetuate human existence, his own and the loved one's. Even so, Shakespeare also knows time through the private pleasure-sadness of memory; as the Englisher of Proust reminds us in his, perhaps slightly inappropriate, title.

> When to the sessions of sweet silent thought,
> I summon up remembrance of things past . . .,

[1] *The Wife of Bath's Prologue*, ll. 469–73. (The 'as' is merely expletive, i.e. it fills out the line.)

[2] v. E. Panofsky, *Studies in Iconology*.

6

this (Sonnet 30) comes nearer Wordsworth's way of responding to time than Proust's insistence on 'involuntary memory' – though much of Wordsworth's most significant remembering is unbidden too, at least initially unlooked for. But for Shakespeare, in the *Sonnets*, any victory against time is won by looking to the future, not the past.

Spenser, in *The Faerie Queene*, explores the mysterious nature of time more deeply, more philosophically. In his account of the Garden of Adonis, in the Mutabilitie cantos, he fuses the destructive and the generative aspects of time in a mode of thinking which remained workable at least up to the age of Pope. In *Epithalamion*, where the poet's celebration of his own marriage certainly helps towards a personal note, it is again, as with Shakespeare, the poet's own work, the poem itself, which helps to conquer time: it becomes 'for short time an endless monument',[1] the triumph of art here combined with the obvious principal theme of human generation; as it is, in an exhortatory way, in the opening sequence of the Shakespeare sonnets. But the subjection of life to time, and the overcoming of it by art or by procreation, all finally remain within the general terms of a philosophical notion. And however the Shakespeare tragedies exemplify 'individualism', a 'new' sense of human identity, the implications of individual life set against time are not worked out there; other forces, inner faults, drive the characters. We see irresponsibility, anger in action, destroying Lear: Shakespeare's interest in, or use of, time in this play is confined to the brilliantly disturbing sense of historical pre-Christian remoteness – 'This prophecy Merlin shall make, for I live before his time' (III, ii). However, it is part of the greatness of the last plays that Shakespeare should manage to combine in them ideas about Art and Nature and continuity by generation with a distinctly 'personal' reading of time. How this personal quality comes through might not be easily demonstrated; but various readers have always felt *The Tempest* anyway to be making some sort of private 'in-confidence' statement; and *The Winter's Tale*, too, has something of this air. It is overtly a play about time. Its central meaning is contained by, can only be made explicit by, the passage of time, of sixteen years. It interprets, mystically but comprehensively, it allegorizes the motto (from its source tale, Greene's *Pandosto*) *Temporis Filia Veritas*. Truth is the daughter of time because, for Leontes, it is only the passage of

[1] l. 433. v. A. Kent Hieatt, *Short Time's Endless Monument* . . . , New York, 1960.

7

years, of prolonged human suffering with all the awareness of duration this implies, that can bring him to understand truths about human relationship, the loss of innocence, the power of growth – truths about time itself. Shakespeare, towards the end of his own career and life, *embodies* the human experience of time in his work. He incorporates the passage of time as a reality – partly of course through the nature of the story he chooses, partly through the themes and symbols he works with, partly through his continuous skill in making time felt to be something affecting the characters 'in action', in their progress through the play. And the archaic formal device of Time personified is very effective in at once drawing attention to, and overcoming, the difficulty and strangeness of actually portraying long time-stretches in drama. It reinforces the sense of duration embodied in the story from the beginning.

> We were, fair Queen,
> Two lads, that thought there was no more behind,   [beyond
> But such a day tomorrow, as today,
> And to be boy eternal.   I, ii

The reminiscing of Pollixenes to Hermione about childhood, its timelessness, its innocence, feelings now superseded but still remembered, this scene immediately sets the tone and places the subsequent events in a symbolic or mystical time-context. *The Winter's Tale* strikes an unexpected note in its knowledge of time; and when in *The Tempest* (its unities-obeying companion-piece) Prospero tests Miranda about her earliest memories and then asks 'What seest thou else/In the dark backward and abysm of Time?' (I,ii), the question seems to strike again surprisingly, in advance of its age. But the feeling that a private sense of the past could fully be given meaning in drama does not really appear till Ibsen. There the action, particularly from *Ghosts* onwards, evolves by way of brooding retrospective emotion and information. In Shakespeare there is just a suggestion that remote or 'backward' time could be a dimension of revelation. Nearly all Shakespeare's action is, dramatically speaking, 'in the present'. In Ibsen the whole process is more expository – the past is revealed and the plot unfolds.

Time is a revealer of truth in different ways and at different levels: it may confirm facts (justify an oracle), it may uncover the sins of the fathers, it may be equivalent to a sum of human experience, reaching happiness through suffering and endurance. In *The Winter's Tale* it also acts in conjunction with Nature. Nature, the process of life, is there to be understood as creative time.

> The child was prisoner to the womb, and is
> By Law and process of great Nature, thence
> Freed, and enfranchis'd . . .[1]

The survival and recognition of posterity, this, as much as the healing of a former breach, represents a true victory over time. Shakespeare deals with both destructive and regenerative time, devouring time and redemptive natural time. And by playing them against each other, he suggests also a private, almost mystical experience of time, a reading of human time. It remains submerged, an intimation not a statement; but more satisfying, nearer the vital mysteries, than the slightly shrill, evidently factitious claims made in the Sonnets.

Time as an aspect of Nature's creativity is an important factor in the general continuity of the idea of time throughout the Seventeenth century. It would be extremely complicated, if fascinating, to trace the time-consciousness of that age: the nature mysticism which one finds in Marvell combined with distinctly personal meditation and the sense of place (and of political actualities) would certainly provide one key. It might be a fair generalization about the idea of time that from being either an admonitory or a mystical force, in neither case strictly related to individuals, it became primarily a philosophical problem in the strict sense of having to do with consciousness and identity. That is naturally the main line of development in philosophy itself: Descartes is the revolutionary and the representative figure – and one of great interest even when approached from a purely literary angle.

While pursuing abstract inquiry in the exploration of identity, Descartes concentrates very much on his own mind, his own sensations. 'My design', he says in the *Discourse on Method*, 'has never stretched further than the attempted reform of my own thoughts and a reconstruction on foundations that belong only to me.'[2] In the second section, he is

---

[1] II, ii. Wordsworth perhaps echoes this, certainly carries on the essential meaning and gives it a personal context, when he says 'The Child is father of the Man': v. *PW* 4, p. 466.

[2] Penguin edn., 1960, transl. by Arthur Wollaston; p. 47.

careful to present himself in a circumstantial manner – he is in Germany, it is winter, the famous day of illumination on which he felt the essential unity of knowledge is spent 'in a stove-heated room'. And he continues to present his speculations in a careful autobiographical tone. One might say that Descartes' philosophical problem of identity – roughly, how is it maintained at all in a time composed of 'durationless instants'? – is firmly if unwillingly related to a sense of 'literary' identity, the embodied self particularly, temporally placed. The *Discourse on Method*, Arthur Wollaston points out,[1] is primarily 'a sort of memoir . . . a revival of the past in the light of the present'. And although it marks a revolution in philosophy, 'it is by no means the formal treatise which its title suggests . . . Descartes' first intention had been to call it "A History of my Mind" . . .'. This projected title makes one think of Wordsworth's conception of the *Prelude* and Coleridge's designation of it as a 'Poem on the Growth and Revolutions of an Individual Mind'; however different the ultimate character of their work, both Descartes and Wordsworth present their qualifications, their credentials by a review of, and an awareness of, their own selves in time.

Descartes' three-fold dream, which took place on the evening of the day described in the *Discourse*, is another biographical document, obviously less deliberately put forward but nonetheless one which he made available. It is described in the Abbé Baillet's *Vie de Descartes* (1691). M. Poulet has an exciting and detailed interpretation of it,[2] too long to summarise here, but based on showing how Descartes experienced a terrifying discrepancy between his philosophical sense that time does not exist and his human awareness of it, of past occasion and experience in his life. Descartes is seen as having a 'terror of *failure in time*', of being really sure of getting from one moment to the next only 'by a veritable leap to God'.[3] In his first dream Descartes is moving towards a college chapel: symbolizing, says Poulet, an attempted return towards God – but an unsuccessful one because it is also a return to the past. As Descartes proceeds, he realizes that he has walked by 'a man of his acquaintance' without greeting him: 'he wanted to retrace his steps in order to pay him his compliments, and he was violently driven back by the wind which was blowing against the chapel.'[4] This

[1] Penguin edn., 1960, p. 12.
[2] *Studies in Human Time*, pp. 50–73.
[3] loc. cit., p. 58.
[4] ibid., p. 59, quoting Baillet.

man, says Poulet, is Descartes himself: a Descartes to whom he can no longer turn back – because he has at one stage missed the point about memory, he has not recognized 'at the right moment the tie that binds our actual being to our antecedent being . . . For time is not made only of isolated "present moments" but also of a past situated at the back of consciousness . . .'. For Descartes this has become inaccessible; his mind, like 'the wind', thrusts him towards the future.

Memory, philosophically speaking, is virtually no use; but the man whom he failed to recognize, who was himself coming out of the past, whom he cannot now reach – this man, a sort of Doppelgänger, admonishes him, a symbol of the everyday experience of life in time. However much one tries to subdue time by defining it, a sense of its flow still continues; however one acknowledges the pastness of experience and the onwardness of time, the subjective possibilities of memory persist. Descartes describes his winter's day in Germany some seventeen years later in the *Discourse*, when 'he was more concerned with the long train of reflections by which he sought to justify his philosophical position than with the dramatic character of the underlying experience'.[1] But he had responded to it, had remembered it. And if he stressed the continuity, the similarity of his ideas then with those at the time of writing, he nonetheless recognized that in writing the history of his thoughts he was inevitably recording a development. Time was *needed*: as he recognized when he deliberately put off the task of formulating his principles until he reached a more mature age.[2] He knew that he had both to accumulate material and strengthen his mind. Descartes 'knew' time, and he knew that the young Descartes in the stove-warmed room was part of him – though he might never need to return to him, he could not do without him. In his dream, at least, he had once been touched by that feeling of double identity which so disturbed the Romantic mind – the paradox of feeling continuity with one's past self, that one is the same person, and feeling separation, that one is, through time, a different person. The latter feeling is in general perhaps the stronger. Heine's poem *Der Doppelgänger* expresses how there can be no absolute return to the past, even for those who most long for it, and aim, perhaps dangerously, most near it. In this respect, Heine's Doppelgänger, no less than Descartes', is a symbol of an irrevocable past – with the significant difference that there is, to begin

---

[1] *Discourse*, Introduction, p. 14. [2] *Discourse*, p. 52.

with, a wilful turning in the direction of the past. The poet, already fixed on something irredeemable, stares at the house where his love used to live; she has long ago left the town.

> Da steht auch ein Mensch und starrt in die Höhe,
> Und ringt die Hände vor Schmerzensgewalt;
> Mir graut es, wenn ich sein Antlitz sehe –
> Der Mond zeigt mir meine eigne Gestalt.
>
> Du Doppelgänger, du bleicher Geselle!
> Was äffst du nach mein Liebesleid,
> Das mich gequält auf dieser Stelle
> So manche Nacht, in alter Zeit?[1]

This is a classic bodying-forth of one state of the Romantic self in time; a classic exposition of how nostalgia can be felt as a tangible implacable regret which is part of oneself, which sometimes *is* oneself totally, physically identified – and yet which is separate too, separated by years, by time.

But, though literature only comes to express violently subjective time-feelings like this after the end of the Eighteenth century, it can be found at the beginning of the century continuing to foster more general ideas about time and nature: diffused literary-philosophical ideas, in an older, non-Cartesian tradition, which grow directly, though mostly underground, towards particular feelings of identity in relation to nature and landscape. Pope, as an autobiographer, brings himself forward almost entirely in the present. But he knows the passage of time and he has definite ideas about the relative permanence of society and the visible world around him, and that Nature which is its context. A particular place is seen in relation to man who, in turn, is related to that principle of nature which governs landscape and society equally. When Pope prophesies over Timon's Villa (not a particular place, but a very circumstantially described type), he implies a reading of time, a

---

[1] Another man stands there too, staring upwards, wringing his hands, possessed by grief. Terror grips me when I see his face – the moon shows my own shape to me. You Doppelgänger, pale companion, what do you want, mirroring the pain of my love that tortured me on this same spot so many nights in times gone by?

principle of withdrawal and return, a temporal *discordia concors*, which
is at the heart of his social criticism.[1]

> Another age shall see the golden ear
> Imbrown the slope, and nod on the parterre,
> Deep harvests bury all his pride has plann'd,
> And laughing Ceres reassume the land.[2]

Wordsworth too can be found thinking in these terms. At the end of
Hart-leap Well (we return to this in Chapter IV) he contemplates a
dreary hollow marked by some ruins: the activities of man have produced a waste land. But, he says (ll. 171f.), 'Nature, in due course of
time, once more/Shall here put on her beauty and her bloom'. The
ruins are left as an admonishment: 'But at the coming of the milder
day/These monuments shall all be overgrown.' As in Pope, Nature is
related to man, a principle of growth in time of larger than human
dimensions. In either case the contrast of human and natural time embodies a redemption by reversion to nature. The differences are instructive too: it is worth noting in the lines from Pope that Ceres would not
reassume the land autonomously; the harvests would still be the product partly of man's hand, of his necessary co-operation with nature.
Wordsworth treats nature more mystically and more generally; his
forward-looking is vaguer than Pope's – 'the milder day' has chiliastic
rather than practically prophetic overtones. It may include a political
note (a relic from the French Revolution), but Wordsworth leaves it in
a deliberately tentative, ideal form, and connects it with the outside
world, if at all, then privately: Pope, on the other hand, is able to be
confidently political in his use of philosophic ideas – as he is for example
throughout *Windsor Forest*, where he 'uses' a particular place both
historically and prophetically, the woods 'harmoniously confused',
the 'unbounded Thames' flowing into the ocean, symbolizing peace
and prosperity at a number of different levels.[3]

It is somewhere in the mid-Eighteenth century that chiefly philosophical approaches to time and nature become firmly involved with
other feelings of identity and of flux – personal 'poetic' feelings, though
they parallel the problems exercising formal philosophy. This is a further development, which again would be hard to account for syste-

[1] v. E. R. Wasserman, *The Subtler Language*, Baltimore, 1959.
[2] *Epistle to Burlington*, ll. 173–6. [3] v. Wasserman, op. cit.

matically, in thinking about time as part of nature's creativity. One possible approach would be to see nature in terms more and more of landscape – landscape as the version of nature *in* which man most fully experiences himself, both in place and in time. Landscape (as the title of this study tries partly to indicate) is certainly a key concept in the shift towards subjective time-consciousness. The individual response to particular place sets a number of new attitudes in motion; Gray's response to the Thames at Windsor – a subjective, exclamatory view – makes an instructive contrast with Pope's symbolic politics and pastoral diffidence about his own role. Gray, in the second verse of the *Ode on a Distant Prospect of Eton College* (1742), cries out:

> Ah happy hills! ah pleasing shade!
> Ah fields beloved in vain,
> Where once my careless childhood stray'd
> A stranger yet to pain!
> I feel the gales that from ye blow
> A momentary bliss bestow,
> As waving fresh their gladsome wing,
> My weary soul they seem to sooth,
> And, redolent of joy and youth,
> To breathe a second spring.

Gray's manner is self-indulgent; he uses the place for his own private emotions, and a good deal of rhetorical moralizing. One can understand Johnson's irascibility – in his 'Life' – at the whole poem ('His supplication to Father Thames, to tell him who drives the hoop or tosses the ball, is useless and puerile'); but, in complaining that Gray uses the word 'redolent' (in the stanza quoted) so that it reaches a little beyond 'the utmost limits of our language', the lexicographer takes over from the critic who might have recognized an experience – or an attempt to express it – essentially new in poetry. The language of course *contains* the quality of the experience, and one might say the verses were mainly interesting as an early example of a feeling which had to wait for Wordsworth to find full poetic expression. But Gray makes his meaning clear enough: the 'momentary' happiness, if it does not quite have a Proustian 'redolence' of involuntary memory, is nevertheless an authentic experience in a new genre. There is just a hint of physical identification with the place and with the memory. In looking back to childhood, Gray feels the wind blowing from fields which lend to the 'gales' a doubly-intensified redolence by their being both remembered and presently experienced. The whole scene, of course, is 'present' not only subjectively but with a kind of remoteness too – it is a poem on a *distant* prospect of Eton College; but the distance is appropriate, referring almost as much to time, to the separation between Gray and his schooldays, as to place, the ground lying between Gray and his old school. The association of past experience with present locality, the one durable, the other fleeting, grows throughout the century; in this particular key becoming perhaps more openly regretful, more aware of, though not more submissive to, time. Gray would not say, for example, with Hazlitt in 'My First Acquaintance with Poets', 'Would that I could go back to what I then was! Why can we not revive past times as we can revisit old places?'[1] Gray goes on to look gloomily at the future and contents himself with deciding in the last verse that the schoolchildren should be kept in blissful ignorance of the coming pains of life.

The sense of time connected with a particular place, a known landscape, develops variously: if in one direction it produces Gray, using the Thames 'privately', in another it continues that line of thought in which Pope used the Thames publicly and philosophically; it becomes involved with the growing historical sense. A glance at the century's great historian conveniently suggests a sort of illustrative link between personal reflectiveness and the dignified large-scale exposition of human affairs, the showing of time in action. Gibbon writes his autobiography; he does it, of course, soberly, without rhapsody. He is, for a start, scathing about childhood: he feels 'tempted to enter a protest against the trite and lavish praise of the happiness of our boyish years, which is echoed with so much affectation in the world'.[2] He did not enjoy them, partly, it seems, because he was the wrong shape: he adapts with some bitterness the lines about schoolboy athletes from Gray's poem on Eton. But if he could only complain that 'the felicity of a schoolboy consists in the perpetual motion of thoughtless and playful agility', he seized eagerly on his introduction to university life; and, though he was soon to be disillusioned, he records that 'at the distance of forty years I still remember my first emotions of surprise

---

[1] *Works*, vol. 17, p. 114.
[2] *Autobiography*, World's Classics edn., 1907; p. 33.

and satisfaction'. He naturally does not elaborate on this. But for a man interested both in the historical and the personal past, it is not surprising that he has a sense of occasion, a feeling for 'the local moment', the significant union of place and person.

> It was at Rome, on the 15th of October, 1764, as I sat musing amidst the ruins of the Capitol, while the barefooted friars were singing vespers in the Temple of Jupiter, that the idea of writing the decline and fall of the city first started to my mind.[1]

Again, there is no elaboration; the solemn moment is presented quite casually, it seems almost thrown away: but Gibbon is an artist, the style is heightened and points up the ironic historical vignette to make the occasion memorable. And his account of the close of his work has the same significant precision.

> I have presumed to mark the moment of conception: I shall now commemorate the hour of my final deliverance. It was on the day, or rather night, of the 27th of June, 1787, between the hours of eleven and twelve, that I wrote the last lines of the last page, in a summer-house in my garden.

And he goes on to treat this a little more fully, describing how he took several turns in a walk of acacias, savouring the view, the temperate air, the moonlight, his emotions of joy and then melancholy. He is sobered, as he puts it, 'by the idea that I had taken an everlasting leave of an old and agreeable companion, and that whatsoever might be the future date of my *History*, the life of the historian must be short and precarious'.[2] In his life, although Gibbon had no childhood golden age on which he could look back, he develops a time-sense from his own experience and feels the appropriateness of recording the terminal moments of his work in his own personal history. In his art, he is a more than representative figure; and, as R. G. Collingwood points out, his beginning the *Decline and Fall* with his own conception of a golden age, the Antonine period, gives him 'a rather special place among Enlightenment historians and assimilates him on the one hand to his predecessors, the humanists of the Renaissance, and on the other to his successors, the Romantics at the close of the eighteenth century'.[3]

[1] edn. cit., p. 160.   [2] edn. cit., p. 205.
[3] *The Idea of History*, London, 1946; p. 79.

After Scott, Byron is the greatest exponent of an Augustan-cum-Romantic view of history. An admirer of Gibbon,[1] his sense of the historical past and present is more important to his poetry (in *Childe Harold's Pilgrimage*, in parts of *Don Juan*) than his half-autobiographical pose of guilt and strange heredity. Someone once pointed out how his vision, or reverie, of the dying Gladiator[2] gets its power not only from the vividly imagined occasion and dramatic identification, but from the historical feeling that his question ('Shall he expire/And unavenged?') is not a rhetorical one. 'Arise! ye Goths, and glut your ire!' – history, he knows, will provide the vengeance asked for. Byron, in his character of reflective historian, 'saw in the past a monument and an admonition'.[3] The sense of history contributes to various Romantic attitudes to the past: it does not perhaps add anything essential to Wordsworth's time-sensibility, but, as we shall see, long before he embarked on the *Ecclesiastical Sonnets*, he responded to historical promptings and emotions. He naturally thought of them as being idealistically subordinate to the poetic impulse; but they were circumstantial enough and very different in quality from, say, the ideal pasts, 'Grecian' or 'Charlemagnish', of Keats. There is in Keats a tension between the claims of a remote, other-worldly past, and a feeling of continuity, historical and biological. Madeline and Porphyro, for example, at the end of *The Eve of St Agnes* are completely distanced from reality:

> And they are gone: aye, ages long ago
> These lovers fled away into the storm.

They have no representative human quality; the pathos is everything There is in them nothing, to point the contrast, of the lawyer in *Joseph Andrews* (III, i), who 'is not only alive, but hath been so these four thousand years; and I hope God will indulge his life as many yet to come'. Where Fielding recognizes time as the element in which the consistency of human nature displays itself, Keats *experiences* time. And he also combines his feeling for remoteness with a sense of the organic onwardness of life. The nightingale of the *Ode* ('The voice I hear this passing night was heard/In ancient days by emperor and clown:') is the same and not the same, is representative, in a different sense from

---

[1] v. *Childe Harold*, III, cv, cvii.   [2] *Childe Harold*, IV, cxl-cxli.
[3] Mario Praz, *The Hero in Eclipse*, London, 1956; p. 463.

Fielding's lawyer. If it is 'the self-same song that found a path/Through the sad heart of Ruth . . .', then in this it represents for Keats *time* rather than nightingales; the bird itself to which he is listening has an animal innocence of human knowledge, including the flow of human time, which is what Keats envies. The 'hungry generations' are all too human in their stretching backwards in history and forwards in time and hope; Nature is above this turmoil: serene, unified, Nature *is* generation, answering time – as Art does too in its colder way: the Grecian urn, 'sylvan historian', remaining 'When old age shall this generation waste'.

This sort of time-sensibility is marginal to Wordsworth's experience. It is different from the unabashed personal feeling for time which is the characteristic of Wordsworth, and of Hazlitt and de Quincey. And as it develops historically, it continues to be fused with an idea of, and feeling for, nature, the visible landscape world. Tennyson perhaps carries on the tradition in poetry. But both the earnest contemplation of self in Wordsworth and the frank nostalgia of Hazlitt seem turned to a generally more wistful, though pronounced and varied, time-sense. Tennyson's Ulysses puts forward the value of experience accumulated in time:

> I am a part of all that I have met;

(At least he seems to mean by this: I am *composed of* parts of all that I have met – which is perhaps the equivalent of: All that I have met is part of me. It could just mean that he has scattered his personality about the world, that he has left parts of himself behind; but, if it does, then he has not lost anything in the process – accumulated experience makes up for what has gone out from him.)

> Yet all experience is an arch wherethrough
> Gleams that untravelled world, whose margin fades
> For ever and for ever when I move.

The feeling here is forward-looking, restless – perhaps helped by the slightly confused diagrammatic quality of the 'arch': the value of a personal past lies only in giving direction to the future; and in giving it this ideal or endlessly receding quality. The whole poem is informed by the idea of fading powers – that things are not as they were, that we are 'Made weak by time and fate' – and the restlessness, the forward-

18

looking, draws its strength, its quality of something 'willed', from this elegiac feeling of decline. *In Memoriam* is, of course, essentially elegiac; and it combines an almost Eighteenth-century melancholy in contemplation of landscape with a slightly more 'Victorian' sense of nature continuing remorselessly into the future – as for example in the hundredth section. 'Unwatch'd, the garden bough shall sway . . .', the place will be unloved, untouched by particular human care: or so it seems. But life goes on; the place will be taken over, until

> . . . year by year the landscape grow
> Familiar to the stranger's child;
>
> As year by year the labourer tills
> His wonted glebe, or lops the glades;
> And year by year our memory fades
> From all the circle of the hills.

Work, human but impersonal, is set against private feelings: nature's time, circling 'year by year', may not for Tennyson subdue emotion; but it will inevitably supersede it. Tennyson meanwhile, continuing to meditate about 'the well-beloved place', discovers it has two contending claims on his memory: that he enjoyed his boyhood there, and that later he spent time there with his now 'lost friend'; these two facts mix, he says, 'To one pure image of regret'. This kind of regret – not only for the person, but for the place and past time – is in some ways a Wordsworthian emotion, typified, presented at its best, in the elusive Lucy poems; here, it seems almost over-indulged – simply, perhaps, over-explicit: though the comparison is not really a fair one, being relevant only to the quality of the time-sense, not to the full respective characters of the poems.

A much more directly and essentially Wordsworthian connection can be made with George Eliot – who was, of course, a great Wordsworth enthusiast, and was touched by his thinking in many ways. She knows the value of memory and of early years – of how, at the simplest level, memory could help one's understanding of childhood: she recognizes the sympathetic virtue of 'anyone who can recover the experience of his childhood, not merely with a memory of what he did and what happened to him, of what he liked and disliked when he was in frock and trousers, but with an intimate penetration, a revived consciousness of what he felt then . . .'.[1] In *The Mill on the Floss* she shows and uses the experience of childhood as effectively as it has ever been used. She understands the difficulty of truly reviving that time; but she also knows how it is almost physically identified with ourselves, and how this can make a deep ultimately reassuring continuity. She describes it at the end of the first chapter in Book II:

> There is no sense of ease like the ease we felt in those scenes where we were born, where objects became dear to us before we had known the labour of choice, and where the outer world seemed only an extension of our own personality: we accepted and loved it as we accepted our own sense of existence and our own limbs.

The power of early life to shape our whole being is decisive; and its value often lies in its commonplace quality, in a familiarity which is most intense simply because it was familiar from the start: 'the loves and sanctities of our life' have inevitably 'deep immovable roots in memory'. And she goes on to point out how 'One's delight in an elderberry bush overhanging the confused leafage of a hedgerow bank . . .' is based on subjective reasons which would make no sense to a nursery-gardener.

> And there is no better reason for preferring this elderberry bush than that it stirs an early memory – that it is no novelty in my life, speaking to me merely through my present sensibilities to form and colour, but the long companion of my existence, that wove itself into my joys when joys were vivid.

Memory has to do not only with specific emotions but also with *states* of being, continuities of feeling; and George Eliot shows how connections can be made, almost physically perceived, between nature, time, and the sense of self. This comprehensive and characteristically sensuous mode of memory is very evident in Wordsworth; and has been made familiar by Proust – who was, in his turn, a great admirer of George Eliot and who recorded that two pages of *The Mill on the Floss* could make him cry.[2] There is a community of experience stretching from Wordsworth through George Eliot to Proust which is all the more fascinating because there is no immediately obvious intimate

[1] *The Mill on the Floss*, I, vii.
[2] v. André Maurois, *The Quest for Proust*; Penguin edn., p. 34.

point of contact between the Lake Poet and the novelist of Combray and Paris, of aristocracy and decadence as well as of provincial life. Of course, they have in common the large area of memory in general; and comparisons of various emotional situations could show them to be psychologically correspondent – but the 'tonal' quality is so different that it would say more about memory than about either Wordsworth or Proust. But a more extended general comparison of their attitudes to art and to time could well be made. Proust, like Wordsworth, is concerned with the relationship – its value at first only vaguely apprehended – of memory and subjective experience to creation. And they both understand the recovery of the past as a mixture of moments and duration – an alertness to heightened moments is tempered by a submission to the passing of time as the element which contains these, without which they could neither have existed nor *come* to have significance. But for both Wordsworth and Proust memory is inherently so personal a business, so much a matter of subjective unity, that comparison of instances between the two should perhaps be kept short or avoided altogether.

Between Proust and George Eliot various affinities have been pointed out,[1] some in Proust's case reinforced by direct transmission. André Maurois has suggested how the opening chapter of *The Mill on the Floss* can be compared with the opening of *Swann's Way*. George Eliot leads in to her material by evoking and contemplating a remembered landscape through sleep; and Proust begins with an elaborately extended version of this. Marcel, lying in bed, closely relates the business of sleeping and some of the activities of memory; it is partly a matter of physical position and sensation. George Eliot uses a similar sort of starting-point: having dozed off, she wakes to find her arms numbed by her chair, having imagined she was leaning on the cold stone of 'the bridge in front of Dorlcote Mill, as it looked one February afternoon many years ago'. The landscape, and with it a sense of the past, is established.

Among other things Proust could have derived from George Eliot, Mario Praz suggests a confirmation of 'monotony as a source of deep-seated sensations'. Monotony is a mode of time which accords with much in the general celebration by Nineteenth-century novelists of the humdrum, of the commonplace and the everyday (a theme of Praz's

[1] v. Praz, op. cit., pp. 376–83, 410.

book): and George Eliot deliberately illustrates the connection. When, for example, she says about the elderberry bush that there is 'no better reason' for preferring it than that it stirs a memory, the ambiguity – it is at once the best reason, and also a slightly deprecatory one – sharply points up the power, the value of this time-feeling in its relation to the commonplace. She indicates at once the novel's essential stuff (what is ordinary) and an important perspective in its scope (early years, the remembered past).

Her insistence on the value of childhood and a response to landscape and visible nature can fairly be called Wordsworthian if one realizes how it is also entirely her own, native to her experience. Tom and Maggie, who as children thought life would never change,

> were not wrong in believing that the thoughts and loves of these first years would always make part of their lives. We could never have loved the earth so well if we had had no childhood in it – if it were not the earth where the same flowers come up again every spring that we used to gather with our tiny fingers as we sat lisping to ourselves on the grass – the same hips and haws on the autumn hedgerows – the same redbreasts that we used to call 'God's birds' because they did no harm to the precious crops.[1]

The flowers, the hips and haws, the redbreasts – these are the 'same', they embody a continuity, in a more personal, more Wordsworthian way than the nightingale for Keats. The feeling tends willingly backwards into its *own* past; the present is not anguished but, rather, subdued to this past. George Eliot adds 'What novelty is worth that sweet monotony where everything is known, and *loved* because it is known?' Praz suggests that the two pages which made Proust weep were those containing the passage just quoted, and adds, 'The gentle flow of the first part of *The Mill on the Floss* must have left a deep imprint on the mind of the author of the *Recherche*.'

It is of course the novel as a form which especially embodies this flow of time – which, one could almost say, was invented to contain it. The detailed unfolding of life, the gradual progress of a story which automatically creates a feeling of time, this was something new in the Eighteenth century. Ian Watt, in *The Rise of the Novel*, gives a succinct and authoritative summing-up[2] of the importance of the various roles

---

[1] *The Mill on the Floss*, I, v.   [2] v. pp. 21–6, Penguin edn.

time plays in the novel compared with those it plays in ancient, medieval, and renaissance literature. A good deal of literary *interest* in time has evolved by way of the novel: the representation of time is one of the novel's tasks – just as is circumstantial description and the portrayal of ordinary people and the value of everyday events. And the connection of these various tasks lies in the simple fact that the novel, in quite a literal sense, has time for such things.

It is the novel which would dominate any full discussion of the relationship of time to the full representation of reality in literature. The novel has naturally become *the* form for solving some of the problems of time; to say that time is implicit in any novel is perhaps the easiest way of pointing to the central place of both in our literary thinking. The accumulation of experience by way of temporal progress affects the characters in a novel – and the reader of it too. One becomes 'immersed' in a novel – and its scale has something to do with the degree of immersion. The novel is essentially a 'long' form. One does not, unless one's attention is drawn to it, necessarily have to think about time; like St Augustine, one simply knows what it is. However, time can be treated imaginatively in various ways. The novelist's recognition of time, and the closely connected problem of how to represent it, to show it as one aspect of reality, these bring their own rewards. But a concentration on expressing time through memory (or some sort of historical pathos), a concentration on the experience of time, this is the response with which we are here particularly concerned – which the distinction made between Fielding proposing his lawyer and Keats describing his medieval lovers helps to illustrate. Fielding recognizes time, objectively – as, in a different but related way, he recognizes it in the business of constructing his novels. *Tom Jones*, for example, obeys a realistic time-scheme and was apparently plotted with the help of an almanac.[1] Keats, throughout *The Eve of St Agnes*, is experiencing time subjectively, is responding to it as distance, something at once evocative and felt; he relies on the reader's sympathetic time-sense. Perhaps one should simply distinguish between cases where the *problem* of time contributes to the *form* of a work, and cases where the *feeling* of time contributes to the *quality* of a work. But the distinction is not as sharp as it may at first seem: Wordsworth, for example, throughout the *Prelude* is conscious both of the

---

[1] v. Watt, p. 26.

growing past that he is recording and of the shape, and the direction, that his narrative is taking. And though the sense of time also builds up autonomously, Wordsworth deliberately focuses on deeply remembered experience, so that the structural and the emotional sense of time work together. The record and the life recorded are fused; the poet obeys memory, and directs his poem.

Wordsworth is conscious of relating both subjective feelings about time and a general recognition of it to the progress and structure of the *Prelude*; but it remains a personal matter, there is nothing 'literary' about it. However, time easily can become a matter for literary self-consciousness. The Twentieth-century consciousness about time has produced some remarkable attempts at puzzling over it and 'playing' with it, experimenting with its representation; but, though these are often stimulating, keeping you alert, it is a mental or technical not an emotional approach. And although 'streams of consciousness' or D. H. Lawrence, say, exclaiming about 'the poetry of the sheer present'[1] testify to the significance of time in Twentieth-century literature, these ideas seem outside the Wordsworthian range and certainly provide little in the way of illuminating comparison. The sophisticated use of time as a literary theme has something unsatisfactory about it; it is possible to prefer, say, Thomas Mann's straightforward embodiment and commonsense discussion of time in *The Magic Mountain* than more flexibly paradoxical versions – though sometimes these can be very effective. Mann discusses the nature of tedium: and *Waiting for Godot* (however much of an interpretation-trap it may be) can quite happily be explained as having something interesting to say about this aspect of time. It is, after all, a play about waiting – a time-situation of which there are two conditions, expectation and endurance, where if in one tomorrow is a reality, in the other today is reality, something to be 'got through' somehow, a struggle based on experience, on previous endurance, which is continually demonstrating that you can make today into yesterday but never today into tomorrow. Life is habit, boredom; an awaited point in the future disturbs habit, provoking anxiety, suffering, which is the too-conscious awareness of time. One should not reduce it to formula; but such an epigrammatic or 'theoretical' interpretation (and its terms – Habit, Suffering, Boredom) can be

---

[1] Preface to the American edn. of *New Poems*.

quite justly extracted from Beckett's early essay (1931) on Proust.[1] The play provides a clearer, and more objective, exposition of the time-idea put forward in the essay – which tends to be more illuminating about its author than about its subject. Beckett rather overemphasizes the sheer malignity of Time, its 'poisonous ingenuity in the science of affliction'; Proust is too fully immersed in the medium to be gratuitously defiant of it.

Proust of course offers theorizing and criticism about time, but his total reading of it is a closely, personally involved one. And yet, simply because he is a novelist, a measure of impersonality must be accorded to his work. There is a considerable difference between Marcel the narrator and Proust the author; and the distinction to be made is, for example, very much more marked than that between the selective but consciously autobiographical Wordsworth who is the hero of the *Prelude* and Wordsworth as a man writing about himself. Proust sets a whole society in motion; and the 'subjective' speculative parts of his novel are structural and to that extent depersonalized. The 'petite madeleine', initiating the whole search for the past, shaped as though it had been 'moulded in the fluted scallop of a pilgrim's shell', makes an appropriate symbol for the quality of Proust's memory and marks the beginning of a pilgrimage into the far recesses of self and society, a measuring back which is at the same time leading forward both in self-clarification and in the clarification of form, the creation of the novel.

Proust takes subjective-cum-structural time-consciousness about as far as it will go. It could be noted that Anthony Powell, in his deliberately sub-Proustian picture of English society, deliberately makes impersonality the dominant note. The opening of Powell's sequence (*A Question of Upbringing*, 1951) skilfully introduces the importance of the sense of time, including the subjective past, while also indicating the reserved, non-subjective use to be expected of it in what is after all a first-person novel. It begins with a studied time-complex: various images, emotions, characteristics are worked in. Firstly, there is a tableau: some workmen beside a brazier – it is winter, snowing, the day getting dark, the scene quite elaborately composed and contemplated. Then in the second paragraph the narrator introduces himself – discreetly, and combining his objectivity with just a hint of the emo-

---

[1] v. pp. 4–5, 16, Evergreen edn., New York, n.d.

tional weight the present description has for him. 'For some reason, the sight of snow descending on fire always makes me think of the ancient world . . .' ('For some reason' – that is, he implies, for a private one, probably not explicable, and not worth consideration here.) He thinks of legionaries, mountain altars, centaurs – 'shapes from a fabulous past, infinitely removed from life; and yet bringing with them memories of things real and imagined'. Memory is already conditioned, and confused, by a vaguer sense of time. However, his thoughts continue from one point to the next. These 'classical projections', together with the physical appearance of the workmen, bring him to think of Poussin's *Dance to the Music of Time*. 'Classical associations made me think, too, of days at school . . .' And so, by a process of reminiscence, he moves into roughly the same sort of pattern displayed in George Eliot's opening to *The Mill on the Floss*; he describes the landscape around the school (which is presumably Eton), and the buildings themselves, where his story is going to begin. And here again he brings in a sense of the past, again fusing the inevitable hint of subjectivity with a generally objective view; his feeling for the personal past is 'projected' into the medieval buildings and the water-meadows that he mentions. He does not yet actually recall himself being there, he merely implies it by evoking a perhaps over-general sense of former times. Indeed, when he talks about 'the sombre demands of the past becoming at times almost suffocating in their insistence', he manages to obscure to whom or what or when they precisely refer. He is the opposite of Thomas Gray contemplating the same school, the same underlying landscape, a little over two centuries earlier. Anthony Powell's sense of time here has an objective, contemplative richness which he derives from a carefully controlled personal feeling, and which he uses to dominate any possible self-indulgence. It is an altogether more complicated mixture of the personal and the impersonal than was available to the nostalgic poet. The two are opposite also in their imprecisions: Gray shoots out his emotion too obviously, over-vocatively, Powell wraps himself in muffled prose which decently subdues personality but may also unduly hide it. And if these opening paragraphs are an invitation to descend into the past (through the tableau, into the 'abyss in the road' leading 'down to a network of subterranean pipes') then it is one whereby the whole personal past and the remembered landscape are straightaway subdued to, and presided over by, Poussin's calm, admonitory, yet somehow reassuring picture (Panofsky has described[1] how Poussin presents both the relentlessness and the creativeness of Time).

The subjective *use* of time may never again completely disappear; but it may well spread into a more impersonal manner, out again into history. The recognition that man exists in time is perhaps a more lasting development from the individual feeling that one is a creature subject to duration. But any larger 'historical' recognition is almost inevitably made first of all by, and continuously related to, one's own sense of time, 'stretching before and after'. 'Time present and time past/Are both perhaps present in time future,/And time future contained in time past.' In the opening lines and throughout the *Four Quartets*, T. S. Eliot brings a philosophical largeness, at least a firmly generalised air, to his meditations on time. And although there is also a strongly personal feeling in the Quartets, it works in a curious way: less through the first-person than through seeming to be firmly subordinated to the metaphysics or religion, and yet coming to the surface in spite of this. The tone of voice and the movement of the verse effectively distance any very great intimacy or autobiographical element; yet there seems to be quite a lot of suppressed emotion, mainly to do with the past. It is not at all like the *Prelude*, although comparisons could be made. Despite the occasional circumstantiality (the tube, 'the gloomy hills of London') the general impression is one of a fairly confident symbolism, a standing-back from the object. And this in its turn reinforces the contrasting oddity of the Quartets being 'local' poems, about particular places.

Meditations on time at this level tend to be self-sufficient; they point out the possible directions and conditions of thought on the matter. There is no question of saying anything merely neat or systematic; but the time-eternity formula to which the poem corresponds is one of the great mystical commonplaces. There is a feeling here of standing-back from any too subjective involvement with the ideas about time he is rehearsing; one is to feel that the statements are arrived at through the intensity of *contemplation* devoted to the ideas. The theme is worked out and presented in terms of eternity, and of a quietistic freedom from

[1] *Studies in Iconology*; v. also his contribution to *Philosophy and History*, Essays presented to Ernst Cassirer, ed. Klibansky and Paton, Oxford, 1936: a useful compendium of thinking about time.

time, a worked-for release from the tension of *The Waste Land*'s 'mixing memory and desire'. In the fourth Quartet, Eliot talks about 'indifference' – something half-way between 'Attachment to self and to things and to persons', and detachment from these (it is a concept something like Beckett's 'habit').

> This is the use of memory:
> For liberation – not less of love but expanding
> Of love beyond desire, and so liberation
> From the future as well as the past.   *Little Gidding*, III

Wordsworth (as we shall see) discovered his own form of deliverance from time; but it is worked out in terms very different from Eliot's. Wordsworth speaks altogether more personally; he might at one stage in his career have understood this 'use of memory' – but he never expresses anything about it in such general religious terms: though he does in the 'Immortality' *Ode*, almost it seems in spite of himself, come to a mystical interpretation of the nature of memory and its function in human life. The religious theme of the Quartets of course insists on an ultimate impersonality – or fusion of self with larger forces; and in fact Eliot achieves a remarkable synthesis of the personal and the impersonal, of subjective and philosophical thinking about time. He is not temperamentally tuned to the Wordsworthian kind, though he has evidently read Wordsworth carefully; but he achieves his own ideal impersonality in a field of meditation which is almost bound to include a certain amount of temporal self-consciousness.

Eliot's time-consciousness reaches naturally into all departments of his thought and all the themes of the Quartets. In the circular pattern of renewal-with-metamorphosis Eliot includes religion and history and the aesthetic problem of musical form – of form as duration, at once organic, cumulative, retrospective, and unified. Most of this seems to extend from Eliot's early, mainly historical notion about literary criticism and tradition, that no one should be surprised 'that the past should be altered by the present as much as the present is directed by the past'.[1] Eliot, in seeing all aspects of culture 'in time', is closely connected with much Twentieth-century speculation of the more metaphysical sort. Collingwood and others, for example, have puzzled over the problem developed from F. H. Bradley (Eliot's philosophical

---

[1] *Tradition and the Individual Talent* (1917).

master) of the historian in the present altering his authority (the past) by the simple act of putting himself in a working relationship to it.[1] The personal and the philosophical work together. 'Every present has a past of its own . . .'[2] is a truth about the study of history which extends very naturally from, or into, remembered experience.

By submitting to the Christian historical tradition Eliot clearly gained any additional help he may have needed to resolve his own temporal problems. One can be made aware of the cumulative onwardness of life not just through the personal past but also in many ways through the social, historical past. Eliot's quest towards Christianity, reflected in his poetry, might, for example, be paralleled in the opposite direction; Ortega y Gasset, having been brought up in the Christian faith, but no longer subscribing to it, puts it thus,[3] in what is both a personal and historical perspective: '. . . of course I am still a Christian, but in the form of having been a Christian'. A contemplation of Christianity in its historical and its mythical terms can obviously influence both a social and a personal sense of time. Arnold Toynbee observes the peculiar and powerful time-sense embodied in Christianity. There is, he says,[4] 'one feature of the Christian mythology which seems to have no precedent'; this lies in the concept of the Second Coming, 'the future return to Earth of an historical figure who had already lived' there. This fuses the 'timeless past' of myth and the 'timeless present of the agrarian ritual' which are involved in the story, and translates them into 'historical striving'. Christianity is, in fact, a religion of time: it constantly directs itself to the future by dwelling on, putting its faith in, the past – while concentrating also on the present. It is not 'weighed down' by history – though its history is part of it, this is not just an accumulation. And as it demands personal involvement, so does any act of thinking about the past which is beyond mere antiquarianism – of submitting experience to 'the historical imagination' which, says Collingwood, 'is properly not ornamental but structural. Without it the historian would have no narrative to adorn'.[5] What he calls 'the autonomy of historical thought'[6] is bound to be a private force, using a time-sense which obviously transcends memory

---

[1] v. *The Idea of History*, pp. 238–40.   [2] Collingwood, p. 247.
[3] In *Philosophy and History*, p. 307.
[4] *A Study of History* (abridged edn.), p. 223.
[5] *The Idea of History*, p. 241.   [6] ibid., p. 236.

itself but not that personality which memory alone maintains.
As a fine example of how the historical sense and a more personal
sense of time can modify each other, one might look at Chekhov's
favourite among his short stories, *The Student*; noting how in this case
a response to time which sees nothing but dreary persistence, sameness,
can be countered by one which feels continuity, living tradition. The
student is coming home from snipe shooting on Good Friday: the
weather suddenly worsens.

> And now, as he shrank with the cold, he was thinking of how just
> such a wind had blown in the days of Rurik, and Ivan the Terrible,
> and Peter the Great, and there had been the same grinding poverty
> and hunger, too; the same holes in the thatched roofs, the same
> ignorance and frustration, the same empty wastes, the darkness, the
> feeling of persecution – all these horrors had always been, were now,
> and always would be, and so even when a thousand years had passed,
> life would be no better.[1]

He stops at a market-garden, kept by two widows, mother and
daughter. A fire is blazing. ' "The apostle Peter warmed his hands at
a bonfire just like this one night," said the student . . . "That means it
must have been cold then, too." ' And he tells the story of Peter before
the Crucifixion, his third denial and the cock crowing, and how 'he
went out, and wept bitterly'. The older woman sobs, her daughter is
disturbed. The student goes on his way, and reflects:

> . . . what he had just been telling them about something that hap-
> pened nineteen hundred years ago plainly had some relation to the
> present – to both women and probably to this isolated village, to
> himself personally and to all mankind.

It was not just that he knew how to touch the old woman's heart 'with
a story' – 'her whole being was concerned with what happened to
Peter's soul'. This realisation produces in him a sudden welling-up of
joy. He sees the past linked with the present unbrokenly, 'events
flowing one from the other'. And as he watches the wintry sunset 'he
was thinking that the truth and beauty which had guided human life
there, in the garden and the chief priest's palace, had continued without
a break up to the present day'. He is filled with happiness: 'and life

[1] Transl. by Jessie Coulson, World's Classics edn., 1963.

seemed to him delightful, miraculous, and full of high significance.

It is a story of a subjective response to history; of how history is illuminated, temporarily transformed by emotion. The student who feels the same wind, the same poverty and hunger stretching back in the Russian past and a thousand years forward, feels a more outwardly historical version of Keats's pessimism at hearing the nightingale's 'self-same' voice. And it is not a case of pessimism being converted to optimism (it is perhaps finally a pessimistic story – the truth and beauty which inform the continuity are evident but they are represented by Peter's feeling of the bitterest remorse). The sudden illumination is more valuable than facile optimism because, by recognizing the past, it makes time valuable – the vast stretches of misery have been, *are* worth while: and will be. Another continuity reassures the student; a past outside the personal past – which nonetheless affects him personally.

The permanence of reality, of human emotion, provides a reassurance about time. And this experience is presented as something 'in time' – obviously enough, in the context of the historical reflections: but also because it is presented as a short story. The short story is especially designed to deal with time being vividly experienced; time flows *through* the short story, it is not embodied as in the novel. A significant moment continues beyond the limits of the form containing it: the container is strictly limited (the brief episode is shaped, given finality), but the feeling contained is one of onwardness. Here, there is something impermanent in the student's happiness ('he was only twenty-two' Chekhov says in parenthesis) – but incorporated with history, its value is not diminished because it may disappear from him. Some of the story's impact comes from the irony, almost, of using the form of the passing incident to illumine a nineteen hundred years continuity. And much of the story's impact comes from that essential quality of the form, the feeling it creates of managing to express an inherently inexpressible emotion or state of mind. The 'significance' that life is full of, the student's expectation of 'mysterious unknown happiness', the source of these is made clear; but their sense of being something greater than any statement can produce or pin down is what the story really creates.

This is a kind of feeling, one might almost call it 'the sense of something', that Wordsworth was one of the first to use: a sense of the indefinable which is self-sufficient, self-justifying by its very intensity–and by being written down. Wordsworth makes quite explicit the height-ened value of certain moments – of what he calls 'spots of time', those experiences which become *loci* of memory. And if this emphasis on the episodic touches one characteristic aspect of the short story, though *used* very differently by Wordsworth, it makes it possible to think of him as also having in this connection a short story writer's approach to the hidden significance of *ordinary* events – what he makes clear when, after painting a picture of Simon Lee the old Huntsman ('the more he works, the more/Do his weak ankles swell'), he addresses his audience thus:

> My gentle Reader, I perceive
> How patiently you've waited,
> And now I fear that you expect
> Some tale will be related.

> O Reader! had you in your mind
> Such stores as silent thought can bring,
> O gentle Reader! you would find
> A tale in every thing.

Wordsworth continually alternates between the commonplace and the numinous – heightened moments and simple observations are equally remembered. Here he suggests how the accumulated 'stores' of 'silent thought' can always be given meaning in time and by way of it.

The general relationship of time to the circumstantial and the every-day is seen in the rise of the novel: its special relation to the short story has been made explicit in Joyce's notion of the epiphany, described in *Stephen Hero*.[1] A trivial fragment of overheard conversation makes a sudden strong impression, makes Stephen 'think of collecting many such moments together in a book of epiphanies. By an epiphany he meant a sudden spiritual manifestation, whether in the vulgarity of speech or of gesture or in a memorable phase of the mind itself.' In *The Student* the 'manifestation' is obviously of the last sort: the treat-ment could be said to imply how such a memorable illumination as the student had comes suddenly and unexpectedly, almost as a gift of time, as a reward for having *endured* boredom or, in this case, depression.

[1] London, 1956, p. 216.

Joyce believed that the artist should 'record these epiphanies with extreme care, seeing that they themselves are the most delicate and evanescent of moments'. And here the literary theorist can be heard beginning to share the idea of time with the artist, recognizing a technical, aesthetic problem. In that direction, or in the ultimately more significant direction of history, self-consciousness about time may continue. But the full awareness of the self in time by way of memory is a special matter, a theme without which further time-thinking could not have taken place, and which in Wordsworth receives a full (definitive, if the word were not so inappropriate to the idea) poetic treatment and expression.

(ii) *Eighteenth-century Literature and the Personal Past*

To approach the subject, then, a little more directly: a consideration of Wordsworth's poetry and his use of memory is obviously not concerned with the simple faculty of retention and recollection possessed in varying degrees of power by everyone; neither with the quality of Memoria, as it was understood in ancient psychology, nor with the old rhetorician's discipline of ordered recollection, nor, of course, with any system of mnemonics or 'artificial' memory; while a consideration of, say, Wordsworth's powerful verbal memory, or of his retention of Miltonic echoes, though interesting, would be only marginally relevant to a study of that distinctive way of thought which produced his greatest poetry. It is the *idea* of memory, large, evocative, and ill-defined, with which we are now concerned: a literary idea to which we immediately respond – as a narrative mode, as an approach to the passing of time, as a particular way of understanding events, almost, in the case of Proust, as a complete system of personal experience – yet an idea whose workings have not always been prominent in literature, and whose importance in Wordsworth is one of the most interesting aspects of his achievement. It might be generally agreed that memory can be used, and understood, as a particular mode of literary feeling; the nature of memory is a recognizable literary problem. And it would almost certainly be agreed that a retrospective attitude to personal experience is a distinctive feature of Wordsworth's best poetry. Any attempt to isolate and analyse the idea of memory as it appears in the poetry, to examine it as a literary mode, to find out in what manner, and with what degree of literary consciousness, Wordsworth used his sense of the personal past, should beware of 'sophistication' – of attributing to Wordsworth a perceptiveness about memory which, over one and a half centuries ago, he might not be expected to have had. But in fact Wordsworth is quite clear about its importance; and partly because of its subsequent development we can pursue the idea in its historical past with added clarity. It might be as well to begin by making a few preliminary qualifications and distinctions, and by indicating very briefly, and in slightly more particular historical terms, the intellectual position of the concept at the start of Wordsworth's career.

Memory in Wordsworth's poetry is an important aspect of his individual genius; it is also present in the spirit of the time, the idea at once intuitively felt and enlarged, in the way a great writer furthers sensibility. To Wordsworth, in writing the *Prelude*, it was 'a thing unprecedented in literary history that a man should talk so much about himself',[1] and in poetry this was certainly true. When, in those first spontaneous lines – spontaneous both apparently and actually[2] – which introduced the *Prelude*, he cried (l. 15) 'The earth is all before me', the two basic changes in the Miltonic phrase[3] (present tense, first person pronoun) might have suggested two fundamental changes in the epic relationship of the poet to his task – it had become personal, and the narrative was to be continuously related to the writer in the present. When, by the end of Book I, Wordsworth could write (l. 668) 'The road lies plain before me', the autobiographic and consciously retrospective nature of the work, its point of greatest originality, was fixed. A whole trend of Eighteenth-century sentiment connected with the individual and with a kind of emotional nostalgia is realized in Wordsworth; it was in the nature of his undertaking that memories of his own life should seem to him permissible: but it was in the nature of his entire poetic character that his work should owe its chief strength to the evocative power of these memories. The sense of the past, of the individual man in relation to his earlier years, might almost seem to have been created by Wordsworth; yet it had been growing throughout his native century, and the depth to which some of his younger contemporaries, notably Hazlitt and de Quincey, are imbued with this

---

[1] *EL*, p. 489.   [2] v. *Prel*, p. 510.
[3] 'The World was all before them, where to choose . . . ' (*Paradise Lost*, XII, 646).

sense, the degree to which they are explicit about the workings of memory, demonstrate both his influence and his sensitivity in the first place to an idea very much of the age.

Throughout the Eighteenth century, memory received considerable attention from various literary theorists, frequently in the light of Associationism; but the distinction which must here be emphasized, between memory considered as a mental faculty, and memory considered as a literary idea, would not then have been readily apparent. Memory, indeed, was scarcely recognized as an independent force, being usually compared with Imagination, and contrasted as more vivid or less powerful. It might be said, in general terms, that the extreme view of Hobbes, 'Imagination and Memory are but one thing . . .',[1] was gradually modified until Memory came to be considered as referring to real events, Imagination to thoughts not immediately connected with actual experience; while the mutual dependence of the two faculties was also recognized: how, 'in some cases Imagination may become Remembrance', and how, further, 'Remembrance will sometimes decay, till it be nothing more than Imagination'.[2] Memory, then, was thought about seriously; Beattie's views deriving from lectures to his students, where he was deliberately avoiding 'all matters of nice curiosity', may be taken as typical of the period in which Wordsworth was growing up. As a critic, Beattie is intelligently aware of those problems of the mind closely connected with literature; as the author of *The Minstrel*, he conveys something of that subjective interest in poetic emotion working on its own medium, and something of that introspective sensibility about the nature of the poet which is at the root of the *Prelude*; but about the nature of the personal past and its poetic force there is nothing yet to be said. The nature of the Imagination was already becoming one of the great problems of literary theory; but speculation about memory remained firmly within the bounds of empirical psychology.

Here we must make a fundamental distinction: memory in Wordsworth cannot be studied as an aspect of the Imagination; it is an independent force, and it is an independent literary idea. To put it as briefly as possible, memory is concerned not with the relationship of subject and

---

[1] *Leviathan* I, ii.
[2] James Beattie: *Dissertations Moral and Critical* (2 vols.), Dublin, 1783: 'Of Memory and Imagination', p. 9.

object, but with the relationship of the subject and Time. It is concerned not with the reaction of the mind to static material but with the attitude of the mind to time passing. It is a purely inward working of the mind, producing a simultaneous awareness of past event and present thought; and in Wordsworth's poetry the synthesis of present and past is an expressive force as great as the synthesis of, or the attempts to distinguish between, internal and external worlds. For Wordsworth, memory is at once mode and subject matter; and to examine the idea in this light will not be to make the elementary confusion between the mental activity of remembering and the past event thus recalled. The principle of unity in Wordsworth's thought includes the unity of present and past; the mode of action of his poetry sometimes achieves this unity.

Primarily, Wordsworth's use of memory comprises the act of creation related to the emotion impelling it:

> I would give,
> While yet we may, as far as words can give,
> A substance and a life to what I feel:
> I would enshrine the spirit of the past
> For future restoration.   *Prel* **XI**, 339–43

He understood the continuous nature of memory in time, and some of the problems it raised; the difficulty, for instance, of distinguishing 'in truth' between 'naked recollection . . . And what may rather have been call'd to life/By after-meditation'.[1]

He knew the continued influence and the accumulated power of memories held in the mind; and he understood how they generated new emotion, so that if some poetry seemed to be the immediate result of a particular experience or observation, it nevertheless owed something to all Wordsworth's previous experience, to his past in general – and much of his finest poetry was, he knew, only possible as the result of past experience long and deeply held in the mind. A strong sense of time is inherent in such a way of thinking; in Wordsworth's poetry it expresses itself by way of memory in a variety of complex forms; the past may be felt as a distance which memory can bridge, a gap which memory can close, a course which it can trace, it may be felt as a complete emotion in the present, or as something almost totally lost, exist-

---

[1] *Prel* III, 645–8.

ing only in remembrance. Basically, each act or experience of memory in Wordsworth is unique, and relevant only to the poetry by which it is expressed. Wordsworth himself does not often try to distinguish absolutely between past experience and present being; it is the sense of remembering, of memory becoming poetry, which is important to him.

For example, in Book I of the *Prelude*, having recalled the 'fair seed-time' (l.305) of his soul, Wordsworth exclaims (ll. 517–21):

> Unfading recollections! at this hour
> The heart is almost mine with which I felt
> From some hill-top, on sunny afternoons
> The Kite . . . Pull at its rein.

This is a straightforward identification by way of memory with a past experience – one of the classic delights of memory working as a creative power; it is inherent in the 'species of re-action' which follows on 'emotion recollected in tranquillity'. Near the beginning of Book II, Wordsworth, having 'measured back' (l. 3) and reflected on the way he travelled in his growing childhood, writes (ll. 27–33):

> A tranquillizing spirit presses now
> On my corporeal frame: so wide appears
> The vacancy between me and those days,
> Which yet have such self-presence in my mind
> That, sometimes, when I think of them, I seem
> Two consciousnesses, conscious of myself
> And of some other Being.

This seems to be partly in antithesis to the preceding example: instead of Wordsworth's feeling that the 'heart' of his former experience is almost the same now as then, he seems to insist on a complete separation between the past emotion, the former 'heart', and the present one; and yet, while seeming to feel 'two consciousnesses', he is also insisting on the 'self-presence' of those past days, so that there is in fact some confusion between the memory, the time remembered, and Wordsworth himself, the remembering consciousness. It is worth noticing here two points which will be of some importance in understanding Wordsworth's use of memory: the strongly sensuous nature of its working – a tranquillizing spirit 'pressing' on his 'corporeal frame', together with

37

a seeming palpability, the 'self-presence' of the past; and the fact that this past, although felt as a 'vacancy', is yet finally unified, the gap is closed, by memory, by Wordsworth's self-awareness and a sense of bodily continuity.

Although this 'wide vacancy', then, seemingly contradicts the idea of continuity, the chiefly spatial image is corrected by the strong time feeling inherent in the act of remembering. Memory, experienced both in terms of distance and of sensuous continuity, led Wordsworth, as we shall see, more and more to a reflective sense of time; but in the earlier stages of his poetic life Wordsworth's temporal way of thinking most often expressed itself in active remembering, related to particular occasions – as for example in 'Tintern Abbey'. Here, the most immediate emotion is concerned simply with the length of time between his first visit and the second.

> Five years have past; five summers, with the length
> Of five long winters! and again I hear
> These waters . . .

The extent of time gone by is emphasized, and throughout this opening passage the emotion of returning is stressed: 'Once again' he sees the cliffs, 'once again' the hedgerows, 'the day is come' when 'again' he lies under the sycamore. But this simple apprehension of length of absence and of return to a known scene is followed by an account of the five years' influence on the poet of memories inspired by this scene; it is to these memories that he has owed not only feelings of 'tranquil restoration' but also 'that serene and blessed mood' (l. 41) of his deepest insights, and Wordsworth here pays tribute to the continuous value of a remembered past – O sylvan Wye! . . . How often has my spirit turned to thee!' He goes on to describe the act of remembering, 'the picture of the mind revives again' (l. 61), and this act is coupled with a strong awareness of both the function and the power of memory, and of its relation to his personal sense of time, so that he looks on a past scene

> not only with the sense
> Of present pleasure, but with pleasing thoughts
> That in this moment there is life and food
> For future years.

This awareness leads him to recall the difference between memories implanted five years ago and those being implanted now; and the implication is how his attitude to nature has been changed and enlarged at least partly by virtue of those previous memories. The final passage addressed to Dorothy owes some of its force to that devotion to the past which knowledge derived from memory of it must induce: although his own development is recognized, his former self is too real, too strongly with him, to be dismissed:

> Oh! yet a little while
> May I behold in thee what I was once . . . (ll. 119–20

An awareness, then, of the autonomous power of memory, or its mode of action, and, above all, of its deep moral influence, is exemplified in 'Tintern Abbey'; and this awareness is closely related to Wordsworth's personal sense of time. So introspective a reading of time was something new in English literature, and if only to emphasize this originality, a few indications of immediately previous attitudes may be useful.

Eighteenth-century attitudes to time occasionally display an awareness of memory, though with no great feeling that it is important. In theoretical writings, memory, as we have said, was considered only as a mental faculty; it had no temporal implications except in the most elementary sense of dealing with ideas in ordered or random succession. Time is perhaps most explicitly dealt with in the juggling and Lockean sophistication of *Tristram Shandy*;[1] though, as we have suggested, a fundamental concept of time is implicit in the structure, the full and ordered narrative revelation, of the more typical novel throughout its development in the Eighteenth century. In poetry, however, there are moments of more immediate sensibility, in which recollections of past events and a knowledge of passing time are set off against each other.

Akenside (Wordsworth's 'classical predecessor', as Hazlitt recognized him) had produced his *Pleasures of Imagination* in 1744; we find, among his observations, that he had experienced

> the secret union, when we feel
> A song, a flower, a name, at once restore

---

[1] Three volumes of which together with 'two or three papers of the *Spectator*, half subdued', Wordsworth stated to be, in 1791, his only 'incursions into the fields of modern literature'; v. *EL*, pp. 55–6.

> Those long connected scenes where first they moved
> The attention;

he knew how, consciously looking backwards,

> The prospect from that sweet accession gains
> Redoubled influence o'er the listening mind.
>
> III, 338–41, 346–7

Although this is a generalized account, not a particular experience, like Gray's, there is just a 'sense of the madeleine' here, some recognition of how what is momentary and slight can not only summon up entire periods and areas of past existence, but also, by virtue of this evocative power, imbue them with added significance and pleasure. In Cowper we can find this same sensibility further developed. In 'The Winter Walk at Noon', Book VI of *The Task*, he describes himself listening to the music of the village chimes: 'With easy force it opens all the cells/Where mem'ry slept'. The feeling here (ll. 11–12) is intensified to the extent that it is treated as a particular dramatic moment; it is given the context of a winter walk, and when Cowper goes on to make it a matter of general observation and reflection, it is still with reference to himself.

In general, the backward glance was an opportunity for melancholy; many writers in this vein might have taken their text from Burke on *The Sublime and Beautiful* (I, 5):

> It is the nature of grief to keep its object perpetually in its eye, to present it in its most pleasurable views, to repeat all the circumstances that attend it, even to the last minuteness; to go back to every particular enjoyment, to dwell upon each . . .

Eighteenth-century melancholy was fostered on retrospection, and the sense of time and its relation to private feeling grew steadily; our own time-sensibility (which, despite Wyndham Lewis's polemic, *Time and Western Man*, remains one of our deepest emotional sources) stems directly from this period. But it was only with Wordsworth that the true relation of time and memory found expression, as it was only with Wordsworth that the moral and total value of memory was recognized – its capacity to furnish not merely a wilful literary attitude, but 'invigorating thoughts' (*Prel* I, 649) and influences of natural goodness. While memory was invoked simply as an aspect of melancholy – and was not deeply experienced as a way of feeling – it remained a matter of entirely commonplace sentiment. 'Of Joys departed/Not to return, how painful the Remembrance!': this, from Robert Blair's *The Grave* of 1743, was a sentiment echoed, in equally undistinguished lines, by many others. Yet, if there was a certain lack of mental vigour, an air of acceptance or lassitude about this sense of the past, when it was actually expressed in literature, the feeling for time – as the medium of both past and future – was everywhere deeply if obscurely felt; it was perhaps only occasionally expressed in words, as in this aphorism of Shenstone's:

> The words 'no more' have a singular pathos; reminding us at once of past pleasure, and the future exclusion of it.[1]

But in that larger world of nature-sensibility, of which Shenstone the gardener and landscaper was a famous inhabitant, the past had an ideal significance which was basically moral. The past of classical antiquity, and of primal, newly-created Nature, was evoked and recalled in the landscape, in ruins and distant horizons, as it was discovered in, and inspired by, the paintings of Claude Lorrain and his successors – the past represented a perfection which it was the business of art to recover as nearly as it could. And the impulse behind this was one of nostalgia, a feeling for a past country, a past state of life, which at once grew from, and, much more, furthered, a sense of the personal past, of the individual human life in time.

This connection between landscape and a sense of the past was understood chiefly in associative primitive-historical terms; but it came to be felt also more personally and more topographically. James Beattie, for example, understood the associative value of landscape in this way: 'With what rapture, after long absence, do we revisit the haunts of our childhood, and early youth!'[2] And he goes on to explain how this accounts for love of country and for homesickness – feelings, he adds, which are particularly strongly felt in mountainous districts.

For precipices, rocks, and torrents, are durable things; and, being more striking to the fancy than any natural appearances in the plains,

---

[1] *Works* (2 vols.), London, 1764; II, p. 187.
[2] *Dissertations* . . . vol. I, p. 106.

take faster hold of the memory; and may therefore more frequently recur to the absent native, accompanied with an idea of the pleasures formerly enjoyed in those places, and with regret that he is now removed to so great a distance from them.

The landscape of Wordsworth's childhood, his 'dear native regions', was firmly fixed in his memory; partly for the reason, as Beattie goes on to suggest, that 'the daily contemplation of the grand phaenomena of nature, in a mountainous country, elevates, and continually exercises, the Imagination of the solitary inhabitant'. For Wordsworth, however, it was not so much a matter of his mind becoming 'in a peculiar degree susceptible of wild thoughts, and warm emotions'; as we shall see, 'the grand phaenomena of nature' impressed themselves on Wordsworth in a more continuously active sense, becoming emotionally intensified, and working also with a cumulative moral power. In Wordsworth, a feeling for landscape, the sense of time, and the dynamic discipline of work, of poetry, are all closely connected with memory.

A detailed study of Eighteenth-century time-sensibility would have to include the rise of historicism, of romantic antiquarianism, of the beginning of an interest in the child. But, although a sense of the past, both general and subjective, was developing, it was little related as yet to personal memory. This was the great enlargement brought to the concept of memory by Wordsworth: a way of thinking which was temporal and personal, rather than psychologically objective. The doctrine of the Association of Ideas may be invoked to explain some aspects of Wordsworth's awareness of memory, as of course may that whole trend of literary aesthetics based on the self-consciousness of the mind following on Hobbes and Locke; but the theory can have had little effect on Wordsworth's essentially retrospective way of thinking, and, despite his one-time admiration for Hartley, it could never have been for him, what Sir Walter Scott sarcastically described it as having once been, 'the universal pick-lock of all metaphysical difficulties'.[1] The transcendental nature of Wordsworth's thought could not long be satisfied with so rationalistic a system, and the theory was soon dismissed. Wordsworth, in the *Prelude*, explicitly rejected any suggestion that the mind's growth could be simply explained in terms of accumu-

[1] Quoted in Lockhart's *Life* (1850 edn.), p. 229.

lated sensation, or, indeed, that any ideas could be traced to their
origin. In a passage addressed to Coleridge, he asked

> Who knows the individual hour in which
> His habits were first sown, even as a seed . . .?   *Prel* II, 211–12

It was, he knew, and insisted,

> Hard task to analyse a soul, in which,
> Not only general habits and desires,
> But each most obvious and particular thought,
> Not in a mystical and idle sense,
> But in the words of reason deeply weigh'd,
> Hath no beginning.   *Prel* II, 232–7

The problem, then, of examining Wordsworth's use of memory is
not basically a psychological one. A temporary concern with Associationism is an expected part of Wordsworth's interest in his own mind;
but it was not a cause of any serious change in his thinking. (The
valuable work of Professor Beatty (*William Wordsworth . . .*, Wisconsin, 1927) in drawing attention to the ideas of Hartley has been suitably
modified by later criticism (e.g. M. Rader, *Presiding Ideas in Wordsworth's Poetry*, California, 1931). For Wordsworth, memory was not
something to be classed in 'the cabinet of sensations';[1] it was a whole
mode of feeling. A brief comparison with Samuel Rogers's *The Pleasures
of Memory* (1792) will point the difference between a sentimental faculty,
something to be switched on more or less at will, and the autonomous
urgency and compulsive emotion with which Wordsworth responded
to his past.

Rogers's poem was immensely successful (it had reached its fourteenth
edition in 1803),[2] and may be taken to exemplify both an immediate
contemporary responsiveness to the idea of memory and the limitations of popular sensibility. While the second part of the poem deals
with what he calls the 'higher province' of memory, the preservation,
for man's use, of 'the treasures of art and science, history and philosophy', the first part is mainly nostalgic in tone, presenting instances of
'pleasing melancholy'.[3] As must have been evident to popular

---

[1] cf. *Prel* II, 228–9.

[2] v. P. W. Clayden, *The Early Life of Samuel Rogers*, London, 1887, pp. 210–7.

[3] v. 'Analysis' of pt. II, and of pt. I (pp. 16, and 3 in *The Poetical Works*, Aldine
edn., London, 1875).

43

sensibility, 'this mixed sensation is an effect of the Memory'.

> Childhood's loved group revisits every scene;
> The tangled wood-walk and the tufted green!
> Indulgent Memory wakes, and lo, they live!
> Clothed with far softer hues than Light can give.

The easy undisturbing emotion, the suggestion of mere elegant luxury in the waking of memory, these have only to be compared with, say, Wordsworth's account of his return to the Wye, or of his first return from Cambridge (of how, former walks remembered,

> Those walks did now, like a returning spring,
> Come back on me again . . .), *Prel* IV, 126–7

to display not only the difference between a minor poetaster and a great writer responding to the same emotion, but also the fundamental difference between any approach based on a limited psychology and the direct approach of imaginative intuition – and the consequent difference between superficial description and the dynamic working-out of memory in action.

For it is only in the movement itself of Wordsworth's poetry that the true nature of memory in his work is to be understood. A main question we must attempt to answer is simply this: in what manner and how consciously did Wordsworth use his memory? The development of his literary awareness of memory may be followed in three stages, from a more or less Picturesque, or visual, attitude, as in his letter to Dorothy from Switzerland, describing his 'stations' and how he returns to them 'in the hope of bearing away a more lively picture';[1] towards the deeply personal and often sensuous emotions involved in the act of remembering and of describing – his joy in 'the mighty world/Of eye, and ear, – both what they half create,/And what perceive . . .'[2] – those emotions perhaps most fully expressed in 'Tintern Abbey', and nearly always including a strong feeling for their placing in time, the relationship between the past event and its present evocation. These emotions lead in their turn to a third, more general, almost mystical feeling for the relation between time passing and human awareness of it by way of memory. In *The White Doe*, for example, Emily seems, in a spiritual

[1] *EL*, p. 35.   [2] 'Tintern Abbey', ll. 105–7.

sense, to be 'delivered' from time: she is 'Sustained by memory of the past/And strength of Reason'.[1]

Tracing the idea under these three headings, picturesque, 'sensuous', and mystical (and bearing in mind the essential unity at any given moment of Wordsworth's accumulated feelings), we will be able to examine along the way the various other aspects and problems of Wordsworth's memory which arise, to further examine in some detail his reading of time, as a redemptive force in Nature, as a destructive force in human life, and to consider the relationship of landscape in memory to his fundamental imagery.

In setting out to examine the nature of Wordsworth's use of memory, we have tried to eliminate one or two irrelevant problems, and to give a few indications of how the idea of memory stood towards the close of the Eighteenth century. The largeness of the idea today both illuminates and complicates the study of it in Wordsworth. The awareness of memory was conspicuously increased by Wordsworth: an idea growing throughout the century and brought to consciousness largely by way of literary aesthetics was given new significance by his poetry. Memory is no longer merely an aspect of the Imagination; it represents a personal attitude to time, and Wordsworth's intense awareness of time passing in relation to memory is adumbrated only faintly in the Eighteenth century. The essentially retrospective nature of Wordsworth's thinking is individual and temporal, grounded in self and in poetry, not in any study of psychology; Associationism has little connection with his modes of thought; for Wordsworth, memory is an autonomous power of the mind, evoking past experience, and adding new experience in the evocation, but uncovering no origins.

We can look firstly, then, at some of Wordsworth's earlier poetry. Our inquiry will take us as far as *The White Doe*; after that, memory is no longer a great force. It could be followed in the Duddon Sonnets, in isolated moments throughout his later work. But the past was no longer the living power it had once been: the deepest current of feeling in his nature, the continuous presence of his own past, had gone; or, at least, it was no longer the essential mode of his poetry.

[1] ll. 1624-5.

CHAPTER I

Poetry and the Picturesque Eye

THE early stages of Wordsworth's development are involved mainly with his feeling for nature in landscape, and with his various ways of seeing it: with a growing knowledge of how events and impressions in memory were formed by these ways of seeing: and with a consciousness of how the action of such ways influenced the growth of his poetry.

In telling Miss Fenwick about *An Evening Walk*, Wordsworth drew her attention to the image of 'the darkening boughs and leaves' of an oak tree silhouetted against the sunset, and, while remarking that it was 'feebly and imperfectly expressed', he added:

> I recollect distinctly the very spot where this first struck me. It was in the way between Hawkshead and Ambleside, and gave me extreme pleasure. The moment was important in my poetical history; for I date from it my consciousness of the infinite variety of natural appearances which had been unnoticed by the poets of any age or country, so far as I was acquainted with them; and I made a resolution to supply, in some degree, the deficiency. I could not have been at that time above 14 years of age.[1]

He claimed, indeed, of *An Evening Walk*, 'there is not an image in it which I have not observed; and now, in my seventy-third year, I recollect the time and place where most of them were noticed'. Wordsworth, in this recollection, has naturally enough not drawn attention to a great amount of borrowing, conscious or otherwise, from literary sources – from earlier Eighteenth-century poets, from Milton, from French descriptive poets, from current travel books about the Lake District: however, as de Selincourt points out, many of

[1] *PW* I, pp. 318–19.

these borrowings disappear from the revised texts, and much of the imagery, despite the diction in which it is presented, obviously derives from first-hand experience. Wordsworth, then, early on (fourteen is the age from which he dates his whole poetical career)[1] made a habit of observing nature closely, of associating his observations with their particular occasion, and of storing them in his memory as future poetic material.

The three aspects or stages of this habit were combined closely in Wordsworth and went to form a large part of his response to nature. Such primarily visual records were of course made in conjunction with those deeper responses to nature which were already entering and forming his memory, and which he was to evoke in the *Prelude*, the great *Ode*, and elsewhere – those records of emotion, rather than of observation, which grew out of each particular event and the accumulated memories of all its predecessors. 'For', as he was to point out in the *Preface* of 1800, 'our continued influxes of feeling are modified and directed by our thoughts which are indeed the representatives of all our past feelings . . .'. However, a habit of considered visual observation, and its consequent committal to memory, was an early and distinct feature of Wordsworth's poetical development. As we shall notice, this visual discipline was to be augmented – partly by way of contemporary fashion for the Picturesque, more through Wordsworth's own state of mind – and to become predominant during a short formative stage: a stage in which, as he put it, 'the eye was master of the heart',[2] and which to Wordsworth represented an aberration in his understanding of nature; although it was perhaps unavoidable, and certainly of some value in his poetical training.

In looking at nature, in thinking about it, Wordsworth was guided almost entirely by his own direct responses; but in the writing of poetry it was only natural that throughout most of his formative years (that is, up to 1798) he should also reflect the various attitudes of contemporary sensibility. In literature, observing nature and responding to it was carried out in terms of the sentimental descriptive poetry of the Eighteenth century; it included Gothic scene-setting and the Picturesque view, as well as a more generally deployed reflective nos-

---

[1] v. 'Idiot Boy', ll. 337–8: and cf. *Prel*, pp. 582–3. *Prel* V, 575–6 makes it 'Thirteen years/Or haply less': and v. note, p. 548.
[2] *Prel* XI, 172.

talgia about rural places and landscape. It reached perhaps its most typical expression in Rogers's *Pleasures of Memory* (1792): or in those sonnets of William Bowles which Coleridge once admired. That kind of time-sense which expressed feelings of looking forwards or backwards over, and in close connection with, an extent of landscape was often evident in poetry. Eighteenth-century landscape was an associative milieu, and farewells to a particular spot were taken in the understanding of the memories they would provide; for the man of sensibility,

> whene'er of pleasures flown
> His heart some long-lost image would renew,
> Delightful haunts! he will remember you . . .:[1]

while time and memory were often thought of in terms of the landscape which inspired an awareness of them. Bowles, for example, describes himself journeying on 'from day to day', admiring 'the rich landscape', which yet, in the distance, he must compare to 'life's goodly prospect' – for, in general, he seems to think, the promise is not attained: for 'the children of the earth' disillusionment lies ahead;

> And soon a longing look, like me, they cast
> Back o'er the pleasing prospect of the past.

Wordsworth inherited this way of thinking, and to understand the development of his poetry through remembered images and impressions of landscape it will be worth while to look at *The Vale of Esthwaite*, the most considerable fragment surviving from his youth. It had been, he stated, a poem 'of many hundred lines, and contained thoughts and images most of which have been dispersed through my other writings'.[2] This he remarked apropos of the 'Extract', first published in 1815, beginning 'Dear native regions . . .' (which is a version of ll. 498–513 of *The Vale of Esthwaite*), and he seems to have attached particular importance to 'the beautiful image', as he calls it, 'with which this poem concludes', an image of the setting sun casting its light on those eastern hills from which it had first risen. This – the image and the thought to which it gave rise – was another experience dating from the age of

---

[1] *Sonnets, written chiefly on Picturesque spots, during a tour*, 2nd edn., Bath, 1789: p. 15.
[2] *PW* I, p. 318.

fourteen,[1] and at the time Wordsworth apparently felt it to be something unusual, something extraordinary; but it had lodged permanently in his memory as a poetic influence. In his earliest use of this remembered moment – which made its final appearance in the 1850 *Prelude* (Book VIII, 458–75), which had at one time been intended for Book II and which appears in several manuscripts connected with the work from 1799 onwards[2] – Wordsworth imagines himself dying far from the Vale which is the subject of his poem:

> My soul shall cast the wistful view
> The longing look alone on you.
> As Phoebus, when he sinks to rest
> Far on the mountains in the west,
> While all the vale is dark between
> Ungilded by his golden sheen,
> A lingering lustre softly throws
> On the dear hills where first he rose.[3]

Wordsworth early recognized the true significance of the 'wistful', the 'backward' view.[4] If his first expectation of its power seemed to come 'in a casual access/Of sentiment',[5] then three years later, in composing *The Vale of Esthwaite*, he was fully aware both of what it now meant and what it would continue to mean: that the area of reference most firmly established in his memory was the landscape of his 'dear native regions' and that it was here he would return for restoration; that the eastern mountain-tops were an image of lost childhood and that distance of time was more absolute than distance of place; that the past, and more particularly the past of his youth, which might not be regained, might be illumined by memory only.

There is nothing here of sentimental nostalgia: the image (Phoebus or not) was observed accurately; and, in addition, it was felt deeply, and permanently, as a symbol. It became a living thing of memory; and it is true poetry, even in this early version, because it not only is, but, by its precise, if diagrammatic quality, seems to be, derived from particular experience: the best parts of *The Vale of Esthwaite* owe more

---

[1] v. *Prel*, p. 583.   [2] v. *Prel*, pp. 582–3.
[3] *The Vale of Esthwaite*, 506–13.   [4] cf. 'Dear native regions . . . ', l. 7.
[5] *Prel*, p. 583.

49

to a direct descent from what Johnson called 'local poetry'[1] (in which description of 'some particular landscape' was embellished with 'historical retrospection or incidental meditation') than to any youthful display of Picturesque sensibility or Gothic machinery. There is already in this early fragment one of the basic sources of Wordsworth's inspiration – a known landscape fixed in memory, and used with a sense of its relationship to the poet and his place in passing time.

The earlier of the surviving parts are the more 'literary' in content; (though we may notice at ll. 95–102 the first rough version of the image of the oak-tree against the sunset). 'Superstition' and 'her druid sons', 'Twilight', 'Melancholy', are all in attendance. In particular, that sort of nostalgia or generalized memory closely connected with this last personification colours many of the passages. Yet when he tells (ll. 121–4) how

> holy Melancholy throws
> Soft o'er the soul a still repose,
> Save where we start as from a sleep
> Recoiling from a gloom too deep,

the qualifying couplet suggests that he was fully aware both of the limited, and literary, nature of melancholy, and of the more personal and more compulsive emotions out of which true poetry is written. And, for the moment, literary falsity must not be taken to destroy the actual truth.

> No spot but claims the tender tear
> By joy or grief to memory dear.   ll. 416–7

Wordsworth responded to nature with thoughts that worked on him more deeply than by the evocation of 'the tender tear'; but a principle of much of his best poetry is stated in these lines, a recognition of the power of landscape to fix and to evoke a particular memory, to fuse a remembered occasion and a present emotion.

These lines here stand at the beginning of a passage which tells of the incident later described with great effect in Book XI of the *Prelude*, (ll. 345f.), the incident of his waiting for a horse to take him home from school, a few days before his father's death.

---

[1] 'Life of Denham' (*Lives of the Poets*, Oxford, 1905; I, p. 77).

> One Evening when the wintry blast
> Through the sharp Hawthorn whistling pass'd
> And the poor flocks, all pinch'd with cold
> Sad-drooping sought the mountain fold
> Long, long, upon yon naked rock
> Alone, I bore the bitter shock;
> Long, long, my swimming eyes did roam
> For little Horse to bear me home,
> To bear me – what avails my tear?
> To sorrow o'er a Father's bier.   ll. 418–27

The landscape is just particular enough (the 'sharp Hawthorn', the 'naked rock') to be identified with the grief Wordsworth feels; and, further, to be identified with the grief he felt on his recollection of the place at the time of his father's death. It is noticeable how, in memory, grief has flowed backwards to colour the admittedly dismal waiting; the retrospect here is more pitiful, and the two past occasions are emotionally more fused, than in the *Prelude*.[1]

In the *Prelude*, Wordsworth remembers the elemental properties of the landscape, and their continuing influence:

> All these were spectacles and sounds to which
> I often would repair and thence would drink,
> As at a fountain.   *Prel* XI, 383–5

In *The Vale of Esthwaite* Wordsworth revisits the actual source of this fountain of memory. Here, his renewed grief, evoked and intensified by the landscape and the time it recalls, finds a proper release:

> Flow on, in vain thou hast not flow'd,
> But eased me of a heavy load;
> For much it gives my heart relief
> To pay the mighty debt of grief,
> With sighs repeated o'er and o'er,
> I mourn because I mourned no more.   ll. 428–33

The present feeling of mourning is emphasized, made more particular

---

[1] Wordsworth was not, according to the *Prelude*, alone but with two brothers – in his maturity, this sort of personal fact was, when possible, admitted: conversely, a fact of purely poetic significance is likely to be made more telling – here, 'the poor flocks' become 'a single sheep'. *Prel* XI, 359.

than it might otherwise have been, by 'placing' its past occasion, by discovering it at its point of origin.

If this sense of the past seems more personal, more true, than anything of its kind yet seen in the Eighteenth century, it seems so, of course, in the knowledge of the *Prelude* and Wordsworth's other great and original poetry to come: yet an awareness of memory, a consciousness of the special value and power of his own past, is already developed in Wordsworth, although it has not yet taken a predominant role in his poetry. It is seen growing here in particular association with landscape. In *The Vale of Esthwaite* Wordsworth goes on to hope that in his declining years he might be able to fix his gaze there,

> As on a Book, companion dear
> Of childhood's ever merry year,
> Retrace each scene with fond delight
> While memory aids the orbs of sight.   ll. 486–9

That was his first wish, to return bodily to this scene of his youth; and if that were not to be, he knew that memory would still return him there, by way of 'the wistful view' and 'the longing look' (ll. 506–7). In old age, memory was to assist his eyes or his deepest wishes. In youth, among his general awareness of the future value of his continuously accumulating past, a more immediate problem was how his eyes might assist his memory. He may well have considered how memory, that way of feeling whose power he had already recognized, might be intensified by diligent looking. He may well have thought how close observation of nature might lead not only to accurate recollection but to deepened emotion.

We have already noticed how Wordsworth's resolution to make good the deficiency, in poetry, of observed natural appearances implied a certain visual discipline; whatever practice it required was an entirely personal matter. His way of looking at nature, however, must also have been influenced by an interest in Picturesque values; although it is unlikely that this fashionable and explicitly pictorial way of responding to landscape can have had much immediate effect on him before he went to Cambridge in 1787. Certainly he claims in the *Prelude* that up to that time he had shared with Dorothy a complete simplicity of vision:

> before I was call'd forth

From the retirement of my native hills
I lov'd whate'er I saw.   *Prel* XI, 224–6

However, as we know, he was already well acquainted with not only
the more substantial poetry of the century but also with that of many
of the fashionable descriptive and Gothic poets – mainly, it seems,[1]
through the help of William Taylor, headmaster of Hawkshead school,
who was the owner of a good library and probably lent volumes from
it to the young Wordsworth. He may also have been at this time
familiar with some of the earlier traveller's accounts of the Lake
District – Thomas Gray's Journal of his visit to the Lakes, published in
1775, or Dr. John Brown's celebrated letter describing the Lake at
Keswick, printed at Newcastle in 1767, and in London the following
year: this he might also have seen reproduced in *An Excursion to the
Lakes* (1774)[2] by William Hutchinson, or in the second edition of
West's *Guide to the Lakes* (1780)[3]. He may also have read William
Gilpin's account of his Lakeland tour,[4] which had appeared in 1786;[5]
but, before going to Cambridge, he must have read this work and the
others like it more out of local interest than from any desire to become
a connoisseur of the pictorial qualities of landscape. However, the
Picturesque movement was certainly familiar to him. Visitors to the
attractions of the Lake District were already frequent while Wordsworth was still at school, and he would be aware of their walking and
sketching; at that age, he may have regarded 'These Tourists' with a
little more sympathy than 'the homely Priest of Ennerdale' would be
made to in 1800.[6]

[1] v. Moorman, *William Wordsworth*, pp. 50–1.

[2] 1776 (as in *PW* I, p. 320) is the date of the second edition in which the text
had been enlarged with more archaeological detail, illustrations added, and the
tour prolonged.

[3] This was the most successful (and according to Wordsworth the best) of the
various accounts of the District. The first edition appeared in 1778 (not, *PW* I,
p. 320, 1779): addenda to the second included, as well as Dr. Brown's letter,
a popular verse description of the Lake of Keswick from a poem by Dr. Dalton,
and the text of Gray's Journal.

[4] *Observations, relative chiefly to Picturesque Beauty, made in the year 1772, on
several parts of England: particularly the Mountains, and Lakes of Cumberland, and
Westmoreland.*

[5] Not, as stated by Moorman (p. 115n.), in 1789. This was the year of publica-
tion of his *Observations . . . on . . . the High-lands of Scotland*: (pp. 147–78 of
vol. II take in the Lake District on his way home).

[6] v. *The Brothers*, ll. 1–16.

But it seems to have been during his period at Cambridge, and, most evidently, for a short time after, that Picturesque values were of some importance to him, in the impression that landscape made on his creative memory. Such values were derived from a way of looking Wordsworth was later to repudiate as 'a strong infection of the age';[1] but he admitted that he had given way to it, and indeed 'the picturesque'[2] was the sort of fashionable preoccupation which, in any kind of university, could scarcely have been avoided. Although the heyday of argument about the Picturesque (and its attendant disputes about 'the Gothic') had not yet arrived, the notion had become increasingly familiar throughout the century. It had, by the time of Wordsworth's going to Cambridge, been crystallized and given full popular expression in the first two of Gilpin's 'Observations, relative chiefly to Picturesque Beauty', those on the Wye (1782) and those on the Lake District (1786).

The development of this idea has been thoroughly examined by Christopher Hussey.[3] It had grown from a feeling for nature encouraged by travel, by an acquaintance with landscape painting, especially that of Claude Lorrain and that of Salvator Rosa, by an interest in gardening and landscape scenery. It found expression in a great body of descriptive verse, stemming mainly from the work of Thomson and of Dyer (who, besides being a poet, was also an unsuccessful painter, a pupil of Richardson). It became more clearly formulated by way of a general awareness of a pleasurable landscape category not covered by either the sublime or the beautiful of Burke, a category which included effects (derived from Dutch landscape painting) of light and shade, of the massed, ragged forms of clouds and trees, together with anything, including the conventionally beautiful, which could be composed into a picture. Such effects, supplemented by an historical feeling for ruins, were what Gilpin meant by the Picturesque; its chief concern was pictorial, to determine whether or not landscape would, according to 'the rules of picturesque beauty',[4] make a good painting. However,

---

[1] *Prel* XI, 156.

[2] The word was used as a substantive by William Gilpin in his *Observations on the River Wye* . . . (1782), p. 93, where he speaks of 'an ingenious friend, Col. Mitford, who is well-versed in the theory of the picturesque . . . ' (O.E.D.'s earliest example quotes the title of Uvedale Price's *An Essay on the Picturesque* . . . (1794)).   [3] *The Picturesque*, London and New York, 1927.

[4] *Observations on the Wye*, pp. 1–2.

it was difficult to write about landscape solely in terms of picture-making; the emotion experienced before it was an essential part of the total impact. Gilpin, as the illustrations to his books show, was no great artist: the forms of mountain, rock, and tree are generalized to the point of nonentity, and composed into some sort of order by theatrical lighting effects; they owe less to a regard for 'general properties, and large appearances' – he quotes in support of himself Johnson's statement in *Rasselas* about the business of the poet[1] – than to an evident incapacity. However, his vignettes were scarcely intended to do more than illustrate his ideas, and in his writing he was, if a misleading theorist of art, an accurate observer of nature.

The impulse behind his description was emotional rather than formal; and, in terms of general sensibility, it was also literary. Hussey has emphasized[2] the power of landscape in the Eighteenth century to produce a *unity* of attitude to nature in all the arts, and, if only because amateur sketching is troublesome, takes time, and is likely to be unsatisfactory in its results, a combined pictorial and poetic feeling for scenery was the most general kind of response: it was enough to examine a view in pictorial terms, and to leave it at that, assured of an underlying poetic influence. That the pursuit of an ideal landscape, assisted by remembered experience, was perhaps the deepest satisfaction to be gained from the Picturesque way of looking is suggested by Gilpin in a passage of his Wye tour, where he describes how he was 'benighted', while approaching Monmouth, by 'the grey obscurity of a summer-evening'; he goes on to say:

A light of this kind, though not so favourable to landscape, is very favourable to the imagination. This active power embodies half-formed images; and gives existence to the most illusive scenes. These it rapidly combines; and often composes landscapes, perhaps more beautiful, than any, that exist in nature. They are formed indeed from nature – from the most beautiful of her scenes; and having been treasured up in the memory, are called into these imaginary creations by some distant resemblances, which strike the eye in the multiplicity of evanid surfaces, that float before it.[3]

[1] *Observations on the Mountains and Lakes*, vol. II, addenda, p. xvi.
[2] Op. cit., pp. 4 and 96.
[3] *Observations on the Wye*, p. 45.

Gilpin describes here a much more generalized interplay between remembered landscape and present emotion than that which impels Wordsworth's poetry; but he shows, with a slightly more than conventional understanding of its closeness to personal experience, that sensibility which required a landscape setting and which knew the delights of retrospection.[1] In fact, this sort of ideal concern is not typical of the movement: or rather, an active form of reflection towards an ideal was not the aim of the Picturesque traveller or thinker – he was concerned with the immediate apprehension of an actual landscape in ideal pictorial terms: it was the activity of looking which was important. However, the pleasures of reflection obviously belonged to the Picturesque experience. A taste for Picturesque values in landscape implied a taste for polite melancholy in literature: the close Eighteenth-century connection between melancholy and memory has already been suggested; and a growing feeling for identification[2] with some known landscape by way of remembered experience was certainly encouraged by Picturesque sensibility.

That the Picturesque spirit was felt quite early by Wordsworth, even that to some extent it influenced him, is not unlikely; he must be assumed sensitive to one of the most popular ideas of the time, one which was particularly at home in his native regions. However, it also seems unlikely that before Cambridge he made any deliberate use of the idea; for, although Gilpin had formulated a kind of visual discipline, the aims of this discipline, despite its literary and emotional impulses, were entirely pictorial. Wordsworth, as well as his enthusiasm for le Brun's 'Magdalene', had a more sustained interest in painting and visual art than might be immediately suspected: though, as de Selincourt observes, he never acquired any very sound taste.[3] It is worth noticing the persistence of Wordsworth's 'connoisseurship' of landscape – greatly encouraged by Sir George Beaumont, but also very much of the age: his concern, for example, about the whitewashing of buildings,[4] the production of his Guide to the Lakes, the garden he

---

[1] The 'retrospect' – the view of a place after it had been visited – was an important feature of Gilpin's picturesque. e.g. *Obs on the Wye*, pp. 19, 68, 92.

[2] Not necessarily gloomy: Wm. Hutchinson wrote of a spot near Kendal: 'the pleasures of the scene were enhanced to me by my recollection of past felicity, which I had enjoyed from an evening ramble in these sequestered walks'. *An Excursion . . .* (1774), pp. 190–1.

[3] v. *Prel* IX, 77: and cf. note, p. 587.   [4] cf. *EL*, p. 425.

planned at Coleorton,[1] all were activities to be expected of someone with an eye for landscape at least partly Picturesque. One of Rawnsley's informants, 'one of the most well-informed of the Westmoreland builders', told him: '. . . Mr. Wordsworth was a great critic at trees. I've seen him many a time lig o' his back for long eneugh to see whether a branch or a tree sud ga or not'.[2] But the converse approach – more representative of Wordsworth's true ideal attitude to Nature, and his reluctance to criticize – can be illustrated by the reminiscence of a serving man at Rydal Mount: '. . . he wasn't a man as would give a judgment again' ony mountain. I've heard girt folks 'at come to the Mount say, "Now, Mr. Wudsworth, we want to see finest mountain in t'country," and he would say, "Every mountain is finest". Ay, that's what he would say.'[3] However much Wordsworth may have been influenced by the general landscape preoccupations of his day, he did not need any prompting in the understanding of his own countryside – it is hard to imagine him looking at his native hills with a telescope or a 'landscape mirror': however, a way of seeing so closely related to literature may be expected to have claimed his interest at some time.

It was perhaps on his Alpine tour of 1790 that he first appreciated, in the face of completely new scenes, the kind of looking, the method almost, which a concern for the Picturesque required. In a letter to Dorothy, he wrote:

I am a perfect enthusiast in my admiration of Nature in all her various forms: and I have looked upon, and as it were conversed with, the objects which this country has presented to my view so long, and with such increasing pleasure, that the idea of parting from them oppresses me with a sadness similar to that which I have always felt in quitting a beloved friend.[4]

The sadness, the 'melancholy regret', was genuine enough: Wordsworth knew the value of the impressions made upon him, and his meditation, his 'converse' with the landscape, had been to absorb its

[1] v. an article in *The Times*, August 12, 1960.
[2] 'Reminiscences of Wordsworth among the Peasantry of Westmoreland', 1882. *Transactions of the Wordsworth Society*, No. 6, p. 178: or in *Wordsworthiana* (ed. Knight) 1889, p. 102.
[3] ibid., p. 191 (*Wordsworthiana*, p. 116): and cf. *Prel* XI, 207–9.
[4] *EL*, p. 34.

forms and influence as much for future benefit as for present delight. He goes on to say:

> Ten thousand times in the course of this tour have I regretted the inability of my memory to retain a more strong impression of the beautiful forms before me; and again and again, in quitting a fortunate station, have I returned to it with the most eager avidity, in the hope of bearing away a more lively picture. At this moment, when many of these landscapes are floating before my mind, I feel a high enjoyment in reflecting that perhaps scarce a day of my life will pass in which I shall not derive some happiness from these images.

Wordsworth is here fully aware of the continuous nature of memory, of its value in creating a permanent past in time to come: he expresses much of the same feeling he was to describe in 'Tintern Abbey', of looking at a scene

> not only with the sense
> Of present pleasure, but with pleasing thoughts
> That in this moment there is life and food
> For future years.   ll. 62–5

In Switzerland, Wordsworth has consciously tried to intensify his memories; and although he made the attempt not perhaps so much in the interests of pictorial accuracy as because he recognized the emotional value of the scenes as they were being recorded, he seems to owe something to the Picturesque way of looking: he sees himself, with only very faint irony, as 'a perfect enthusiast', and the technical word 'station', by which writers about Picturesque landscape denoted a viewpoint, comes easily enough to his pen. Yet in Wordsworth these conscious attempts at a deeper pictorial impression suggest that he knew his primary feelings for landscape were always still deeper, always more diffused, and their value more permanent, than those contained in the mere bearing away of 'a more lively picture'. He knew these were scenes he was unlikely to revisit for a long time: they were also scenes which he wished Dorothy to share with him, and in telling her of them, he feared that on account of their great difference from English scenes 'it may probably never be in your power to form an idea of them': so that it was natural he should devote to them a special intensity of observation. But in the presence of nature, the pictorial qualities of a landscape were the least permanent, and Wordsworth was already perhaps aware that often the most valuable impression on his memory was that which led to his soul

> Remembering how she felt, but what she felt,
> Remembering not . . .   *Prel* II, 335–6

Though he was well able to associate particular landscapes with particular occasions, it was the 'obscure sense of possible sublimity' (ll. 336–7) which was really important, not the accurate retention of a view.

Yet that Wordsworth later considered himself to have been unnecessarily preoccupied with the pictorial and the mainly visual aspects of landscape – that he was, for a time, a devotee of the Picturesque – is clearly shown in a passage of the *Prelude* in Book XI, 'Imagination, how impaired and restored'. Speaking of a period when his growing mind was most pleased with Reason, the reason of 'logic and minute analysis' (l. 126), he regrets that this power became for a time predominant and inhibited his response to nature:

> Oh! Soul of Nature! that dost overflow
> With passion and with life, what feeble men
> Walk on this earth! how feeble have I been
> When thou wert in thy strength! Nor this through stroke
> Of human suffering, such as justifies
> Remissness and inaptitude of mind,
> But through presumption, even in pleasure pleas'd
> Unworthily, disliking here, and there,
> Liking, by rules of mimic art transferr'd
> To things above all art.   *Prēl* XI, 146–55

For Wordsworth the Eighteenth-century idea that art, though a gift of nature, could help to reveal nature, was ultimately unthinkable. Rules had no place in man's response to the natural world about him: acceptance of what was there was all that was required. Wordsworth goes on to regret that he not only found himself liking and disliking to rule, when he should have been content to find his own response self-sufficient, when, like Dorothy (l. 207) he should have 'welcom'd what was given, and craved no more', but that by further application of rule he found himself meddling with nature, giving way to that arrogance which presumed to improve on what was there, and blinding himself, as it were, to the less visible, more deeply penetrating qualities of a landscape:

> But more, for this,
> Although a strong infection of the age,
> Was never much my habit, giving way
> To a comparison of scene with scene
> Bent overmuch on superficial things,
> Pampering myself with meagre novelties
> Of colour or proportion, to the moods
> Of time or season, to the moral power
> The affections, and the spirit of the place,
> Less sensible.
>
> ll. 155–64

All this refers quite plainly to the Picturesque attitude – that connoisseurship of landscape which had certainly grown from a desire to be true to nature, and to receive her restorative gifts, but which now perhaps consulted the genius of the place with less humility and understanding than it had in the time of Pope and Kent.

This positive allegiance to the Picturesque does not in fact colour Wordsworth's poetry in any very obvious or, at least, significant way. Although the Picturesque influenced that whole literary sensibility of which *An Evening Walk* and the *Descriptive Sketches* are both evidently products, a more immediate interest lies in its effect on his way of seeing, of how it deepened his sense of landscape impressed on memory, and his sense of the value of this. *An Evening Walk* had been more or less completed by the time Wordsworth left Cambridge; it probably incorporated a large number of the better lines and the more closely observed images taken from *The Vale of Esthwaite*.[1] It is a substantial achievement, in its detailed imagery, its strong if elaborate diction; but the inlay of literary allusion imparts its character to the whole poem, and there is no essential advance in feeling from the more youthful work. Its melancholy cast seems conventional enough: it is not so surprising that the poet feels it his lot 'to rove …

> Where twilight glens endear my Esthwaite's shore,
> And memory of departed pleasures, more.   ll. 1 & 15–16

It seems a matter of purely literary sensibility that

[1] v. *PW* I, p. 319.

> While, Memory at my side, I wander here,
> Starts at the simplest sight th'unbidden tear.   ll. 43–4

Wordsworth's greatest poetry, as we know, was not written out of such excessive tearfulness: nor indeed with 'memory' at his side – that power was in him, part of him, permanent and working continuously. Yet the poem shows, and, at times, expresses the strong connection, for Wordsworth, between remembered landscape and poetry.

The *Descriptive Sketches* are more 'literary' and less successful than *An Evening Walk*: their main character is that of a sort of poetic Guide to the Alps. In his letter of dedication to the companion of his tour Wordsworth incidentally reveals the two principles, one 'literary', the other more personal, which underlie his early local poetry: he expects from Robert Jones both a conventional sort of melancholy, and something of that recollection and identification in memory between landscape and past experience which was his own mode of thought. Wordsworth is confident that his verses 'must certainly interest' Jones, 'in reminding you of moments to which you can hardly look back without a pleasure not the less dear from a shade of melancholy'; he adds, 'You will meet with few images without recollecting the spot where we observed them together; consequently, whatever is feeble in my design, or spiritless in my colouring, will be amply supplied by your own memory.'[1] In a work which almost of necessity required strong pictorial description, it is perhaps not surprising that Wordsworth should supplement his memories of the tour with descriptive information taken from various French topographers, notably Ramond, whose help he acknowledges. Wordsworth's inspiration flagged throughout the poem, and it is already evident that description by way of accurately remembered details was never his talent, or indeed his intention. Here, he almost admits that, on occasion, he is relying more on the evocative power of Jones's memory than of his own poetry. In his great poetry, it is the sense of landscape, the general effect, the spiritual contours and the play of light, which he *must* get down: in writing the *Descriptive Sketches* he seems already to have recognized this. To a passage (ll. 332–47) describing a magnificent sunset, he appended a note in which he stated:

I had once given to these sketches the title of Picturesque; but the

[1] *PW* I, p. 43.

Alps are insulted in applying to them that term. Whoever, in attempting to describe their sublime features, should confine himself to the
cold rules of painting would give his reader but a very imperfect
idea of those emotions which they have the irresistible power of
communicating to the most impassive imaginations.

Wordsworth, by this time, knew that the impression made on him by
mountain scenery was never essentially pictorial. 'Had I wished', he
says, 'to make a picture of this scene I had thrown much less light into
it. But I consulted nature and my feelings.' He declined 'any intrusion
of shade' (which would have accorded with the Picturesque recipe),
and concentrated on 'the unity of the impression'. The power of these
mountains, he says, 'that controuling influence, which distinguishes the
Alps from all other scenery, is derived from images which disdain the
pencil'. What he has applied here particularly to the Alps would, with
even less faith in Picturesque values and a further knowledge of his own
feelings, become generally true of his attitude to landscape. The 'cold
rules of painting' contributed little to his understanding of either nature
or poetry: the note implies Wordsworth's basic contempt for the
Picturesque, as well as his interest in it at the time, and a recognition of
its popularity.

We can learn, from Book VI of the *Prelude*, how Wordsworth's
memories of the Alps became both generalized and intensified: in
longer retrospect the emotional presence of the great mountains was
felt scarcely at all in pictorial terms. It was enough for him to be able to
say:

> Ye have left
> Your beauty with me, an impassion'd sight
> Of colours and of forms,   ll. 607–9

without detailing these any further. And at the time Wordsworth was
probably aware, amidst all the excitement of new scenery, that he was
not merely 'rich one moment to be poor for ever' (l. 665). The power
of his mind to retain the emotional essence of a scene was already fully
developed: the power of ideal vision seems already to have been
recognized. Wordsworth describes his reaction to his first view of
Mont Blanc: how he grieved

> To have a soulless image on the eye
> Which had usurp'd upon a living thought
> That never more could be.   ll. 454–6

(It makes an instructive contrast with a typical Picturesque approach, Gilpin's reaction to his first sight of Skiddaw:

> We had heard too much of this mountain to meet it properly: it has none of those bold projections, and shaggy majesty about it, which we expected to have seen in this king of mountains. It is a tame, inanimate, object...[1]

For Wordsworth, a living ideal had disappeared – but one, he says, for which the scene next day made 'rich amends/And reconcil'd us to realities';[2] for Gilpin, a picture had not lived up to prescribed expectations).

In Book XI of the *Prelude*, at the end of the section describing his committal to the Picturesque, Wordsworth indicates that he was not troubled in this way during his Alpine tour: he carried with him, he says (l. 242) 'the same heart' which ruled the innocence of vision he shared with Dorothy. (The syntax is slightly ambiguous here: at least it creates an ambiguity of emphasis, so that it is just possible 'the same heart' refers not to his simplicity of vision, but to his entanglement with Picturesque sophistications.) But it is, anyway, some time later that he was most intensely concerned with Picturesque values, that way of seeing which he afterwards felt as a 'degradation' (l. 243). In this period – probably, as de Selincourt places it, in 1793 – Picturesque values worked in conjunction with personal limitations to his own way of seeing: it was a time of preoccupation with immediate visual delight whose 'sensuous' quality he came to feel as a betrayal of his deepest vision.

In fact, that Wordsworth saw the Alps with a general sense of the literary Picturesque is, if only on the evidence of his letter to Dorothy, evident enough. That for some years he was familiar with Picturesque values and principles, and that he applied them, we know from the *Prelude*. But, for Wordsworth, there was another way of seeing besides the straightforward Picturesque way; besides 'sitting thus in judgment',

---

[1] *Observations on the Mountains and Lakes* (1786): vol. I, p. 174.
[2] *Prel* VI, 460–1.

there was another related but less easily explained interruption of his deeper feeling, something

> That almost seems inherent in the Creature,
> Sensuous and intellectual as he is,
> A twofold Frame of body and of mind;
> The state to which I now allude was one
> In which the eye was master of the heart,
> When that which is in every stage of life
> The most despotic of our senses gain'd
> Such strength in me as often held my mind
> In absolute dominion.   *Prel* XI, 168–76

This difficulty is much more closely related to Wordsworth's personal vision, to his own sensuous way of looking, of feeling himself in and part of a landscape, untroubled by any specifically pictorial considerations. He declined here to enter 'upon abstruser argument' which would explain how Nature unifies the senses by making them work upon each other so that no one should have uninterrupted predominance, but he adds, indeed, he insists, of this period,

> that my delights,
> Such as they were, were sought insatiably,
> Though 'twas a transport of the outward sense,
> Not of the mind, vivid but not profound:
> Yet was I often greedy in the chace,
> And roam'd from hill to hill, from rock to rock,
> Still craving combinations of new forms,
> New pleasure, wider empire for the sight,
> Proud of its own endowments, and rejoiced
> To lay the inner faculties asleep.   ll. 186–95

This period of visual pleasure, whether pictorial or sensuous, Wordsworth also described in 'Tintern Abbey'; as de Selincourt has noted,[1] it was at its most intense during the time of Wordsworth's first visit to the Wye in 1793. In this period of, for Wordsworth, general moral disturbance it is possible that in sensing that the foundations of his way of life – his memories of childhood and his feeling of past certainty – were shaken, he also sensed a desire for new, immediately apprehended

[1] *Prel*, p. 611.

memory-landscapes: partly as a distraction from guilt, remorse, political and moral doubt – more in implicit recognition of his need to assimilate imagery, to flood his memory with landscape and with 'beauteous forms',[1] for their virtue both as moral influence and as future creative impulse. Five years after, in a deepened and matured understanding of nature, Wordsworth finds it hard to recollect his past state of mind:

> I cannot paint
> What then I was. The sounding cataract
> Haunted me like a passion: the tall rock,
> The mountain, and the deep and gloomy wood,
> Their colours and their forms, were then to me
> An appetite; a feeling and a love,
> That had no need of a remoter charm,
> By thought supplied, nor any interest
> Unborrowed from the eye.   ll. 75–83

Such an attitude to nature – the pleasure in immediate seeing, while coming to it as though 'flying from something that he dreads' (i.e., says de Selincourt, 'in reaction from his moral sufferings') – represents perhaps a kind of disturbed visual equivalent to the 'coarser pleasures' and the 'glad animal movements'[2] of his boyhood. That the sensuous element in this feeling was both strong and disturbing seems evident from Wordsworth's great concern about it: whatever a Picturesque discipline of looking may have contributed to it, it had become transformed and intensified by deep emotion and violent personal need. It certainly made for a time of 'aching joys' and 'dizzy raptures',[3] and such a way of looking moved him, if, as it seemed, immediately and without moral reflection, also deeply and with lasting effect. It was a necessary stage in his development, and we can see how this exclusively visual appetite, 'greedy in the chace',[4] laid up stores of imagery, and laid out whole spiritual internal landscapes in which Wordsworth's memory could move and create.

What produced in Wordsworth his revulsion from the Picturesque was not so much its concern with pictorial values as its inherent falsity – not the technical differences between its way of seeing and his, but the difference in the relation it implied to nature: this, together with the

---

[1] 'Tintern Abbey', l. 22.   [2] ll. 73–4.
[3] 'Tintern Abbey', ll. 84–5.   [4] *Prel* XI, 190.

fact that it seems to have actively assisted his over-sensuous vision. A Picturesque landscape was always seen through an imaginary frame; its parts were compared, and perhaps censured and rearranged: the spectator was before it, rather than in it. Ideally, he saw it in two dimensions; he could scarcely see the landscape for the picture: the landscape-mirror, the 'Claude glass', tended to be more important than direct seeing. Such preoccupations would soon deaden any true feeling for the living world. But it was the whole idea of criticizing and judging this world which was so alien to Wordsworth. It found its most marked expression in Gilpin: he made the conventional admission that nature must always have the final word, but, in the interests of 'picturesque beauty', his chief concern was to criticize and to give directions on how to hide, if possible, whatever he found 'displeasing', 'disagreeable', 'disgusting'. In his anxiety for the ideal of picturesque correctness, he seems moved less by piety to nature than by something like Victorian prudery; indeed, as Hussey puts it, he makes a comical figure, 'first abasing himself before nature as the source of all beauty and emotion; then getting up and giving her a lesson in deportment'.[1] For Wordsworth, such unnatural behaviour, the search for prescribed forms and outlines, the desire to 'improve', was not only absurd but wrong. It prevented and destroyed any feeling for the deep moral influence of nature.

The emotional falsity of the Picturesque might be indicated by a reference to any of Gilpin's illustrations. As in his writing, there is no true respect for the natural contours and dispositions of landscape. The most noticeable quality of his little scenes is their emptiness: though preoccupied with composition, Gilpin can give them no form; despite his concern for outline, there is no sense of control. What is left is vague emotion, expressed in shadowy mass and luminous haze. Interest is centred on evocative, not formal, content: such unity as the illustrations have is one of purely emotional mood.

And yet, some slight resemblance might be noticed between Gilpin's lighting effects and Wordsworth's vision of 'gleams' and 'flashes' – though what in Gilpin is an arbitrary patch of illumination on a rock, or a valley, or a mountainside, is in Wordsworth a momentary glimpse of mystical insight. That Wordsworth had thought of this kind of poetic vision as having at least some connection with the painter's art

[1] *The Picturesque*, pp. 113–14.

is suggested in 'Peele Castle',[1] composed in 1805; he looks back to the time of his first visit there, in 1794, a summer of perfect calm, 'So like, so very like, was day to day!'

> Ah! THEN, if mine had been the Painter's hand,
> To express what then I saw; and add the gleam,
> The light that never was, on sea or land,
> The consecration, and the Poet's dream;
>
> I would have planted thee, thou hoary Pile
> Amid a world how different from this!
> Beside a sea that could not cease to smile;
> On tranquil land, beneath a sky of bliss.

Gilpin's was certainly 'the light that never was'; it had a kind of nostalgic visionary charm, which would appeal to poetic sensibilities, including Wordsworth's. But it is the contrast in total attitude between the industrious sketcher and the poet which is instructive. Many of Gilpin's effects derive, as does much of the Picturesque tradition, from Seventeenth-century Dutch landscape painting: it is only by way of Wordsworth that we may think back to Rembrandt. Hazlitt had understood this mode of luminous vision in Wordsworth;[2] adding, sarcastically enough, that in this connection the poet liked to compare himself with the painter. After describing Wordsworth's enthusiasm for Poussin's landscape-compositions (for their 'unity of design', their 'character of wholeness'), Hazlitt goes on to say:

> His eye also does justice to Rembrandt's fine and masterly effects. In the way in which that artist works something out of nothing, and transforms the stump of a tree, a common figure into an *ideal* object, by the gorgeous light and shade thrown upon it, he perceives an analogy to his own mode of investing the minute details[3] of nature

---

[1] *Elegiac Stanzas suggested by a picture of Peele Castle, in a storm, painted by Sir George Beaumont.*

[2] *Works*, vol. 11, p. 93.

[3] Hazlitt is thinking more, say, of the Lesser Celandine, or the Sparrow's Nest; but his insight refers equally to those larger, more mystical gleams which light up Wordsworth's inner landscapes:

> Those bright blue eggs together laid!
> On me the chance-discovered sight
> Gleamed like a vision of delight.

with an atmosphere of sentiment; and in pronouncing Rembrandt to be a man of genius, feels that he strengthens his own claim to the title.

We have been concerned with pictorial vision if only to emphasize the distinctive nature of Wordsworth's own visual experience and its incorporation in memory: we have considered the Picturesque, and its most popular exponent; and while it has been unnecessary to break a touristic 'butterfly' (v. 'The Brothers', l. 4) on a wheel of rigorous artistic criticism – William Combe deals with it all very justly in *The Tour of Dr Syntax* (1812) – it is important to understand both the powerful literary appeal of the Picturesque and the essential falsity of its vision. It is then possible to account both for its influence on Wordsworth, more or less in spite of himself, and for the reason why he revolted so strongly from it.

As a poetic way of seeing, it was attractive to Wordsworth: the emotions from which it all derived were predominantly literary ones. But its technical criticism was distasteful to him; and it is this split between literary impulse and pictorial aim which accounts for the inherently unsatisfactory nature of the Picturesque ideal. It was, indeed, a highly artificial way of looking, and had consequently little real value either to poetic vision or to painting.

It offered, to Wordsworth, nothing memorable, nothing for memory to hold. Ultimately, its forms were not merely vague, but non-existent, for they achieved neither pictorial finality nor poetic permanence. They were the antithesis of how we must imagine those most vivid but intangible forms which Wordsworth sensed; the way in which the great features of Wordsworth's landscape presented themselves to the Picturesque eye was the antithesis of how, for him, they worked in memory: these, half natural shapes, half spiritual presences, were actually and totally experienced, and then sensuously, continuously remembered.

> Above, before, behind,
> Around me, all was peace and solitude,
> I look'd not round, nor did the solitude

This experience is a microcosm of such a one of which he can say
Gleams of light flash upon me from the east . . .

Speak to my eye; but it was heard and felt.
O happy state! what beauteous pictures now
Rose in harmonious imagery – they rose
As from some distant region of my soul
And came along like dreams; yet such as left
Obscurely mingled with their passing forms
A consciousness of animal delight,
A self-possession felt in every pause
And every gentle movement of my frame.
                                   Prel IV, 388–99

For Wordsworth, the deepest experience of nature, of landscape, was always unified – the experience was a sensuous and a spiritual totality, of past forms remembered, working with present forms, these not so much seen as 'heard and felt'. The forms, the 'beauteous pictures' of Wordsworth's inward landscape, did not, to begin with, conform to any ideal, pictorial or otherwise: they were given by nature, and by Wordsworth taken up, with a belief in their continued influence towards an inner visionary ideal: that vision which came in gleams and flashes, within the 'self-possession' of physical being.

Fundamentally, then, the Picturesque view of landscape was pictorial and emotionally literary, while Wordsworth's view was immediate, visual, and sensuous. That is to say, Wordsworth is always much more aware of the *presence* of landscape, of its surrounding influence, than of any pictorial qualities it might have. His sense of being not merely related to it, but of being *in* it, part of it, precludes any very objective view. Besides, the fundamental landscape of his best poetry is not at all detailed: the unifying force of nature is what creates it and holds it together, and this force is conveyed by Wordsworth's emotion rather than by his observation. He responds to a landscape rather than observes it: he feels it, almost, rather than sees it: the eye, for Wordsworth, was a sensuous medium, predominant, but actively part of his whole presence in the landscape, not a mere ocular instrument for observing data to be correlated with literary emotions.

Despite his repudiation of all Picturesque ideas, and his more personal feeling of release after having been for a time enslaved to pure seeing, the idea of visual discipline was nonetheless of great importance to Wordsworth. In his account, in *The Ruined Cottage*, of the Pedlar's

69

early years (which it seems fair to represent at at least one aspect of Wordsworth's) he describes how

> While yet a child, and long before his time
> He had perceived the presence and the power
> Of greatness, and deep feelings had impressed
> Great objects on his mind, with portraiture
> And colour so distinct [that on his mind]
> They lay like substances, and almost seemed
> To haunt the bodily sense.[1]

This sums up one aspect of that distinctively Wordsworthian way of seeing, the sensuous and total apprehension of nature, visual, but not purely ocular, in which the impressions of sight predominate but become immediately transmitted to the other senses, become transfused through the whole body. Wordsworth at this time was specially interested in the way the various senses conveyed an understanding of nature to the mind: the feeling of unity with nature came most evidently through the sense of sight, though it did not owe its existence to it. There is a fragment connected with the *Prelude* in which he considers this problem:

> There is creation in the eye,
> Nor less in all the other senses; powers
> They are that colour, model, and combine
> The things perceived with such an absolute
> Essential energy that we may say
> That those most godlike faculties of ours
> At one and the same moment are the mind
> And the mind's minister.[2]

Wordsworth goes on to consider how often

> Have we to Nature and her impulses
> Of our whole being made free gift . . .

This sensuous abandon he speaks of as a 'trance': 'the impressions which it left behind' may then be considered, and something of our nature learned. He goes on to emphasize that those first hours of reflection did not destroy

[1] ll. 79–85 (*Excursion* I, 134–9).   [2] *PW* 5, p. 343.

The original impression of delight,
But by such retrospect it was recalled
To yet a second and a second life,
While in this excitation of the mind'
A vivid pulse of sentiment and thought
Beat palpably within us, and all shades
Of consciousness were ours.

This is a clear recognition of the continuous and cumulative power of memory. For the moment, the points to be noticed are the primacy of the eye, or rather, the implication that the eye is the sense of greatest immediacy, and the subsequent diffusion, through memory, of a kind of unified sensuousness.

Of the physical or 'sensuous' nature of Wordsworth's memory, there will be more to say in our next section. Here we must notice this quality of diffused but unified sensuousness in the Pedlar (how great objects lay on his mind 'like substances, and almost seemed/To haunt the bodily sense'), and how Wordsworth goes on to say of him:

He had received
A precious gift, for as he grew in years
With these impressions would he still compare
All his ideal stores, his shapes and forms,
And being still unsatisfied with aught
Of dimmer character, he thence attained
An *active* power to fasten images
Upon his brain, and on their pictured lines
Intensely brooded, even till they acquired
The liveliness of dreams.[1]

We must emphasize here that Wordsworth derives a conscious method of visualization from the comparison of ideal forms with remembered impressions. It is, of course, ultimately an ideal visualization, but it works, and is formed, in the closest conjunction with actual impressions from nature. Wordsworth does not concern himself with the Eighteenth century problem of how ideas were formed other than through the sense of sight: the important elements here are sight and memory, and the implication of these lines is that through the interplay of the

[1] *Ruined Cottage*, ll. 85–94: (*Excursion* I, 139–48).

continuously accumulating visual impressions on the mind, the actual and the ideal become more and more integrated, and that the ideal forms grow as a result of this continuous influx on earlier impressions held in memory. It is an '*active*' power (the stress is Wordsworth's) of fastening images on the mind, and this implies continuous observation and conscious memory. The 'ideal stores', in fact, become progressively more lively insofar as by comparison, and integration, with actual 'shapes and forms' the 'pictured lines' become more deeply permanent.

Wordsworth, then, looked closely at nature and consciously bore away his observations in memory, though his aims were not primarily mnemonic. He had in fact to preserve a continuous interplay, a constant balance, between the ideal and the actual: anything which was of 'dimmer character' – allowance must be made for the slight imprecision inherent in the Wordsworthian comparative – seems to have been any impression which did not partake of both ideal and actual together.

The act of seeing must always have had a distinct poetic significance for Wordsworth: sight, always 'the most despotic of our senses',[1] was for Wordsworth a gateway into the world of nature which threatened, by its immediacy, to overwhelm reflection and poetry; but its early and conscious association with landscape, and with memory, brought him a full awareness both of its powers and of its limitations, and turned what seemed to be merely ways of looking into poetic discipline.

In conclusion, two factors should be mentioned which help to account indirectly for Wordsworth's concern with visual matters: the emphasis, throughout the Eighteenth century, placed on the sense of sight in literary and aesthetic psychology; and, a parallel development, an interest in descriptive poetry of all kinds. About the importance of seeing, Addison expressed what was to remain popular aesthetic opinion: 'We cannot indeed have a single Image in the Fancy that did not make its first entrance through the Sight; but', he goes on, 'we have the power of retaining, altering and compounding those Images, which we have once received, into all the Varieties of Picture and Vision that are most agreeable to the Imagination . . .'[2] Here he has indicated how this elementary use of memory leads to delights predominantly descriptive: and as these delights became in literature gradually personal and more pictorial, the emphasis on actually seeing,

[1] *Prel* XI, 174.
[2] *On the Pleasures of the Imagination*: *Spectator* 411, June 21, 1712.

on looking, mainly at landscape, in terms of pictures, is understandable. (Perhaps Burke's more generalized emphasis on the immediate impact of beauty, by way of the senses, and not by thought, has the most direct aesthetic relevance to Wordsworth's mode of seeing.)

At the end of the century descriptive poetry received a very extreme justification from Erasmus Darwin. Wordsworth and Darwin were, for a short time, admirers of each other's work: Wordsworth would scarcely have agreed with much of the brief critical interludes in the fourth edition of *The Botanic Garden* (London, 1799): in a comparison between prose and poetry, Darwin wrote: '. . . as our ideas derived from visible objects are more distinct than those derived from the objects of our other senses, the words expressive of these ideas belonging to vision make up the principal part of poetic language. That is, the Poet writes principally to the eye, the Prose-writer uses more abstracted terms.'[1] Darwin went on to quote a line from Pope, 'And Kennet swift for silver Eels renown'd', which he thought could be improved by re-writing it 'And Kennet swift, where silver Graylings play'; then, he suggested, 'it becomes poetry, because the scenery is then brought before the eye'. To this sort of foolery Wordsworth was temperamentally opposed: his chief poetic aim was not to evoke scenery but to re-create emotion within himself. He later referred to Darwin as 'an eye voluptuary';[2] any excessive concern with mere seeing, let alone with mere picture-painting, was for Wordsworth a distinct hindrance to true poetry. However, it is not surprising that in his formative years he should have felt impelled to write 'descriptive' poetry and to express his sensuous nature in an active and deliberately intensified way of seeing.

In tracing the effect on Wordsworth's memory of his ways of looking at landscape we have seen how he recognised the immediate power of the eye, and how disturbed he was by its sensuous predominance. For a time he owed so much of his direct pleasure in nature to the plain fact of seeing that he seemed to have been diverted from all reflection, all responsiveness to nature's moral influence: yet, despite his pre-occupation, he was storing up imagery and emotions for future benefit. In 'Tintern Abbey' he described the change in his way of looking which had taken place between his first visit and that on the occasion of the poem, five years later: and he described how 'the beauteous

[1] Part II, *The Loves of the Plants*: p. 63.　　　　[2] v. Legouis, p. 137.

forms' of the landscape had worked in his memory, so that he felt not only 'sensations sweet' and 'tranquil restoration', but also that 'serene and blessed mood' in which the mysterious nature of the world seems about to be explained,

> Until, the breath of this corporeal frame
> And even the motion of our human blood
> Almost suspended, we are laid asleep
> In body, and become a living soul:
> While with an eye made quiet by the power
> Of harmony, and the deep power of joy,
> We see into the life of things.   ll. 43–9

This was the reward of diligent looking, of observation which had been assimilated, reflected upon, and allowed to mature in memory: to see 'into the life of things' was the vision only of an 'eye made quiet'. It was a vision which grew continuously from the remembered forms of an actual landscape transmuted by reflection to ideal forms: it was the true vision of both inward and outward understanding.

It was by way of memory, by way of conscious reflection on remembered scenes, that Wordsworth tamed his over-dominant sense of sight, the eye that had been 'master of the heart'.[1] The eye, though perhaps growing in sensuous power, became gradually subordinated to inward seeing.

In the first of the Matthew poems, 'Expostulation and Reply' (1798), Wordsworth's answer begins:

> The eye – it cannot choose but see;
> We cannot bid the ear be still:
> Our bodies feel, where'er they be,
> Against or with our will.
>
> Nor less I deem that there are Powers
> Which of themselves our minds impress;
> That we can feed this mind of ours
> In a wise passiveness . . .   ll. 17–24

Wordsworth was becoming increasingly conscious that his true understanding of nature was by way of remembered impressions. An im-

[1] *Prel* XI, 172.

mediate delight in nature was not enough; only time would reveal which moments of delight were of more lasting significance than the others. He now recognized, what had been true all his life, how

> the visible scene
> Would enter unawares into his mind
> With all its solemn imagery . . .[1]

Therefore the important attitude was one of 'wise passiveness'; it was a development of that same 'active'[2] power which fastened images on the mind: but it was now active in a slightly paradoxical way – trained further, and now calm, more disciplined. His vision of landscape had become less immediately sensuous: it may not be entirely fanciful to suggest that a trace of Picturesque discipline had remained, had helped to control the wilful eye, if only by making it aware of its powers – though here a mode of conscious seeing went not to the inventing of pictures but to the forming of a poetic vision of nature and a deeper understanding of its moral influence.

In a stanza of 'A Poet's Epitaph' Wordsworth writes, of the poet,

> In common things that round us lie
> Some random truths he can impart, –
> The harvest of a quiet eye
> That broods and sleeps on his own heart.   ll. 49–52

Wordsworth's way of looking had progressed steadily towards this ideal of 'The harvest of a quiet eye'. Seeing was turned to contemplation; the eye was made quiet, it became an 'inward eye',[3] an eye of reflective and restorative memory. The sensuous eye remained; but Wordsworth was no longer 'greedy in the chace';[4] he could, whenever possible, give himself over to a 'wise passiveness'.[5]

The relationship between this 'quiet' eye, and a continuing sensuous apprehension of experience, together with a correspondingly sensuous recreation of it by way of memory (mainly in the actual writing of the *Prelude*), is the subject of our next chapter.

---

[1] *Prel* V, 409–11: the passage in which this occurs – 'There was a Boy' – was written in 1798; v. *Prel*, pp. 546–7.

[2] *Ruined Cottage*, l. 91: and v. supra.

[3] 'I wandered lonely . . . ', l. 21.

[4] *Prel* XI, 190.   [5] 'Expostulation and Reply', l. 24.

CHAPTER 2

Self, Memory, and Sensuous Continuity

WE CAN now go on to examine Wordsworth's growing awareness of memory as a mode of experience, and his mature understanding of its importance to his poetry. We shall try to distinguish some of the various qualities memory had for Wordsworth, in particular its unifying quality in relation to the senses, and its relation to his feeling for time. In the previous chapter we noticed how an immediate visual delight in landscape gradually became integrated with the restorative power of memory, how the sensuous eye was made 'quiet' and became an instrument of remembered event and reflective wisdom: here we shall notice Wordsworth (mainly in the initial course of the *Prelude* – that is, up to 1805) not only, by way of memory, arriving at a unified view of the senses, but also, in consequence, achieving a more unified view of self within time present and past.

To approach it from a slightly different angle: the workings of memory seem, in Wordsworth, to be closely bound up with the senses – with the visual sense, and perhaps most completely with what he sometimes called 'the bodily sense'.[1] It is this kind of total sensuousness, partly an amalgam of all the senses, but further involving the sense of 'being', of existing physically in time, which will help us to understand Wordsworth's sense of the past: it is, paradoxically enough, through this physical sense that the underlying moral use of all Wordsworth's poetry and remembering can be demonstrated.

Wordsworth knew how

> Our bodies feel, where'er they be,
> Against or with our will:[2]

[1] v. *Excursion* I, 139: *Recluse*, l. 50: *Prel* (1850) XIV, 88.
[2] 'Expostulation and Reply', ll. 19–20.

and he knew, what he described also in 'Tintern Abbey', how a landscape became

> As beautiful to thought, as it had been,
> When present, to the bodily sense . . .[1]

The continuity between a 'bodily' experience, an experience at once physical and emotional, and its subsequent experience in memory, remained a matter both sensuous and ideal.

In a long, notebook passage[2] (connected with Book VIII of the *Prelude*, though never in fact used) Wordsworth describes how an early love of nature leads to a love of mankind. He traces the growth of perception and delight from infancy onwards: after showing how the child satisfies his sense of wonder in the worlds both of reality and romance, he tells how the man, the growing man, that is, who has remained true to the promptings of nature, is able, 'as his powers advance', to look at the natural world not only with knowledge, but, more importantly, with understanding – how he looks at the stars, and

> Without the glass of Galileo sees
> What Galileo saw; and as it were
> Resolving into one great faculty
> Of being bodily eye and spiritual need,
> The converse which he holds is limitless;
> Not only with the firmament of thought,
> But nearer home he looks with the same eye
> Through the entire abyss of things. And now

(Wordsworth continues, having suggested the initial, but by no means absolute, primacy of the eye in the forming of the mind)

> The first and earliest motions of his life,
> I mean of his rememberable time,
> Redound upon him with a stronger flood . . .
>
> ll. 151–61

The state achieved by the resolution of 'bodily eye and spiritual need', this 'one great faculty of being', is that towards which Wordsworth himself, as we noticed in our last chapter, had been tending: physical seeing and inward vision work unanimously. The most striking point

---

[1] *Recluse*, ll. 48–50.   [2] v. *Prel.* pp. 569f.

in the passage is how this state is explicitly connected with memory.

The earliest 'rememberable' motions of the man's life come flooding back to him with renewed force; and these memories return in conjunction with that unity of 'bodily' and 'spiritual' which has just been achieved. The spiritual power of memory is increased by this unity. Conversely, that Wordsworth considered this unity to be, at least in part, a direct result of the force of memory, is clear from what he goes on to say. (The whole fragment, as de Selincourt points out, 'exhibits the loose and uneven texture of a rough draft', so that strictly ordered argument is not to be looked for; but it is anyway a mistake to enquire too minutely after cause and effect in Wordsworth: synthesis, unity of feeling, are what he continually strives to express. In the relationship which we are to examine between the workings of memory and of the senses, their effect on each other must be taken as simultaneous. Wordsworth's more conscious awareness of one or the other is what we must try to distinguish.) Unity of self in time by way of memory – a state of which Wordsworth becomes increasingly aware – is implied in the present passage. Now that these 'earliest motions of his life' are returning to the man,

> In speculation he is like a Child,
> With this advantage, that he now can rest
> Upon himself; authority is none
> To cheat him of his boldness, or hoodwink
> His intuitions, or to lay asleep
> The unquiet stir of his perplexities . . .   ll. 162–7

The growing mind has become conscious of its sources; the man can now 'rest upon himself', that is, upon his memories of childhood now flooding back, bringing with them all that experience and knowledge accumulated, almost unknowingly, in the past. Memory at once provides the sole authority for self-knowledge and further awakens the sense of unity in outward looking and inward vision – that sense which makes complete understanding possible. At this stage of man's development – Wordsworth calls it 'this season of his second birth',[1] no less – the power of memory (and the feeling of its growing presence) enables him to speculate about his aims and origins, not only with a child's freshness of vision, but with a new inner confidence.

[1] l. 168.

The sensuous manner in which, for a time, Wordsworth responded to the visible world caused him, as we have noticed, some disturbance. But he had sufficient faith in the ultimately restorative power of images impressed on his sight, and therefore on his memory, to weather this apparent distraction; and of course his awareness of all the senses, and his interest in their unity of working, remained: the eye 'made quiet'[1] was achieved by its own co-operation with the poet's other feelings. Perhaps the really troubling thing about the predominance of the eye had been not only its sensuous nature but also its immediacy of effect – with so strong and immediate delight in looking, there had been no time for 'passiveness', for calm reflection and the influence of memory. As the senses became more controlled, and unified, a 'wise passiveness'[2] increased; with it there came more room, and more time, for the influence, the restorative workings of memory; and consequently, there came a greater awareness of time itself – of time passing, of the distance, in memory, between time past and the present time of reflection. Towards this awareness, all the senses contributed.

An awareness of memory, and a deep submission to its power, does not straightaway imply a deeply sensuous mode of experience. Yet if, say, we consider the sensuous nature of memory in Proust, he will be seen to be an exemplar of its mode of action, not an exception to it. In attempting to recall the past by, as he put it, plunging into himself,[3] he seemed to become a literal embodiment of Time. Wordsworth's egocentric interest in himself, and his confidence that he was a fit subject for poetry, grew out of a strong physical self-awareness and led equally to a further, more intellectual, awareness of present being and of past experience. In Wordsworth's poetry lies one of the deepest expressions of this kind of Romantic awareness – an awareness which is still developing; as Hazlitt, in a philosophical context, perceived it: 'Every sensation that I feel, or that afterwards recurs vividly to my memory strengthens the sense of self . . .'[4]. What seems clear enough today, the importance of the personal past, is a key to the understanding of Wordsworth's poetry: in the subjective life of this past, the senses are permanently involved. For Wordsworth, in his poetry, as for any-

---

[1] 'Tintern Abbey', l. 47.

[2] 'Expostulation and Reply', l. 24.

[3] '. . . c'est en moi-même que j'étais obligé de redescendre.' *A la Recherche du Temps Perdu* (Gallimard), 1954, III, p. 1046.

[4] *Principles of Human Action: Works*, vol. I, p. 42.

one given over to the power of memory, a sense of physical continuity is created: the feeling of a sort of bodily presence in time is achieved. Memory has an all-pervading quality which cannot help being sensuous – it pervades the five senses, blending inner and outer; it pervades the sense of time, blending past and present; it unites the physical sense to the sense of temporal flux.

What we suggest, then, is that memory was, for Wordsworth, a sensuous mode of experience – first made apparent to him through the sense of sight, becoming more calm and diffused through a general sense of being, and so becoming concerned with the whole self in relation to time. In illustrating how the 'bodily eye',[1] and its effect in memory, becomes diffused in the whole 'bodily sense', we may seem to overstate the idea of sensuousness – at least, the word 'sensuous'[2] may seem to become a little repetitive; but this is more a limitation of vocabulary than a difficulty of precise meaning. Wordsworth insists on the importance of the senses: and he makes no qualification about how much he owed to them in his response to nature. At the same time he had to avoid implying indulgence, or any excess of mere physical pleasure; a tension between spiritual explanation and sensuous feeling is often noticeable in Wordsworth's writing, more particularly in accounts of his experience of nature. In fact, the senses are, in Wordsworth's poetry, obviously present, and need no emphasizing; but the complexity of their relation to memory must here be demonstrated – how they further his awareness of it, and how, at the same time, memory unifies the senses; how its power continues to be felt sensuously, and how, later, its main concern becomes more purely temporal.

In trying to understand the conflict in Wordsworth between sensu-

---

[1] *Prel*, p. 575: v. supra.

[2] 'Apparently invented by Milton, to avoid certain associations of the existing word *sensual*, and from him adopted by Coleridge; evidence of its use in the intervening period is wanting . . . ' *O.E.D.* (v. quotation of 1814; also absolute use 1809–10). Cf. also *Biographia Literaria*, ch. x; ' . . . to express in one word, all that appertains to the perception considered as passive, and merely recipient, I have adopted from our elder classics the word *sensuous* . . . ' Wordsworth himself uses the word rarely – twice in the 1805 *Prelude*; once however to make an important distinction, where he speaks of man, 'the Creature,/Sensuous and intellectual as he is,/A twofold Frame of body and of mind;' (XI, 168–70). Wordsworth either took the word from Coleridge, or perhaps, considering its Miltonic origin, and his use of it earlier than the first attributed to Coleridge, gave it to him: anyway, quite apart from it subsequent fairly general usage, it is clearly the appropriate word to use in this discussion.

ous feeling and ideal thought, there is a distinction, made by Schiller, which states very clearly both Wordsworth's struggle and his consistent aim: Schiller's concept of nature and of childhood is, in its moral seriousness, in its ideal basis together with its active acceptance of human life, 'as it is', in many ways equivalent to Wordsworth's.

While we were still only children of nature we were happy, we were perfect: we have become free, and we have lost both advantages. Hence a twofold and very unequal longing for nature: the longing for happiness and the longing for the perfection that prevails there. Man, as a sensuous being (der sinnliche Mensch), deplores sensibly the loss of the former of these goods; it is only the moral man (der moralische) who can be afflicted at the loss of the other.[1]

Wordsworth's regret for childhood, his longing for nature, for a world of innocence and harmony, has always this moral sense of loss: and it is this which gives meaning, and poetic power, to his strong physical self-awareness. For Wordsworth, Nature is an idea, continuously embodied and recalled both in his native landscape and his own continuing and feeling self – a state of perfection, once dimly experienced, remembered yet inaccessible: and because it is partly a physical sense, the loss seems the more absolute. Memory recalls the idea, but cannot actively be perfection: the moral man is also continuously alive in body. Nature's perfection, a thing of the past, lies in memory; nature herself, her imperfections seen through our own imperfections, lies about us all the time. This is one reason for the importance of the past, of remembering, to Wordsworth: it is the sensuous element in memory which recalls and preserves such fragments as self-consciousness may of the ideal, the moral perfection.

'The feeling we experience for nature resembles that of a sick man for health.' 'Unser Gefühl für Natur gleicht der Empfindung des Kranken für die Gesundheit.'[2]

The conflict, in Wordsworth, between 'der sinnliche Mensch' and 'der moralische' is resolved, the two parts are unified, in the writing of

[1]*On Simple and Sentimental Poetry*; in *Essays Aesthetical and Philosophical*, London, 1875; p. 276: and v. *Über naive und sentimentalische Dichtung*, ed. W. F. Mainland, Oxford, 1951; p. 14.
[2] op. cit., pp. 280: 17.

poetry, and, perhaps most completely, in the workings of memory. One of the lessons Wordsworth learned from the workings of nature in memory, one which he described perhaps most fully in 'Tintern Abbey', was that of being able

> to recognise
> In nature and the language of the sense
> The anchor of my purest thoughts, the nurse,
> The guide, the guardian of my heart, and soul
> Of all my moral being.   ll. 107–11

The word 'sense', in the comprehensive meaning with which it is used here, implies that unity of feeling towards which he continually struggled: it is one of the most interesting members of that specifically Wordsworthian vocabulary connected with this problem: its complexity and significance has been noticed by Mr. Empson.[1] Here it is enough to insist that it is used in a special way by Wordsworth to suggest a kind of synthesis of the five senses – chiefly, of course (for poetry), the eye, the ear, and, much more enigmatically, the sense of touch. This last is what Wordsworth seems to mean by the 'bodily sense' – a sort of interfused touch, a complete physical self-awareness, a sense of great power and one closely related to that feeling of bodily continuity in time which belongs to the power of memory. In a passage dating from 1798–9[2] he describes this sensuous awareness very accurately – or rather, gives an evocative account of what it meant to him; he is in fact describing a 'Picture of a Child employed in a Cottonmill', one of those who have been defeated by society, deprived of nature, one in whom

> this organic frame,
> So joyful in its motions, is become
> Dull, to the joy of her own motions dead;
> And even the touch, so exquisitely poured
> Through the whole body, with a languid will
> Performs its functions; rarely competent
> To impress a vivid feeling on the mind
> Of what there is delightful in the breeze,

---

[1] *The Structure of Complex Words*, Ch. 14.
[2] *Excursion* VIII, 315–32: and v. *PW* 5, p. 468.

> The gentle visitations of the sun,
> Or lapse of liquid element – by hand,
> Or foot, or lip, in summer's warmth – perceived.
>
> ll. 322–32

Wordsworth recognizes the power of the touch, poured as it is 'through the whole body', to apprehend both the immediately physical and the permanent impact of a delight in nature: what the body registers is also impressed as 'a vivid feeling on the mind'. Wordsworth had faith in his senses, not least in this diffused sense of touch – knowing its extreme 'bodily' nature, but perhaps recognizing that for this reason it was most comprehensively related to his spiritual sense of being, of existence. He knew that his responses to nature were initiated, to a high degree, sensuously, and that they continued to be felt so in the mind. He came to know how memory would maintain and diffuse these feelings – maintain them in time, and diffuse them in his own both physical and temporal being.

We have noticed Wordsworth, in his account of the Pedlar, stating that 'deep feelings had impressed/Great objects on his mind',[1] and going on to describe how

> They lay like substances, and almost seemed
> To haunt the bodily sense.

The physical nature of this inner feeling of the mind is immediately apparent: and there is a noticeable ambiguity of literal and figurative meaning in the word 'impressed' – both here and elsewhere in his poetry: Wordsworth's vocabulary often suggests the complete and physical way in which he experienced and remembered things. The power of this 'bodily sense' both to apprehend and to continue experience leads to a growing awareness of the power of memory, this power which, in its turn, creates a unity of 'sense' and spiritual self.

A passage from Book I of the *Prelude* (related in argument to the section just considered from *The Ruined Cottage*) provides a good indication of how this 'bodily sense' works, and of the way in which sensuous experience retained in memory achieves value through the course of time. After describing some instances of his childhood delight in

[1] *Ruined Cottage*, ll. 81–2.

nature, 'those fits of vulgar joy', Wordsworth tells how, even then, 'Nature spoke to me/Rememberable things': and although, as he remarks, these may sometimes have been the result of mere chance, yet they were not vain

> Nor profitless, if haply they impress'd
> Collateral objects and appearances,
> Albeit lifeless then, and doom'd to sleep
> Until maturer seasons call'd them forth
> To impregnate and to elevate the mind.   ll. 619–24

The absolute use of 'impress'd' perhaps indicates some of the force with which Wordsworth experienced these 'rememberable things': he goes on to say

> – And if the vulgar joy by its own weight
> Wearied itself out of the memory,
> The scenes which were a witness of that joy
> Remained, in their substantial lineaments
> Depicted on the brain, and to the eye[1]
> Were visible, a daily sight.

The physical sense of the joy, its 'weight', is explicit: allied to the 'glad animal movements'[2] of his childhood, it played its part in the shaping, both sensuous and intellectual, of memory; and the more permanent register is, by implication, no less physical – instilled, depicted, as it was, in 'substantial lineaments', by 'repeated happiness' or by 'the impressive discipline of fear'. The whole passage (ll. 609–40) is a clear statement of Wordsworth's belief that only through a presence continued by way of memory can landscape forms and scenes have any value.

We have already quoted (in dealing with the predominance of 'the eye') one of Wordsworth's most explicit statements[3] about the cumulative and sensuous value of memory; it must be recalled at this point if only to emphasize the connection, for Wordsworth at the beginning of his poetic maturity, between the workings of memory and of the senses. 'There is creation in the eye,/Nor less', he adds, 'in all the other

---

[1] This is presumably the physical, seeing eye: his native mountains were (if the rain held off) 'a daily sight' – but there is a latent suggestion of the inward eye working at the same time.
[2] 'Tintern Abbey', l. 74.   [3] v. *PW* 5, p. 343, vi.

senses.' These faculties ('most godlike' he calls them; and in another related fragment he refers to 'the godlike senses') work plastically and dynamically, they 'colour, model, and combine the things perceived', they work with 'such an absolute essential energy' that they seem 'at one and the same moment' to be 'the mind and the mind's minister'. It is within such a unity of creation and perception that the senses work together with memory. We must understand here an awareness of the power of memory (an awareness as it was described in the Pedlar), of how its more immediately sensuous apprehensions evoke in their turn earlier, more ideal, memories. Wordsworth's almost voluptuous delight in the natural world induced a receptiveness which could scarcely help furthering this power of memory.

> In many a walk
> At evening or by moonlight, or reclined
> At midday upon beds of forest moss,
> Have we to Nature and her impulses
> Of our whole being made free gift, and when
> Our trance had left us, oft have we, by aid
> Of the impressions which it left behind
> Looked inward on ourselves, and learned, perhaps,
> Something of what we are.   ll. 8–16

Nor, he goes on to say, is 'the original impression of delight' destroyed by this consciously induced remembering: on the contrary,

> by such retrospect it was recalled
> To yet a second and a second life,
> While in this excitation of the mind
> A vivid pulse of sentiment and thought
> Beat palpably within us, and all shades
> Of consciousness were ours.

The sensuous, no less than the unified, nature of such memory is obvious. Such thinking, conceived of as a vivid pulse, beating palpably, must include, among 'all shades of consciousness', a strong feeling of bodily participation. And if this passage may refer more to immediate or recent memory, deliberately evoked, we know from 'Tintern Abbey' that such memories persist, emotions and 'beauteous forms' working in close conjunction with the bodily sense; imparting not only 'sensations sweet,/Felt in the blood, and felt along the heart', but working, more spiritually, in the opposite direction:

> Until, the breath of this corporeal frame
> And even the motion of our human blood
> Almost suspended, we are laid asleep
> In body, and become a living soul.

This state of 'harmony', by which, as we noticed, the eye is 'made quiet', is a spiritual one – yet one in which the poet remains a *living* soul: it is achieved by way of that bodily continuity implicit in the workings of memory. In whichever way its purpose tends, memory remains a sensuous medium.

Another example of the idea of sensuous memory, of how Wordsworth makes it apparent that he feels the continued presence of forms, of landscape impressions, as something physical, occurs in *The Ruined Cottage*: in the course of a long description of the Pedlar's spiritual development (similar in drift to the ms. connected with Book VIII of the *Prelude*) there comes a stage when

> before his twentieth year was pass'd
> Accumulated feelings press'd his heart
> With an encreasing weight; he was o'er power'd
> By Nature, and his mind became disturbed.   ll. 221–4

These 'accumulated feelings', heavy, pressing, and disturbing, are, as Wordsworth makes clear, the product of a memory stored with forms, no less than with the ideas and speculations to which these forms give rise. Like the 'huge Cliff' which rose up and strode after him when he had taken the shepherd's boat (*Prel* I), the more impressive forms of his native landscape must be thought of as continually looming in his mind: it was through such scenes that his brain, as he said (ll. 419–20), 'Work'd with a dim and undetermin'd sense/Of unknown modes of being'; and it was through such scenes that memory was revealed to him as one of his deepest modes of experience. We shall consider more fully in a later section how landscape is transmuted by memory to Form: here we must notice that any natural object once 'impressed' in memory remained there, for Wordsworth, as a presence – it continued to exist both as idea and as thing. Remembered landscape no less than remem-

bered event contributed to revived emotion. The visible world, taken
up into the mind, retained, in the mind, its physical essence.

Such a mode of sensuous apprehension, though directed more and
more resolutely towards intellectual, not to say spiritual, ends, continued throughout the writing of Wordsworth's greatest poetry. Or,
to put it another way, there is, in his poetry, no real distinction to be
made between a memory of sensuous experience, and sensuously
experienced memory, between say, Wordsworth's particular account
of stealing the boat (an incident deeply impressed), and his more generalized accounts of, and meditations on, his childhood (remembering its
'glad animal movements'). In the writing of the *Prelude*, memory
becomes, as we have suggested, both mode and subject matter. The
poetry must be read as a material embodiment of Wordsworth's past,
no less than as a spiritual reincarnation of its meaning: it must be read,
that is, in support of his own desire to give 'as far as words can give/A
substance and a life to what I feel'.[1] That 'plastic power', the 'forming
hand',[2] which Wordsworth, writing of his school-time, describes as
helping the development of his 'first creative sensibility', remained to
impart a feeling of vigorous life to the story of the *Prelude*, to the
growth, that is, of its author's mind. Wordsworth's childhood was
essentially a time of 'glad animal movements': and a delight in physical
action remained with him throughout most of his life.[3] To his greatest
poetry, the activity of remembering imparts a feeling of sensuousness –
to what, as it were, it half-recalls and half-creates.

In writing of his childhood, then, Wordsworth evokes, as well as
elucidates, the sensuous way in which the natural world is experienced;
and the lessons he learned thus – immediately, at that time – he remembered as one of the many joys of his youth:

> what happiness to live
> When every hour brings palpable access
> Of knowledge.   *Prel* II, 304–6

[1] *Prel* XI, 340–1.   [2] *Prel* II, 381–2.

[3] cf. *Recluse*, ll. 703f., where Wordsworth describes the 'wild appetites and
blind desires' of his childhood, and how even now he cannot read of mortal
battle without being pleased 'more than a wise man ought to be' (l. 724):
however, Nature, he goes on to say, has 'tamed' him – physical ambition has
been turned to intellectual struggle, to poetry.

This sensation of knowledge, 'palpably', almost, as it seems, physically acquired, obviously grew from a delight in the visible world; and Nature not only induced such 'gentle agitations of the mind' (l. 317) but also employed 'severer interventions, ministry/More palpable'.[1] According to Hazlitt, describing his 'First Acquaintance with Poets', Coleridge had remarked of Wordsworth 'that there was a something corporeal, a *matter-of-fact-ness*, a clinging to the palpable, or often to the petty, in his poetry': he had gone on to limit this remark to Wordsworth's descriptive pieces, saying, very justly, 'that his philosophic poetry had a grand and comprehensive spirit in it, so that his soul seemed to inhabit the universe like a palace, and to discover truth by intuition, rather than by deduction'.[2] Yet Coleridge's insight into the 'something corporeal', the 'clinging to the palpable', in Wordsworth's poetry lights upon a condition which permeates all his finest work, and which might be described as a feeling for a corporeal self diffused in nature and in time, in the memory of childhood, and in the act of writing. Wordsworth discovers truth (where no external authority can 'hoodwink his intuitions')[3] because he is able to 'rest upon himself', that is, upon a sensuously experienced self where the union of 'bodily eye and spiritual need' works in conjunction with memory.

Wordsworth, in fact, might have agreed with what Hazlitt remarks in his preceding paragraph: 'In the outset of our life ... our imagination has a body to it.' The sense of self, and the visible world, are felt equally strongly. In connection with these feelings we should recall Wordsworth's account, which he repeated more than once,[4] of how, as a schoolboy, he used to grasp at a wall or a tree. The reason for this was, he said, that he was 'often unable to think of external things as having external existence, and', he added, 'I communed with all that I saw as something not apart from, but inherent in, my own immaterial nature'. This seems to be the direct antithesis of a strong experience of the visible world. It was a feeling which, for Wordsworth, was closely related to his childhood idea of immortality, and we must respect his statement that this idea came from 'a sense of the indomitableness of the spirit' within him rather than from feelings of 'animal vivacity'. Yet he had known, as here he recalled to Miss Fenwick, the true condition of the 'simple child,

---

[1] *Prel* I, 370–1. [2] *Works*, vol. 17, p. 117.
[3] *Prel*, p. 575, ll. 165–6: and v. supra. [4] v. *PW* 4, pp. 463–4, 467.

> That lightly draws its breath,
> And feels its life in every limb,[1]

and this diffused sense of being was the source of all consciousness, of the mind no less than of the body, spiritual no less than animal. Felt by Wordsworth as a disturbing problem, this predominance of the conscious mind in relation to the external world seems to adumbrate something of his later feeling for a corporeal self in relation to the impressions it received from nature. In fact, this childhood feeling that the visible world was an inherent part of his experience, coupled, as he put it on another occasion,[2] with an urge 'to push against something that resisted', suggests rather a hyper-sensuousness of mind than any conscious 'idealism'. The child's mind is diffused in his physical being, and is liable to be overcome by an excess of perceptual energy. This state of animal innocence, the almost paradoxical state of bodily delight uncorrupted by consciousness of it through the individual senses, has been well described by Carlyle: 'looking back on young years . . .' he recalls that time in which

> the body had not yet become the prison-house of the soul, but was its vehicle and implement, like a creature of the thought, and altogether pliant to its bidding. We knew not that we had limbs, we only lifted, hurled, and leapt; through eye and ear, all avenues of sense, came clear unimpeded tidings from without, and from within issued clear victorious force; we stood as in the centre of Nature, giving and receiving, in harmony with it all . . .[3]

This description might be accurately applied to the main feelings of childhood which emerge from Wordsworth's poetry. It sums up that state of unthinking physical being, coupled with a central feeling of pure action, 'lively' motion, in which the problem of 'external things' not having external existence was inherent: it seems fair to suggest that Wordsworth, in his old age, emphasized the spirituality of this childhood problem at the expense of what he admitted to knowing later too well, 'a subjugation of an opposite character'. In explaining a period of his life (during his first vacation from Cambridge) where an increased number of mental distractions led to 'an inner falling-off'[4]

---

[1] "We are Seven", ll. 1–3.   [2] v. *PW* 4, p. 467.
[3] *Essays III* (*Works*), p. 2.   [4] *Prel* IV, 270.

D   89

in his straightforward love of nature, he described it in terms of losing that oblivion of self which is one of the qualities of childhood; it came through an excess of physical awareness.

> The very garments that I wore appear'd
> To prey upon my strength, and stopp'd the course
> And quiet stream of self-forgetfulness. ll. 292–4

Wordsworth, in his greatest poetry, evokes, in remembering his childhood and early youth, that feeling of bodily existence which continues only, but nevertheless actually, in memory. In his maturity, the continuation in memory of this and allied later feelings was the highest reward which could be gathered from sensuous experience.

At times, Wordsworth's growing sense of the physical world, and of its continuing presence in memory, seems to have induced a return to its childhood state of uncertainty between inner and outer worlds – or rather, it was no longer a question of uncertainty, but a feeling of fusion, of recognizable unity, in which all the senses combined with the memory of past experience. An example of this kind of sensuous fusion appears at the beginning of 'Tintern Abbey', where he describes, in what is an act of memory as much as an act of observation, how

> Once again
> Do I behold these steep and lofty cliffs,
> That on a wild secluded scene impress
> Thoughts of more deep seclusion.

Here, the physical 'pressure', as it were, is chiefly outward-going: by a kind of shorthand, he implies that the steep cliffs, having impressed themselves on his mind (in the past, in memory, and at that moment), lead him to transfer this impression, and the 'thoughts' evoked by it, to the whole scene. This is not a sophisticated case of Romantic identification, of deliberate breakdown in subject-object relationship (Keats 'picking' with the sparrow on the gravel). In Wordsworth, thought and image are always ultimately unified, as they are here, in time; both parts, subject and object, landscape and emotion, are maintained in that sensuous unity which is co-equivalent with the power of memory.

A fragment which describes this fusion of inner perception and outer experience also suggests how this fusion is taken up into the memory by way of a sensuous bodily feeling. Wordsworth speaks of the great joy, on summer days, when no breeze, no cloud is stirring, to sit

> Far in some lonely wood, and hear no sound
> Which the heart does not make, or else so fits
> To its own temper that in external things
> No longer seem internal difference
> All melts away, and things that are without
> Live in our minds as in their native home.[1]

Here Wordsworth's physical, beating heart and, as it were, the more poetic heart of perception and inner consciousness are identified. It is in such moments of unity that the mind is most receptive to lasting emotion. There is a close connection between quiet (which is yet a quiet of the senses) and those moments in which the mind is impressed, in which memory is furthered, created. A good illustration of this sensuous quiet is provided in another short note-book fragment: 'I stood', he says,

> Within the area of the frozen vale,
> Mine eye subdued and quiet as the ear
> Of one that listens . . .[2]

Wordsworth's sensitive notation of sound, and his accurate aural memory, have long been remarked.[3] There is a suggestion here that the sense of sight must gradually be tamed to the calmer sense of hearing – or, at least, that it should approach the visual equivalent of that ideal contemplative state in which silence takes on a positive, absolute virtue. Even in a landscape immediately perceived, a complete calm, in which nature is at once motionless and silent, should be possible.

> The clouds are standing still in the mid heavens;
> A perfect quietness is in the air;
> The ear hears not; and yet, I know not how,
> More than the other senses does it hold
> A manifest communion with the heart.[4]

[1] *PW* 5, p. 343, iii.   [2] *PW* 5, p. 346, ii.
[3] v. 'Wordsworth's Treatment of Sound', W. Heard: *Transactions of the Wordsworth Society*, No. 6, 1884: *Wordsworthiana*, pp. 221–39.
[4] *PW* 5, p. 343, iv.

Yet even in this moment of calm, it is the sense of hearing, and the feeling that it is being used, even if only towards silence, which is important to Wordsworth: and in all his deepest responses to nature he conveys in his poetry a distinctly sensuous apprehension of them. These responses do not always take an explicitly aural or visual form, but become expressed by that sense of diffused bodily feeling which was characteristic of his deepest perceptions.

> And I have felt
> A presence that disturbs me with the joy
> Of elevated thoughts . . .[1]

It is the unifying quality of this 'presence' which Wordsworth feels, 'interfused' as it is amongst 'all things', a 'motion' no less than a 'spirit': and it is in conjunction with this presence that he pays tribute to 'nature and the language of the sense'. To say that the presence he feels is an effect of memory, working together with a continued interest in nature – memory working sensuously, unifying inner and outer, past and present – is not to explain it completely: but Wordsworth, as we have seen, experienced the past, in 'Tintern Abbey', as a sensuous continuity, and it is because of *this* presence (alive in memory up to the moment of writing) that actual no less than remembered landscape remains a source of inspiration to him; 'Therefore', he can say,

> am I still
> A lover of the meadows and the woods,
> And mountains; and of all that we behold
> From this green earth; of all the mighty world
> Of eye, and ear, – both what they half create,
> And what perceive . . .

Memory and the unified senses work together calmly in poetry.

A famous passage provides one more example of 'sensuous quiet', of that sort of diffused sensuousness which is characteristic of Wordsworth's deepest experience. Wordsworth describes the Pedlar looking at the clouds touched by the rising sun.

> Sound needed none
> Nor any voice of joy: his spirit drank

[1] 'Tintern Abbey', ll. 93–5.

> The spectacle. Sensation, soul and form
> All melted into him. They swallowed up
> His animal being; in them did he live
> And by them did he live. They were his life.[1]

The forceful words here are the verbs, the ideas of drinking, melting, swallowing – all contained in the idea of living. It describes a state of unity: and one sensuously experienced; 'sensation', no less than 'soul and form' was part of it. And if this particular unity was of an exceptionally spiritual kind, it was yet the result of a deliberate and everyday submission to 'Habits of eye and ear and every sense', and of an awareness that these formed an 'endearing union'.[2] Wordsworth's finest poetry grew from a conscious unity of mind and body, including that unity in time felt by way of memory.

In arguing the basically sensuous nature of even those experiences, in childhood and later, which seem to be the result of complete bodily calm, we must remember that no very clear distinction can be made between types of Wordsworthian feeling – neither at any given moment, nor between past and present. Just as the temporal calm, the 'tranquillity' in which emotion is first recollected, becomes agitated, excited, in order to achieve poetic value,[3] so the bodily calm (in which, it may have seemed, the emotion was conceived) must become disturbed and re-affirm its sensuous nature – without which it could not, in fact, have experienced the original event. Recalling his childhood walks of the early morning, Wordsworth asks

> How shall I trace the history, where seek
> The origin of what I then have felt?
> Oft in those moments such a holy calm
> Did overspread my soul, that I forgot
> That I had bodily eyes, and what I saw
> Appear'd like something in myself, a dream,
> A prospect in my mind.   *Prel* II, 365–71

Such a prospect, this inner landscape, was seen then with a 'quiet eye' of childhood: it is remembered now in the *Prelude* with the new, and hardly-won, 'quiet eye' of maturity. Yet such a calm, if only by being

---

[1] *Ruined Cottage*: ll. 128–33 (*Excursion* I, 205–10).
[2] *Prel*, p. 578, ll. 238–9.   [3] v. *Preface* (1800).

consciously remembered, retains that sense of inward apprehension which is experienced as physical continuity.

The main impulse, and a major problem, of Wordsworth's desire to recall the past lies in the attempt to *explain* sensuous experience. In fact, one of the most original things Wordsworth was doing was quite simply to recognize that highly personal, seemingly incommunicable experiences were fit poetic material, and that poetry might be made out of trying to explain them. Proust tells a story of himself which illustrates the necessity of this kind of explanation:

> The tiled roof . . . dappled the pond with pink in a way that I had till then never noticed. Seeing on the surface of the water, and on the wall, the pale hint of a smile that repeated the gaiety of the high heavens, I waved my umbrella and shouted in my enthusiasm – '*Zut! zut! zut!*' But even while I was doing so, I realized that what I ought to have been concerned with, instead of resting satisfied with the opacity of that inexpressive word, was making an effort to see more clearly into the nature of my delight . . .[1]

Similarly (though perhaps through 'animal' rather than such Gallic 'vivacity') Wordsworth justified elusive emotions; he was self-impelled to get beyond the seeming self-indulgence of momentary ecstasies. In Wordsworth, as in Proust, the explanation becomes a poetic event – an evocation which has a substantial presence in memory, an idealistic weight which it owes to that very sensuousness by which it was both initially implanted and continuously retained. Wordsworth knew this problem or paradox clearly – and knew that such unity of the senses he might achieve would help him to express even the calmest and most seemingly spiritual events.

In Wordsworth's maturity, then, the senses remain: memory works, as he had implied, in conjunction with their growing unity. Memory itself, to begin with chiefly a visual matter, becomes more sensuously unified: and with this unity a feeling for time grows. 'The mighty world of eye and ear'[2] retains its full validity: but for the very reason that it becomes diffused and continued in memory. 'Bodily eye and spiritual need'[3] are one: all experience is now pervaded by memory: the sensuous element achieves value in time.

---

[1] Quoted in Maurois, *The Quest for Proust*, p. 31: and cf. *Swann's Way*, I, p. 213.
[2] 'Tintern Abbey', ll. 105–6.   [3] *Prel*, p. 575, l. 154.

We have emphasized the sensuous element in Wordsworth's experience if only to account for its vivid presence in memory, its continued presence in time during the writing of the *Prelude*. Wordsworth's past maintained a *narrative* existence in memory – it was a presence which shaped the actual writing of the *Prelude* as well as being its source. But as this presence had a sensuous life of its own, it was not of indefinite duration: its vitality began to fade. Wordsworth was perhaps vaguely aware of this in recording the 'growth of his mind' – the sensuous element perhaps only had value during the writing of the poem. After the poem's completion, memory had no value in relation to his art. Memory represented emotion, ideas in action – they were part of a living past. Later, in the *Excursion* for example, the autonomy of these ideas had failed – they were not confidently related to Wordsworth himself: they could therefore have no real poetic life in memory.

In Wordsworth, we do not expect any sophisticated self-consciousness about memory: but a deep awareness that it was, almost, his essential mode of poetic experience is the underlying impulse of much of his finest work. The achievement of the *Prelude* – its originality, its spiritual honesty (rather than material accuracy), not least the art with which its story is shaped – owes much to Wordsworth's awareness of how important the workings of memory were to his poetry. In the actual writing of a long poem a continuing relationship is implied between its author and its progress, and in the course of the *Prelude*'s composition Wordsworth evolved and confirmed many of his notions about time. In embarking on, or, as it seemed to him, preparing for, his great 'philosophic' poem, Wordsworth had from the start, as de Selincourt suggests,[1] an epic conception of his task; the great originality in this conception was that the poet was engaged upon a personal and retrospective poem, a kind of autobiography, and that consequently the narrative would evolve through memory and be particularly time-conscious.

There is a distinction, inherent in imaginative autobiography, between saying, in effect, 'It was so' and 'I remember it was so': Wordsworth consistently implies the latter – the action of memory is important to what he has to say. He not only narrates, he remembers: he is aware, especially in evoking the deep feelings of his childhood, of his position in the present. Of course, some events in his life, usually those

[1] *Prel*, pp. xxxix–xl.

of more recent occurrence, lend themselves to a purely anecdotal treatment. One can sense the difference in tone between those passages describing a more immediate past (e.g. the account of his time in France) and those dealing with his childhood and early career. The narrative tone of the former contrasts quite clearly with the remembered and meditative tone of the latter, a tone which continuously implies that both the narrator and his subject are still present, here, now – in spite of, or rather, because of, time gone by.

Wordsworth never, of course, thought of the *Prelude* as a straightforward narrative autobiography, to him it was always a poem about the 'growth of a poet's mind'. Now, if only because the act of writing the poem immediately clarified that growth (even if it was not actually felt as adding to it), an awareness of passing time in relation to memory must have continually presented itself to Wordsworth. It is such a sense of time which distinguishes the force of memory from an act of mere narrative recollection; and the dynamics of the *Prelude*, its movement by way of memory in relation to its total theme, that is, the growth of its author's mind, illustrate the poetic power, for Wordsworth, of memory in action.

The opening book shows Wordsworth's sense of time operating in all its variety of effect: most strikingly in the manner in which both theme and direction are gradually clarified. The opening lines (1–54, which were first written in 1795)[1] are chiefly in the present tense, and Wordsworth establishes himself in this present, immediately as the poet, and almost, by implication, as his subject-matter – at least, in the context of the whole book (not to say of the completed work) the way he relates a sensuous apprehension of the natural world to his own feelings will be seen to indicate the continuous importance of his own presence to the poem. The breeze which, in the first four lines, beats, as he says, 'against my cheek', is paralleled by an inner creative sense:

> For I, methought, while the sweet breath of Heaven
> Was blowing on my body, felt within
> A corresponding mild creative breeze,
> A vital breeze which travell'd gently on
> O'er things which it had made, and is become
> A tempest, a redundant energy

[1] v. *Prel*, pp. xliii–xlv.

Vexing its own creation.   ll. 41–7

This might be noticed as another example of a sensuous mode of inward experience – and as an example of the synthesizing quality of the
senses related to a dynamic conception of their working. The breeze,
and the feeling of creativity that comes with it, is felt sensuously by
Wordsworth, blowing on his body or within it – seeming, in fact, to be
by way of the senses, both 'the mind and mind's minister'.[1] And while
it is, in this way, 'travelling gently on', the breeze works, in time, in the
manner of memory – the tranquillity of remembered forms and emotions is lost in the continuing creative act of remembering them. For
the moment, the point to be noticed is how Wordsworth establishes
his presence both, as it were, in time and in the material of the poem.

'Not used', as he tells Coleridge, 'to make/A present joy the matter
of my Song', Wordsworth nevertheless introduces himself in the most
effective way possible. In relation to the predominantly retrospective
character of the whole work, this apparently spontaneous 'lead-in' is of
the greatest structural importance. Wordsworth now (ll. 55f.) proceeds
to a section of fairly straightforward narrative, more or less explaining
his situation to Coleridge, and describing his search for a theme. In
this search we can see how important memory, the act of conscious
meditation on his own past, was to Wordsworth. In preparing for his
task he reads or thinks,

> either to lay up
> New stores, or rescue from decay the old
> By timely interference . . .   ll. 125–7

Yet these almost instinctive actions of the mind seem not in themselves
sufficient to give him either the power or the theme he needs:

> But I have been discouraged; gleams of light
> Flash often from the East, then disappear
> And mock me with a sky that ripens not
> Into a steady morning: if my mind,
> Remembering the sweet promise of the past,
> Would gladly grapple with some noble theme,
> Vain is her wish.

[1] *PW* 5, p. 343, vi, ll. 7–8.

We shall see how he comes to recognize that this intermittent vision, these flashes of illumination, are his most penetrating mode of seeing, that they represent in fact the workings of memory and the location of childhood. The gleams from the East, whether direct memories of the dawn of life, or emblems of them in the light of the setting sun, are at once the illumination and essential spark of Wordsworth's poetry. He expresses his realization of this most clearly in Book XI: in a passage to which we shall return he describes (ll. 334-9) how

> the days gone by
> Come back upon me from the dawn almost
> Of life: the hiding-places of my power
> Seem open; I approach, and then they close;
> I see by glimpses now; when age comes on,
> May scarcely see at all . . .

In the whole of this passage we find one of Wordsworth's most explicit statements about the power of memory in his poetry. At the beginning of the *Prelude*, he was perhaps less clear about the importance of this power: or rather he presents himself as having little confidence in it.

When, in casting about for a subject, he remarks that he has found 'plenteous store' of 'time, place, and manners', but that so far he can choose 'No little Band of yet remember'd names' whom he might confidently use, he refers mainly to such characters as might fitly be treated of in an epic; but this diffidence about what, from his own store of knowledge and emotion, should be his essential subject-matter, this self-confessed inability

> to part
> Vague longing that is bred by want of power
> From paramount impulse not to be withstood, ll. 240-2

reveals itself as a careful preparation, an organic introduction, to the main theme of the *Prelude*, the growth of the poet's own mind. As his confidence seems to wane, Wordsworth offers himself (l. 252) a kind of temptation, a relief from his high, self-appointed task:

> – Ah! better far than this, to stray about
> Voluptuously through fields and rural walks,
> And ask no record of the hours . . .

The poet is invited to abandon all thought of his work's progress: he is to put himself outside purpose and human time. But, of course, for the dedicated poet this is unthinkable; and even if work fails him, he will know himself to be

> Unprofitably travelling towards the grave,
> Like a false Steward who hath much received
> And renders nothing back.

The idea of motion forwards, of progress in time, is, perhaps obviously enough, inherent in any worthwhile long poem. In the *Prelude*, in relation to its story, Wordsworth thought of himself as a kind of pilgrim: 'A Traveller I am/And all my Tale is of myself'.[1] He also, here and elsewhere, thought of himself, or the progress of his tale, in the likeness of a river.[2] Both these images, the traveller and the river, emblems at once of motion and of continuity in time,[3] seem to have been images of great power to Wordsworth – if only by way of his native landscape and his native delight in long walks and roads.[4] Certainly it is at this point, where he finds himself 'Unprofitably travelling towards the grave', that these two images come together, and that Wordsworth leads into the real subject-matter of his theme, his self, his past and childhood,

At the thought of his self-doubt he is stricken with shame. 'Was it for this', he asks,

> That one, the fairest of all Rivers, lov'd
> To blend his murmurs with my Nurse's song . . .?
>
> ll. 271–3

And at the same time he finds, almost literally, the source of his inspiration.

> For this, didst Thou,
> O Derwent! travelling over the green Plains
> Near my 'sweet Birthplace', didst thou, beauteous Stream,

---

[1] *Prel* III, 196–7.

[2] e.g. *Prel* IV, 39–55: *Recluse*, ll. 728–32: *Prel* IX, 1–9.

[3] cf. *Prel*, p. 572, ll. 44–6: 'the River that flows on/Perpetually, whence comes it, whither tends,/Going and never gone'.

[4] cf. *Prel* XII, the passage (ll. 145f.) beginning baldly enough, 'I love a public road . . .'

Make ceaseless music through the night and day
. . . giving me,
Among the fretful dwellings of mankind,
A knowledge, a dim earnest, of the calm
That Nature breathes among the hills and groves.

Wordsworth, travelling on in time, thinks of his childhood river: the
memory of the Derwent gives rise to the long, lingering, 'backward
view',[1] to the evocation of his 'sweet Birthplace'[2] (the reference to
Coleridge's lines intensifies the feeling): and so, not explicitly, but by
the force of memory, Wordsworth identifies himself, his present
emotion, with this childhood scene, the river. And it is in this way,
through the backward look, through the moral impulse of a remembered landscape, that Wordsworth finds himself, finds his direction.

Memory of the Derwent recalls particularly the many times he,

a five years' Child,
A naked Boy, in one delightful Rill,
A little Mill-race sever'd from his stream,[3]
Made one long bathing of a summer's day . . .

And this particular memory, of the river, of bathing, and of the other
summer landscapes evoked ('bronz'd with a deep radiance'), leads
immediately to a deepened narrative tone, the 'remembered' tone of
meditation and reflection.

Fair seed-time had my soul, and I grew up
Foster'd alike by beauty and by fear.

Wordsworth, in remembering the Derwent and his bathing in it, has
seemed almost to immerse himself in memory; the river, this 'lapse of
liquid element',[4] becomes both an image of childhood and a medium of
continuity between past and present: and having, by this immersion,
found himself and his theme, and having thereby moved into a tone of

---

[1] cf. 'Dear native regions', l. 7.
[2] From 'Frost at Midnight', l. 28: v. de Selincourt's note, p. 516.
[3] This does not detract from the central idea of the river: rather it enhances
the innocence of the child, isolated partly from the flux of the World, though by
his nature inevitably partaking of it.
[4] *Excursion* VIII, 331: and v. supra. 'Lapse' – from Milton onwards referring to
the gliding or flow of water; becoming also (in Eighteenth century) of time;
v. *O.E.D.*, 6.

rhapsody and invocation, he shows the river to be also an image of man travelling continuously on, working out his human purpose and destiny. With the power of memory and the backward view revealed, with the sense of organic memory felt as something active, creative and developing, the work can now go forward.

And it is by the power of memory that the poem reaches its greatest heights, and remains true to its central purpose. Past experience is both recounted and elucidated, remembered incident becomes poetic event – an event in its own right, revealing, in the elucidation, the poet's mind both then and now.

And so, in the first book, by way of past scenes and present meditation, Wordsworth establishes the theme of his work. He knows the permanence of the natural world, how it has a kind of memorial stability in the face of human transience: he has invoked the 'Wisdom and Spirit of the universe' . . .

> That givs't to forms and images a breath
> And everlasting motion . . . ll. 428, 430–1

He has recognized that he may, in some small measure, participate in this stability by concentrating on himself, on his human past in memory. He has recognized the value of, what he well knows he is 'loth to quit',

> Those recollected hours that have the charm
> Of visionary things, and lovely forms
> And sweet sensations that throw back our life
> And almost make our Infancy itself
> A visible scene, on which the sun is shining . . .
> ll. 658–63

These 'sweet sensations', that take him back to the edge of those earliest days ('Disown'd', as he puts it, 'by memory'), have led him equally to the hope of fetching 'Invigorating thoughts from former years'. By such workings of memory, he says, 'My mind hath been revived'; and by way of such retrospect he finds 'The road lies plain before me':[1] the work will proceed, continuously remembered.

There is no room to deal proportionately with each example of memory's power, or an awareness of its action, within the whole length of the *Prelude*. Some have been noticed already and others will

[1] l. 668: cf. l. 15.

be noticed when we deal more particularly with Wordsworth's sense of time in relation to memory. The poem maintains, in varying degrees of intensity, but from beginning to end, that feeling of having been written out of actively remembered experience, out of

> many wanderings that have left behind
> Remembrances not lifeless . . . :
>
> *Prel* IV, 360–1

wanderings both real and spiritual, creating in their action a sense of living memory. It is in Book XI of the *Prelude* that Wordsworth makes his most complete statement about the significance of memory to his poetry. After his account of his temporary submission to the Picturesque, he describes his escape from it, how his integrity was restored and has been preserved up to the moment in which he is writing: he 'shook the habit off' and

> In Nature's presence stood, as I stand now,
> A sensitive, and a creative Soul.   XI, 256–7

Having established himself in the present, Wordsworth proceeds to enunciate, in a well-known passage, dating from about 1800,[1] what amounts to a fairly explicit doctrine of memory.

> There are in our existence spots of time,
> Which with distinct pre-eminence retain
> A vivifying Virtue, whence . . .
> . . . our minds
> Are nourished and invisibly repair'd.   ll. 258–60, 264–5

Noticing the union of local and temporal in the idea of 'spots of time', we see here a clear statement about the 'vivifying' power, continuous and restorative, of memory. Wordsworth goes on to state:

> This efficacious spirit chiefly lurks
> Among those passages of life in which
> We have had deepest feeling that the mind
> Is lord and master, and that outward sense
> Is but the obedient servant of her will.

[1] Ms.V: v. *Prel*, pp. xxviii–ix.

The conjunction of 'mind' and 'outward sense' in these 'passages of life' is important here. 'Sense', of course, must be subordinate; Wordsworth knew that, ideally, it should never have been otherwise. But in such times when memory is formed, or furthered, 'sense' is undeniably, is naturally there. It is not quite certain if this feeling of the correct dominance of the mind occurs chiefly at the initial 'time-spot' or during the more purely temporal, as it seems, 'passages' within which the spot may be said to have been acting restoratively. However, the slight confusion adds to the Wordsworthian feeling that memory is a continuity, that past moments are firmly within the control of the mind, the '*in*ward sense'. Wordsworth goes on:

> Such moments worthy of all gratitude
> Are scatter'd everywhere, taking their date
> From our first childhood: in our childhood even
> Perhaps are most conspicuous. Life with me,
> As far as memory can look back, is full
> Of this beneficent influence.

It was the consciously 'backward' look of memory which could give poetic value to this influence, and Wordsworth proceeds to tell the story of how he came upon the carved name of a hanged murderer, of how climbing up from the 'bottom' where this was, he saw a 'naked Pool', and a Beacon, and a Girl with a Pitcher, and of how he felt, deeply, the 'visionary dreariness' of the scene. In the original passage (in Ms.V) this story was immediately followed by another[1] (which we have seen he had previously introduced into *The Vale of Esthwaite*), the story of his waiting for a horse to take him home a few days before his father's death, and his later visionary recollections of the place, of the sheep, and the blasted tree, and 'the bleak music of that old stone wall'.

Those two stories are here separated by a passage dating, as does much of the Book, from 1804.[2] In conjunction with the two narrative memories, this passage of invocation and reflection about memory spans from near the end to near the beginning of Wordsworth's years of achieving a completed *Prelude*. As Wordsworth had ended his second story by telling how he would often 'repair' (chiefly, it seems, in memory though perhaps actually as well) to the 'spectacles and sounds' of which

---

[1] v. *Prel*, p. 448n.
[2] Ms. W: v. *Prel*, p. xxix: and n. to ll. 326–43, p. 615.

it had been largely composed, so after his sight of the Pool, and the Beacon, and the Girl, he introduces an account of a similar revisiting, actual and frequent, of the eventful place, a revisiting in which,

> When in the blessed time of early love,
> Long afterwards, I roam'd about
> In daily presence of this very scene,
> Upon the naked pool and dreary crags,
> And on the melancholy Beacon, fell
> The spirit of pleasure and youth's golden gleam.
>
> ll. 318–23

This pleasure came by way of memory of the 'visionary dreariness', a strongly dramatic, not to say disturbed, memory (an example of 'the impressive discipline of fear');[1] the particular memory, the 'spot of time', was fully evoked in the earlier passage (Ms.V), and it is now (1804) realized in all its strength, put to its most significant use – namely, to illustrate the autonomous and visionary power of memory as a mode of experience, and as a poetic medium. It had been 'an ordinary sight'; but he had known its force then, as he had known afterwards its accumulated force in memory. Now, having noted how 'The spirit of pleasure and youth's golden gleam' had fallen in these recollections, he proceeds to account for it: on that place revisited they fell;

> And think ye not with radiance more divine
> From these remembrances, and from the power
> They left behind? So feeling comes in aid
> Of feeling, and diversity of strength
> Attends us, if but once we have been strong.   ll. 324–8

This is the true power of memory – not merely to preserve, but to create emotion, to work within the spirit, and in working, to enlarge understanding and the sense of existence. If the initial experience has been deeply felt (if, in fact 'but once we have been strong') then the memory of it, every subsequent memory of it, and the memory of each similar event, all these create a continuity of feeling and a continuous reserve of restorative power, from which one may at all times draw, not thereby detracting from its power, but thereby adding to it,

---

[1] *Prel* I, 631.

increasing it. The unity of feeling grows in memory; the unity of existence is enlarged by the workings of memory.

This unity is most deeply experienced as a unity of existence in Time. The mystery of the past drives Wordsworth to discover the mystery of being. Here in a moment of evocation he recognizes the kind of understanding that he needs to achieve – at least he recognizes the source of it: 'Oh! mystery of Man, from what a depth/Proceed thy honours! I am lost', he admits,

> but see
> In simple childhood something of the base
> On which thy greatness stands, but this I feel,
> That from thyself it is that thou must give,
> Else never canst receive.   ll. 329–34

Those past moments in which 'we to Nature . . . Of our whole being made free gift',[1] those amongst which feeling would come in aid of feeling, were those in which memory was inherently responsive, actively assisting the present, actively preparing for the future. Now, in this moment of writing, of once more attempting to solve the mystery of past time, Wordsworth feels the power of memory, as he had felt it (in 'gleams of light' flashing from the East)[2] at the outset of the poem; although the sky of childhood memory had more than ripened 'into a steady morning'; it was now almost sunset.

> The days gone by
> Come back upon me from the dawn almost
> Of life: the hiding-places of my power
> Seem open; I approach, and then they close;
> I see by glimpses now; when age comes on,
> May scarcely see at all, and I would give,
> While yet we may, as far as words can give,
> A substance and a life to what I feel:
> I would enshrine the spirit of the past
> For future restoration.   XI, 334–43

Wordsworth here gives full expression to the source of his poetry and to the purpose of the *Prelude* and how it must be achieved. It is a mature realization of the power of memory, what it has meant to him, what

---

[1] *PW* 5, p. 344, vi, ll. 11–12.   [2] *Prel* I, 134–5.

it means even now: together with a fear that it is going to mean less to him. Even as he gives this recognition of childhood and memory, he indicates a further sense of the nature of memory – he implies that because it is a dynamic power, it exists only by virtue of his, Wordsworth's, own poetic energy. The relation, in fact, between time and sensuous existence here becomes apparent. He can only 'enshrine the spirit of the past' by giving 'a substance and a life' to what he feels. When the power to do this fades, then the power of his poetry fades too. Only by the continuous working of memory, feeling coming in aid of feeling, can 'the hiding-places' seem open at all. Memory works by a kind of sensuous energy, it is a force which makes continual demands: here Wordsworth seems to have some inkling of its possible failure. He feels himself travelling onwards in time, further and further from 'The twilight of rememberable life';[1] and distance in time can only be countered by *active* continuity. If this becomes impossible, poetry taking its power from the past disappears.

We see, in this passage, the sense of time evoked by a full understanding of memory. Wordsworth, in the next few years (particularly in *The White Doe*) comes to an almost mystical understanding of Time. It was something which, in Nature, he had long dimly understood, and which in his poetry he had often indicated. But now, it seemed almost inevitable that this more spiritual, more elegiac sense of time, understood by a kind of intellectual observation of nature – of the seasons, of the changing and the unchanging natural world – rather than by sensuous feeling, should take the place of fully experienced memory, a force of the active self in time.

We have emphasized the part played in Wordsworth's poetry by the senses because they are important, as he felt them to be, both in forming and in continuing memory. We have seen how Wordsworth arrived at a unified view of the senses, how memory at once assisted in and partook of this unity. We have suggested that memory maintained an almost 'sensuous' continuity for Wordsworth, in the writing of the *Prelude*, and that both in the actual sense of time implied during the course of its composition and in the sense of time implied in the union of creation, memory, and original event, this 'sensuous' memory was experienced as a kind of physical energy. It began to fail, but not before it had created or furthered a sense of time which was to exist

[1] *Prel*, p. 446, app. crit., Ms.V.

as a power of memory for a few years yet in the creation of Words-worth's poetry. This sense of time, and its relation to memory, we shall attempt to analyse in our next chapter, considering especially *The White Doe* and further considering some of Wordsworth's feelings for organic nature and for landscape in Time.

CHAPTER 3

Wise Passiveness in Time

As WORDSWORTH'S poetry continues to develop, the workings of memory become more closely integrated with the sense of time. We noticed, in our last chapter, how a growing understanding of the poetic importance of memory led to a conscious 'unity of self' within time present and past. Now we can examine other aspects of Wordsworth's time-sense (his feeling for time in nature, for time in human life) and follow its development in his work up to *The White Doe of Rylstone* – showing how this sense of time came to supersede the autonomous creative power of memory, how the remembered personal past was taken up in a larger, more meditative awareness of time. The fundamental characteristic of the 'sense of time' is an awareness of time passing, and of the length of time between present and past action – a primary awareness of distance and flux rather than, as with memory, an awareness of event. The sense of time and a conscious use of memory are, of course, always bound up with each other, and Wordsworth showed this time-sense from his earliest poetry onwards; but while the working of memory was self-sufficient, while its inward subjective power commanded his poetry, he suffered no prolonged exposure, as it were, to the passage of time: he contained and controlled it.

To put it another way, Wordsworth's poetic memory contributed towards an experience of time which 'placed' him self-consciously within its flow: by the act of re-creation in writing, memory was felt to be a medium through which time was continuously passing, as well as one which was an accumulation of what had already passed. But, while memory worked most strongly on particular events and feelings out of Wordsworth's own past experience, it gradually became extended as a reflective, near-mystical power which could be referred not only inwardly to specific occasions but outwardly in a general interpretative sense to the whole world of man and nature. The 'Immortality' Ode expresses this power most fully.

The principal theme of the *Ode* is Wordsworth's sense of a former innocence and vision now lost, and the consolation for this to be found in certain memories of childhood. By saying this we are immediately involved, as we are by the *Ode*'s subtitle, in the ambiguity of reference and the fusion of meaning which is the poem's greatest achievement: for it is at once about recollections of early childhood and about recollections, or intimations, of pre-existence, and so, of immortality. The poem is impelled by recollections, now, of the period of childhood; one of the most important features of that period was what Wordsworth goes on to call 'shadowy recollections',[1] dim memories of some earlier, pre-existing time. For Wordsworth, there are memories *now*, and memories belonging specifically to childhood: it is the fusion of these two kinds of memory which creates the poem.

The *Ode* begins by expressing a change in Wordsworth's present way of seeing. 'There was a time' when the natural world seemed 'Apparelled in celestial light': for Wordsworth this is no longer so; yet, since he remembers – powerfully, as the whole impulse of the verse indicates – the time when it was otherwise, the feeling of change remains active, while the time-sense which impels, and continues, the *Ode* reveals, develops, and creates, out of this remembering, new meaning for Wordsworth's childhood. Wordsworth, as we have suggested, felt memory to be working for him as a kind of continuous creative energy: and he seems further to have sensed, at least by 1804, that this virtue might become exhausted. Such a possibility is closely related to the main theme of the *Ode*: and Wordsworth, somewhere between the beginning and end of its composition (i.e. between 1802–4) achieved an understanding of time which would offer some 'philosophical' answer to the growing failure of dynamic memory. The first four stanzas, which, written in 1802, preceded the rest of the poem by about two years, state the theme of lost vision: 'The things which I have seen I now can see no more.' The poem moves dialectically within these four stanzas between joy and sorrow: any immediate joy in nature is countered by a recent and continuously present sorrow at the thought of past splendour no longer seen:

[1] *Ode, Intimations of Immortality from Recollections of Early Childhood*, l. 150.

> . . . there's a Tree, of many, one,
> A single Field which I have looked upon,
> Both of them speak of something that is gone . . .
>
> ll. 51–3

Clearly enough, there is a problem of memory here; of the 'something that is gone', of 'the visionary gleam', something must be retained, or the force of the regret expressed could not be so powerful as it is: regret (a state we must further examine) is a category of memory.

Indeed, this sense of loss, of regret for past time, becomes, on occasion one of the most radical forms of Wordsworth's memory: it is a regret which is all the more tormenting and more forceful because its object does not seem to be absolutely lost, but lingers in the form of fitful 'gleams' and 'shadowy recollections'[1] – because the object is an emotion, a state of mind which seems to be palpably, though dimly and intermittently, still present in a memory of which it is part. And yet, this kind of regret is almost a paradox of memory; for it is akin also to human grief, the sorrow for something absolutely gone, completely inaccessible – which yet, because it had all the reality of a human life, continues to exist in memory, and, almost, in time.

> She died, and left to me
> This heath, this calm, and quiet scene;
> The memory of what has been,
> And never more will be.[2]

Here, the fusion of quiet landscape and enduring calm is already understood. The heath is at once a reminder of Lucy, a symbol of loss, and a consolation. It stands for memory itself, its workings no less than the object of its strivings; for although it is a symbol of change, and an image of regret, yet it will impart something of its calm, evoking a memory whose value will outweigh the grief it brings.

In the *Ode* Wordsworth regrets the glory of early childhood in the same spirit. What he has lost cannot, by its nature, be completely recollected, re-created: it is a thing of time, a victim of onwardness. Yet he does not in himself grieve for a dead childhood; memory preserves his continuity with those earlier years – though the beauty of

[1] cf. *Prel* I, 134: and *Ode*, l. 150.
[2] 'Three years she grew', ll. 39–42.

nature and landscape is, to begin with, less certainly reassuring: he sees the Rainbow, the Rose, the Moon;

> Waters on a starry night
> Are beautiful and fair;
> The sunshine is a glorious birth;
> But yet I know, where'er I go,
> That there hath past away a glory from the earth.
>
> ll. 14–18

But it is the fact that he *knows* this which is important to him. It is this knowledge, and that regret that goes with it, which creates, in spite of this, a mystical continuity with the past. This sense of the past, of memory distilled in landscape, epitomised in the lines just quoted from 'Three years she grew', is found in much of Wordsworth's finest poetry; it can be found, for example, throughout 'Tintern Abbey', and particularly in the epilogue section addressed to Dorothy. (This part, in its lines of lyrical invocation – cf. ll. 134–7 – is closely related to 'Three years . . .'). In it having invoked the continuity of his past self in the present aspect of his sister –

> Oh! yet a little while
> May I behold in thee what I was once, –   ll. 119–20

Wordsworth goes on to see the mature understanding of nature in direct relationship with memory: he looks forward to the time when, for Dorothy,

> thy mind
> Shall be a mansion for all lovely forms,
> Thy memory be as a dwelling-place
> For all sweet sounds and harmonies . . .

When he goes on to say that

> If I should be where I no more can hear
> Thy voice, nor catch from thy wild eyes these gleams
> Of past existence . . .

he refers immediately to the hope that Dorothy will not 'then forget

> That on the banks of this delightful stream
> We stood together . . .

Yet the whole almost suggests a fusion of a sense of actual memory with that mystical memory which informs the great *Ode*, where the 'gleams of past existence' are from a source outside human time. Here this sense of the past shares the half-actual, half-mystical atmosphere which is the secret of the Lucy poems:

> The memory of what has been,
> And never more will be.

This is what has been left to Wordsworth by Lucy – by a real Lucy, by a spirit of nature, by the 'celestial light'[1] (lux – lucis) which Wordsworth will evoke in the *Ode*: she is all of these, sensed, regretted, and yet, for Wordsworth, still living in poetry.

Wordsworth's Matthew, in 'The Fountain', provides another good example of this particular awareness of memory and regret – and an illustration of how it makes clear the distinction between human time and nature's. Matthew is presented as watching a spring: there is nothing, he says, to check it:

> 'Twill murmur on a thousand years,
> And flow as now it flows.   ll. 23–4

He recognizes nature's time: and contrasts it with human time. He remembers how often, as 'a vigorous man', he used to lie 'Beside this fountain's brink'; at the memory, he is moved, sensing the continuity, in human time no less that in nature's.

> For the same sound is in my ears
> Which in those days I heard . . .

There is continuity in both, but in human time there is not the constancy, the perfect evenness of being, which is nature's time.

> Thus fares it still in our decay:
> And yet the wiser mind
> Mourns less for what age takes away
> Than what it leaves behind.

[1] *Ode*, l. 4.

Human life, sustained in time by memory (here by the stream's same sound over the years), is yet forced by that very power of memory to recognize the fact of human time. What Matthew means here is this: the wise man will not regret mere physical decay, the fact that he is no longer 'a vigorous man': what he will regret, will 'mourn', is that sense of earlier delight which remains in the memory. What age 'takes away' is vigour and youth: what it 'leaves behind' is the sound of a stream in an old man's ears. It is memory that age 'leaves behind': and the meaning comes to the same thing whether thought of in linear terms, some joy left at a point backwards in time, or whether thought of as a deposit remaining in the memory. In fact, the ambiguity nicely illustrates the paradox about regret as memory – the sense of joy expressed still, continuously, by the fountain (or, as he goes on to say, by the blackbird or the lark) is still there in memory, frequently recalled – yet, by way of human time, this joy is now only sensed, as memory of something past, not now, actually, in the present experienced.

> The blackbird amid leafy trees,
> The lark above the hill,
> Let loose their carols when they please,
> Are quiet when they will.
>
> With Nature never do *they* wage
> A foolish strife; they see
> A happy youth, and their old age
> Is beautiful and free . . .

The creatures who live purely in natural time are not subject to human cares or decay: they are innocent of the sense of time.

> But we are pressed by heavy laws;
> And often, glad no more,
> We wear a face of joy, because
> We have been glad of yore.

This seems cold enough comfort: yet it is the best memory has to offer in answer to human time. When the experience of memory goes the same way as the immediate experience of joy, there is indeed little comfort left. Here, there is at least some consolation; Matthew, while understanding that the past can never truly be recalled – he rejects Wordsworth's offer to act as a son for his 'children dead' ('Alas! that cannot be')[1] – seems at least to recover a cheerfulness which is not completely feigned: the 'face of joy' is not entirely a mask, even although, philosophically, he can be 'glad no more'. Matthew, in fact, by refusing Wordsworth's offer, teaches him something of the nature of human time: by his keeping cheerful in spite of his own knowledge of human time, he teaches Wordsworth the true attitude of acceptance to it.

A deliberately unresolved tension between happiness and sorrow persists at the end of 'The Fountain'. The sense of loss, of regret, is still strong: yet Matthew draws some consolation from the enduring time of Nature – as Wordsworth can draw some consolation from the calm and quiet of his Lucy's heath. Regret is inherent in the feeling of change, and at those various stages of Wordsworth's life in which he was particularly aware of change, the idea of regret for the past presented itself to him very clearly. In 'Tintern Abbey' the sense of change is confidently taken: although, he says, the time of 'aching joys' and 'dizzy raptures' is past,

> other gifts
> Have followed; for such loss, I would believe,
> Abundant recompense.   ll. 83–8

In the *Ode* the sense of loss is more absolute; Wordsworth is alive to the delights of a 'sweet May-morning': but, as we noticed, certain objects, a particular Tree, a 'single Field', both spoke to him of 'something that is gone'.[2] Wordsworth, having established his sense of loss by singling out those objects which had particular meaning for him, does not then proceed by way, as we might have expected, of any particular remembered occasion; and from stanza v onwards, till the last one, the thought is meditative and outward-going. The transition from the power of memory to evoke and intensify particular experience – as in 'Tintern Abbey', as in the initial impulse of the *Prelude* and in many of its passages – to the power of memory to evoke a general reflective affirmation (to estabish, in fact, an assured metaphysical tone) is evident throughout the *Ode*: and, as there is a sense of change in

---

[1] ll. 61–4.   [2] ll. 51–3.

Wordsworth's feelings about the remembered past, so there is also a sense of change in his poetic thinking, implicit in the varied rhythms of the Ode form, in 'the transitions, and the impassioned music of the versification',[1] which seem to embody a new achievement, to create a new way of feeling. The philosophical 'control' of the poem is now less the action of memory than an awareness, and acceptance, of Time, of the ever-increasing distance between the present and the earliest rememberable past.

The key to the meaning of the *Ode* is to be found in stanza ix. Stanzas v–viii, which lead up to it, have expressed both Wordsworth's sense of pre-existence and his recognition of human time, a submission – though a questioning one – to the fact that the child must grow, become a Youth, a Man.

> Our birth is but a sleep and a forgetting:
> The Soul that rises with us, our life's Star,
>> Hath had elsewhere its setting,
>>> And cometh from afar:
>> Not in entire forgetfulness,
>> And not in utter nakedness,
> But trailing clouds of glory do we come
>> From God, who is our home:
> Heaven lies about us in our infancy!   ll. 58–66

The Soul enters human time by entering the body at birth; it temporarily disappears from the eternity, the everlasting time of 'God, who is our home', the 'elsewhere' from which it seems to have set.[2] To begin with, the change is barely noticeable: 'infancy' and early childhood is the period of what Wordsworth called 'days disowned by memory',[3] that is, days which are not subject to human time, because their onwardness, their development, passes unnoticed and unregistered; while such a state continues, the infant, the child, is untouched by human time, is still in everlasting time – Heaven lies about him. It is a primary state

---

[1] What Wordsworth, while not venturing to call it an Ode, felt (1800) he had achieved in 'Tintern Abbey': v. *PW* 2, p. 517.

[2] 'Setting' is in antithesis to 'rises': though the ornate suggestion of jewellery may also be present; while limiting, indeed 'placing', to the idea of the Soul, the special mystery associated with jewels is not irrelevant. Wordsworth also thought of the Soul as a kind of precious seed (cf. 'fair seed-time had my soul').

[3] *Prel* I, 642–3.

of this Heaven that the infant, unaware of passing time, unaware of memory, is likewise unaware of self: he has none of that sensuous self-awareness which develops the feeling of being *present* in passing time. But, as we have seen (Chapter II), 'the bodily sense' comes to intrude on unthinking childhood:

> Shades of the prison-house begin to close
> Upon the growing Boy . . .

He begins to be aware of his body, that vehicle of his self in time. The body, the prison-house of the Soul, 'that strong frame of sense in which we dwell',[1] begins to assert itself, creating that sensuous awareness of continuity in time which we have seen as the most powerful element of memory's working. The pure and illimitable mind feels human existence and human substance pressing in upon it.

While the boy advances in life, travels further in time and becomes more aware of it, the pure light of that source beyond the beginning of human time is still visible to him: by its shining, it creates for him a past, a remembered origin, though outside ordinary time and place, of goodness and wonder. Yet, inevitably, he must travel 'daily farther from the east';[2] the close relation which Wordsworth expresses between time and place, between the ideas of travelling and of human life, indicates, as we shall see, the importance of memory in establishing both continuity and distance, both the connection and the separation between present and past. The Youth is still attended by this light and the sense of glory it imparts: but, there comes a point where the source is too far off, the light seems to fail, to become indistinguishable from the light of day-to-day living. Those mountains in the east,[3] which, in *The Vale of Esthwaite*, and earlier, Wordsworth had recognized as the source of his power and as an image of his childhood, are further off, much further, now: yet even now – in the writing of the *Ode* – they are still standing, still remembered and still seen – though it is perhaps a setting sun which illumines them. It is such an affirmation towards which the poem is working: the primal 'light and whence it flows', the vision, must, it seems, 'fade into the light of common day' – unless it can be reillumined by the workings of poetic memory.

---

[1] ll. 153/4 (app. crit.). [2] l. 72.
[3] That east from which 'gleams of light' had flashed upon him: *Prel* I, 134–5: cf. also *Prel* I, 614 and *Prel* XI, 334f.

After suggesting (stanza vi) that the visible delights of the earth are specifically designed to make the man in human time 'forget the glories he hath known', the eternity of the empyrean,[1] and after describing the child at play and, as it seems, reproving his desire and hurry to grow up, Wordsworth goes on to his main, implicit, assertion: the inevitable onwardness of human life is given stability, and value, by the past – a past whose reference both to pre-existence and to childhood, to mystery and to actuality, must be contained and realized, made meaningful, in poetic memory.

Although the four opening stanzas of the poem have been concerned with a sense of lost splendour, it should be emphasized that this loss is merely sensed; it is neither fully experienced nor explained: regret, as we have suggested, is a powerful kind of memory. And Wordsworth's answer to this sense of loss is a continued faith in poetic memory – a new, more philosophical memory, more openly subject to time, yet memory which still compels his deepest emotion into poetry.

> O joy! that in our embers
> Is something that doth live,
> That nature yet remembers
> What was so fugitive!   ll. 130–3

And, he adds (the momentary personal modulation emphasizing the validity of the philosophic 'we'),

> The thought of our past years in me doth breed
> Perpetual benediction . . .

The power of memory returns to counter the notion of time established throughout stanzas v–viii. That much is clear: it is not so immediately clear what, in fact, 'was so fugitive', nor is it explained why it should be 'nature' that remembers it.[2] By itself, the little quatrain is open to a great variety of interpretation; however, the rest of the stanza helps to make it more precise, while enlarging on the theme of 'past years' and their beneficent influence. The thought of this past is with him continually, perpetually: a continuity is implied between the

---

[1] i.e. 'the imperial palace': Wordsworth would be familiar with this C17 and C18 spelling and pronunciation of 'empyreal'.

[2] 'That nature yet *remembers*' =? poetically (though not, at that date, semantically) '*reminds* one of . . . '; Wordsworth might well have sensed this archaic semantic over-tone.

present and that state of childhood and growth described in the fifth stanza. It is a continuity based no longer on immediate experience and consequent reassurance of early splendour but on the continuing memory of such splendour, now felt to be lost, yet leading to a present emotional doubting and questioning, which, if it does not re-create those feelings, is at least something equivalent to them. Wordsworth goes on to qualify his feeling of thankfulness towards this past: the 'benediction', he maintains, is due less to such straightforward and generally accepted concepts as 'Delight and liberty, the simple creed/ Of Childhood', as to certain strange and ambiguous emotions which presented themselves, powerfully and unexpectedly, to the growing child:

> . . . obstinate questionings
> Of sense and outward things,
> Fallings from us, vanishings;
> Blank misgivings of a Creature
> Moving about in worlds not realised,
> High instincts before which our mortal Nature
> Did tremble like a guilty Thing surprised . . .
>
> ll. 142–8

The exact relationship of these disturbing feelings to each other is hard to determine: the 'questionings' may belong to 'sense and outward things', to those aspects of the physical world felt, by Wordsworth, to be asserting their reality, only to be followed by that state of 'idealism', his inability 'to think of external things as having external existence', which he later described more than once:[1] or, these 'questionings' may belong to Wordsworth himself, obstinately enquiring about the reality of those things which continually seemed to be slipping away, vanishing from him.[2] The two processes, 'questionings' and 'vanishings', anyway add up to 'blank misgivings': whether these occur in the face of previously unrealized 'high instincts', which belong

[1] v. ch. 2.
[2] The ambiguities of syntax, or rather, the deliberate lack of syntax (in its literal meaning, of joining), are, in this passage and elsewhere in Wordsworth, one of his surest methods of creating the appearance of explicit statement where no such simple meaning can exist. This is not to imply that he is here subsiding into metaphysical rhetoric (in the pejorative sense) – although he does this on occasions; but rather he creates the impression of simple striving in the face of complexity.

to those worlds of pre-existence and the 'Heaven' lying about the child's earliest years (i.e. assuming 'instincts' to be in apposition to 'worlds') – or whether these 'misgivings' are complemented by the 'instincts' – or whether (assuming the 'vanishings' to be in contrast to the 'questionings') these two are in analogous contrast to each other – whatever the case, the whole, undoubtedly confused, state of mind is summed up in a further defining passage: Wordsworth continues to give thanks

> . . . for those first affections,
> Those shadowy recollections,
> Which, be they what they may,
> Are yet the fountain light of all our day,
> Are yet a master light of all our seeing;
> Uphold us, cherish, and have power to make
> Our noisy years seem moments in the being
> Of the eternal Silence . . .   ll. 149–56

'Shadowy recollections' – these are the immediate key to what is going on in the poem, that working through to an understanding of the truths asserted in stanza v. Here they refer chiefly to that period out of time and place, the realm of pre-existence – for we come 'From God, who is our home' (l. 65). Now, coming, as he does, 'Not in entire forgetfulness', the child may feel the workings of memory to be obscurely present and made known in him. The *first* emotions he experiences are, in fact, 'recollections'. Memory, the backward look, the sense of earlier time, was already implanted in him. And in his childhood, memory worked for him in this inherent way – something felt from the beginning, it worked for him within the time and place of his own living childhood; and as these 'shadowy recollections' are part of the 'eternal silence', are, as he goes on, 'truths that wake,/To perish never', so here they may be referred to those memories of childhood which gave rise to the *Ode* no less than to those earliest days 'disowned by memory' and to the time before birth. Such recollections, of pre-existence, and of joy in childhood, are not entirely separate: 'be they what they may', Wordsworth refuses to be over-specific about either their nature or their subject-matter. They work in a similar manner and to a similar end; and thus Wordsworth has described them in one of the earliest passages (dating from 1798) of the *Prelude*. In

Book II, 'School-Time', after telling of various ways in which he drank 'visionary power' from nature, walking alone, in storm, or at night, or standing

> Beneath some rock, listening to sounds that are
> The ghostly language of the ancient earth,
> Or make their dim abode in distant winds . . . ,
>
> 326–30

(and having thus incidentally imparted to these pure sounds a mystical correlation between time and distance, outside human time and his own experience), he goes on:

> I deem not profitless those fleeting moods
> Of shadowy exultation: not for this,
> That they are kindred to our purer mind
> And intellectual life; but that the soul,
> Remembering how she felt, but what she felt
> Remembering not, retains an obscure sense
> Of possible sublimity, to which
> With growing faculties she doth aspire,
> With faculties still growing, feeling still
> That whatsoever point they gain, they still
> Have something to pursue.

This refers explicitly to the action, afterwards, of memory on a heightened experience of nature: such a mood of 'exultation' is valuable not only because of its affinity with the 'purer mind' – which Wordsworth does not explain, but takes for granted – but because it is kept and is worked upon by memory; because, in fact, this particular mode of memory, by providing material for poetry to work on and towards, creates a continuity with the past – and with the future. The sense of time is in this way fully formed: the soul has something towards which it aspires, something to 'pursue'. The distinction between the soul's remembering 'how' she felt but not remembering 'what' she felt is an awkward one to define: Wordsworth hardly attempts it, but implies it in the relation of the time-sense to work, to the idea of re-creation: something out of the past, a 'shadowy recollection',[1] remains with the poet and creates a worthwhile future – some-

---

[1] v. *Ode*, l. 150.

thing is left towards which he must work. The 'how' amounts to that continuous awareness of memory and the past which the soul has known from the start: the 'what' is something in a sense remembered, but only as the possibility of some later explanation about the nature of the past. It represents a kind of faith. The future, no less than the past, is given value by poetic memory.

Another example of this time-sense forming in relation to work and poetic memory occurs in Book IV of the *Prelude*. The whole book is a tribute to returning memories and to the awakening of poetic creation – to the awakening, in fact, of poetic memory: it incidentally contains Wordsworth's most elaborate simile describing the workings of memory – ll. 247f. where he likens himself to a man in a boat who looks down into the water and is here floating 'o'er the surface of past time ...' The book describes the time of his unconscious dedication to poetry (when 'vows were made' for him, among the mountains at sunrise), and opens with an account of childhood walks which he was making again.

> Those walks, well worthy to be priz'd and lov'd,
> Regretted! that word, too, was on my tongue,
> But they were richly laden with all good,
> And cannot be remember'd but with thanks
> And gratitude, and perfect joy of heart,
> Those walks did now, like a returning spring,
> Come back on me again.   ll. 121–7

One of these, in which Wordsworth makes 'Once more the circuit of our little Lake', leads him on to an experience of self-assessment in preparation for his future poetic task.

>   I took
> The balance in my hand and weigh'd myself.
> I saw but little, and thereat was pleas'd;
> Little did I remember, and even this
> Still pleas'd me more; but I had hopes and peace
> And swellings of the spirit, was rapt and soothed,
> Convers'd with promises, had glimmering views
> How Life pervades the undecaying mind,
> How the immortal Soul with God-like power

Informs, creates, and thaws the deepest sleep
That time can lay upon her . . .   ll. 148–58

The 'little' that he remembered seems to refer to the immediate landscape, the 'external scene': he adds an explanatory qualifying line, which
also appears in several manuscripts, to the 1850 version. What is interesting in this passage is an awareness of memory 'subsumed' by Time:
the *activity* of remembering, where it might have been expected, and
where it had, just previously, been working strongly,[1] is here less
important than the overwhelming and mystical sense of time, the feeling of permanence and continuity which becomes the main theme and
message of the *Ode*. The 'glimmering views' of how the 'immortal
Soul' overcomes, 'thaws', time, refer plainly enough to the pre-
existent or buried past: while the glimpse which Wordsworth goes on
to describe,

how on earth,
Man, if he do but live within the light
Of high endeavours, daily spreads abroad
His being with a strength that cannot fail . . . ,

this forward-looking sense of work suggests the gathering strength of
poetic creation in the recovery of these early memories, both 'glimmer-
ings', and actual events, such as these very walks now 'coming back'
on him, 'like a returning spring'. He is led directly, by an intensification
of memory's working, to a deeper awareness of time and its relation
to work and poetry.

   The faith so established applies equally in the *Ode*: the 'something
that is gone', 'the glory and the dream' which has disappeared, have yet
not disappeared utterly – nor have the glories of 'that imperial palace'.
Enough has been remembered to give temporal life to the workings of
memory: while certainly enough has been forgotten to create a genuine
future towards which, and in which, memory, though further from
its source, will continue to work. This is the real joy which Wordsworth expresses at the beginning of the ninth stanza, the joy 'That

   [1] cf. ll. 126–7, the walks 'coming back' on him 'like a returning spring'. The
'regret' he is aware of in this passage is of a straightforward kind, and is immediately dismissed by his further realization of the continuing influence and value
of these walks. The emotion of returning and remembering is sufficient to com-
pensate for the sense of a past now disappeared.

nature yet remembers/What was so fugitive!' 'Fleeting moods/Of shadowy exultation',[1] 'shadowy recollections',[2] whether of the world of known experience, or of that mystical world before and beyond it, these are what create poetic memory and faith in work. It is in keeping with the close relationship of the worlds of pre-existence and of child-hood that, in this case, it should be 'nature' which 'remembers';[3] the concept of memory is enlarged, so that its impulses seem to come both from within and without. Nature, more permanent than the growing boy, than the man bound to human time, may be thought of as a kind of reservoir, a source of mystically diffused memory, helping the poet in his recovery of earlier years, helping, by her good influence, to intensify his own experience and his own memory of it. This kind of transcendent memory maintains poetic memory: 'shadowy recol-lections' though they may be, they are still 'the fountain light of all our day'. Water and light are the two elements in which the meaning of the *Ode* is suspended: considered separately, water, ever-flowing, mover of streams and rivers, is the human principle, light the radiant principle of eternity: but they never can be entirely separate, and in this 'fountain light' of memory, in this union of water and radiance, the Being, the man in time, and the Soul, are almost One. Poetic memory keeps alive 'the light, and whence it flows' (l. 70): it is poetic memory which answers to the near-oblivion of pre-existence, which returns the sense of immortality.

So it is that memory supports human life on its way from childhood; the workings of memory both increase the sense of time and make it bearable:

> What though the radiance which was once so bright
> Be now for ever taken from my sight,
>> Though nothing can bring back the hour
> Of splendour in the grass, of glory in the flower;
>> We will grieve not, rather find
>> Strength in what remains behind . . .

The splendour, in fact, does remain: no longer as a 'splendour-in-itself', but as a working of memory – the remembrance once instilled by a real and present splendour, it now remains as a 'memory-in-itself'. 'Strength in what remains behind', that is the key to the poetic

---

[1] *Prel* II, 331–2: v. supra.   [2] *Ode*, l. 150.   [3] In one sense: v. supra.

value of memory for Wordsworth. In the *Ode*, the key to its meaning, the consolation which Wordsworth achieved, is this: the workings of poetic memory in life are equated with the 'gleams', the intimations, of a mystical pre-existence.

The two concluding stanzas of the *Ode* seem, in the light of stanza ix, almost tentative in their affirmation of joy: the intimations of immortality (which are after all what the poem is about) are subdued, inexplicit. However, although Wordsworth insists that 'nothing can bring back the hour/ Of splendour in the grass', this reversion to the initial complaint is perhaps only a kind of inner structural necessity; the movement of the poem's meaning has to emphasize both the rarity of the consolation achieved and the fact that the 'philosophic mind' (l. 187) is now established. The initial impulse of the *Ode* was a feeling that immediate delight in 'objects of sense'[1] had disappeared: but, the fact of human growth and development having now been accepted, this 'one delight' (l. 191) in sensuous perception is no longer of any real importance. Nature, and her good influence, continues to exist for Wordsworth, if no longer imparting this sensuous pleasure, yet imparting something of at least equal value, stability in time:

> I only have relinquished one delight
> To live beneath your more habitual sway.

What could no longer be immediate, could yet always be remembered: the 'visionary gleam', the 'radiance' and 'splendour' of childhood experience may be gone – yet the 'Strength in what remains behind' must belong to those 'shadowy recollections' which include now (as they did then, in childhood) both the 'fountain light' and the sense of some former glory now lost.

In that *Prelude* passage (Book XI) where Wordsworth had a strong sense that poetic memory might fail altogether, he felt that while he could, he must 'enshrine the spirit of the past/For future restoration'. This sense of looking forward, the creative time-sense, is also strongly present in the *Ode*. But for the energy of active, sensuous memory, the *Ode* substituted a calmer awareness of the past: a mystical time-sense affords a reassurance about the essential continuity of human life. At the conclusion of the *Ode*, Wordsworth's feeling for nature, for landscape, remains: writing in the seclusion of his home-valley at Town-

---

[1] v. *PW*4, p. 464: Wordsworth to Mrs. Clarkson, 1814, quoted.

end, Grasmere, he is able to contemplate the passing of human time in a setting of nature's time. The prospect of 'man's mortality' is not here too oppressive:

> The innocent brightness of a new-born Day
> Is lovely yet;   ll. 195–6

essentially, this means that Wordsworth still responds to the beauty of the dawn, and further, that each successive day, one after the other, may hold this beauty; but, besides this immediately temporal experience, there is also in these lines a suggestion of that original innocence, that untarnished source of light, which the poem regrets and which by virtue of memory is still understood, and even felt (throughout the poem, and in spite, or perhaps because of, assertions to the contrary) as a permanence, a primeval continuity.

Yet, in the *Ode*, and certainly after it, Wordsworth's way of looking becomes less retrospective, more of the present, and elegiacally forward. The eye that saw the dawn keeps watch also on 'The Clouds that gather round the setting sun'; this progress Wordsworth sums up with the line 'Another race hath been, and other palms are won'; a remark which seems to refer most immediately to a kind of 'getting through' each day, though it is perhaps also a passing epitaph on each human life of which the sunset is an emblem. What it seems to imply is a new sense of time in Wordsworth – sensing, as he did, a change in the force of his poetic memory, he prepares a new, and more 'sober'[1], attitude of day-to-day continuity, an attitude, as we shall notice, he had already observed in others, and already hinted at in the lines which he later put as an epigraph to the *Ode*.

The sorrow which Wordsworth describes in the opening stanzas of the *Ode* was relieved for a while, he says (l. 23), by a 'timely utterance': it seems most likely that it was the famous lyric about the rainbow:[2]

> My heart leaps up when I behold
> A rainbow in the sky:
> So was it when my life began;
> So is it now I am a man;
> So be it when I shall grow old,

---

[1] v. l. 198.
[2] v. *PW* 4, p. 466: and Garrod, *Wordsworth*, p. 113.

> Or let me die!
> The Child is father of the Man;
> And I could wish my days to be
> Bound each to each by natural piety.

This simple response to nature is here explicitly thought of in terms of time past, present, and future: Wordsworth's sense of time, of continuity, is exemplified in nature and his relation to it: the 'strength' of natural time may be imparted to the man bound to human time (and so experiencing a sporadic and essentially dwindling sense of temporal life) if he is a devout and humble worshipper of Nature – if, out of 'natural piety', he keeps the memory of childhood alive, if he remembers that 'the Child is father of the Man'.

Such memory is part of the continuity of human life, of days 'bound each to each', part of that sense of travelling, moving in time further and further from the sources of childhood. What it leads towards, though its energy may be diminishing, is a state of meditative, indeed, absolute, peace. Wordsworth seems to have been aware of this idea, this goal, early on, at least in others if not in himself. The short poem which he published in 1798 called 'Old Man Travelling; Animal Tranquillity and Decay' is a good example of this. 'He travels on . . .' – and everything about him, his expression, his appearance, his shape,

>   all bespeak
> A man who does not move with pain, but moves
> With thought. – He is insensibly subdued
> To settled quiet . . .

He has been patient so long, says Wordsworth, he no longer seems to need patience:

> He is by nature led
> To peace so perfect that the young behold
> With envy, what the Old Man hardly feels.

This 'tranquillity', this state of being 'insensibly subdued to settled quiet', has an almost mystical sense of calm, in relation to time – to the old man's movements in travelling, which are not physical, 'with pain', but seem to make almost a purely spiritual kind of journey, 'with thought'. That Wordsworth, some years later, in the *Ode*, should have a clearer knowledge of this state's relevance to himself, is probable enough. 'Settled quiet' was not his aim: but in his own travelling, 'daily farther from the east',[1] something akin to a 'wise passiveness'[2] in regard to time seemed worth trying for.

We noticed how Wordsworth advocated a 'quiet eye'[3] in looking at the natural world: how he considered the making of active judgments and comparisons merely detracted from a true understanding of nature. He meant that the natural world should be allowed to impress itself more or less unconsciously on the mind, and this state, as far as it was concerned with looking at nature and responding to landscape, he seems to have achieved. Later he seems to have been able to extend what is recognizably the same 'wise passiveness' – an effect of memory, of allowing past experience to form itself and reappear – from the seeing of nature to the experiencing of time.

In the *Ode*, the sense of time is beginning to transcend the declining activity of memory – or rather, the active memory takes on a more elegiac, more purely consolatory mood: it also remains, at least within the poem, closely enough related to landscape and childhood for the human time-sense of working, travelling, going forwards, to be maintained. The poet is engaged in human life no less than in transcendent memory – his continuity remains one of action, that is, of creative, poetic action. Yet 'natural piety' and the sense of time flowing, of days 'bound each to each', includes a further 'wise passiveness' in Time. The 'patience' of the 'Old Man Travelling' looks forward to the patience of Emily in *The White Doe*: although, as we shall see, in the later poem this patience is more closely related to an active time-sense which is integrated with the story, to an idea of time and memory which Wordsworth wants not merely to sense or describe but to work out in action.

The White Doe could be described as a study of 'wise passiveness' in Time. Its story is concerned, as Wordsworth insisted, not with physical, material success, but with spiritual success: the fate of the Nortons, the destruction of family and house in the Rising of the North, is subordinate to the ultimate triumph of Emily in attaining peace of mind, and, even in human life, a real spirituality. 'The mere physical action was unsuccessful: but the true action of the poem was spiritual –

---

[1] *Ode*, l. 72.   [2] v. 'Expostulation and Reply', l. 24.
[3] v. 'A Poet's Epitaph', l. 51: and Ch. 2 supra.

the subduing of the will, and all inferior passions, to the perfect purifying and spiritualizing of the intellectual nature . . .' As Wordsworth further suggested, by the lines from *The Borderers* which began the epigraph he set to it, the poem opposes action (that is, physical action, in this case the Rising) and suffering.

> 'Action is transitory – a step, a blow,
> The motion of a muscle – this way or that –
> 'Tis done; and in the after-vacancy
> We wonder at ourselves like men betrayed:
> Suffering is permanent, obscure and dark,
> And has the nature of infinity . . .'[1]

Two feelings about time are put forward here: the transitory nature of human life, involved in day-to-day activity, and the sense of permanence inherent in a spiritual condition. Suffering is a spiritual state, the endurance of suffering certainly a spiritual achievement. In *The White Doe*, the suffering is Emily's: in the face of action by all the other members of her family, Emily represents patience:

> *Her duty is to stand and wait;*
> In resignation to abide
> The shock, AND FINALLY SECURE
> O'ER PAIN AND GRIEF A TRIUMPH PURE.   ll. 1069–72

This is the master-key to the poem's meaning: Wordsworth, perhaps aware that it was a little difficult to grasp – especially in a poem so closely related to the heroic world and energetic form of the ballad – and plainly anxious to insist on it, added the italics and capitals after the first edition. Patience, then, implies suffering, endurance, and takes place in Time: but has also something of 'the nature of infinity', something of that state which exists outside human time. It is towards this state that Emily moves, thereby transcending suffering, as the lines Wordsworth added to those early six from *The Borderers* indicate – through the darkness of suffering, infinite though it may seem, 'gracious openings lie'; there is a further region, 'the fountain-head of peace divine', which lies beyond all human suffering, and which is accessible, he adds, even in life, even to the soul 'from mortal bonds/Yet undelivered'.

[1] cf. *The Borderers*, ll. 1539–44.

What Emily achieves is a kind of pure patience, like that of the 'Old Man Travelling', the patience of pure thought, outside all pain, either physical or emotional. She achieves it by coming to live, as nearly as she can on earth, in a world outside time. But this is only towards the very end of the poem: for the most part, as we shall see, Emily is bound too closely to human time and circumstances to have yet achieved her state of grace. The spiritual action of the poem is the important one: but the total action must include the various events as they take place, the ballad alarms and warfare no less than the movements and communings of Emily and the Doe. The sense of time runs strongly through the poem's action: the end of this action, as we have suggested, is a form of mystical time-resolution, in which Emily is more or less released from human time, from the sense of onwardness and of the past. Yet there is a sense of the past within the narrative which carries much of the emotional weight of the poem: it is an illustration of Wordsworth's sense of time become not only general and reflective, but seemingly quite external to himself.

This sense of the past shows itself in a number of ways, implicitly enough in the worlds both of northern ballad and historical event in which the poem is set: but it is within the narrative itself that a time-sense is created which leads the more effectively to the ultimate time-resolution. Within the story, a narrative past is frequently evoked – a past, that is, which is particularly antecedent to the characters and events being described. It works most strongly within the relationship of Emily and the Doe, but it appears within the other action too. For example, after Francis has made his stand against his father, he walks in meditation from the hall into the open, to a 'sheltered spot':

> There stood he, cleansed from the despair
> And sorrow of his fruitless prayer.
> The past he calmly hath reviewed . . .   439–41

The 'past' here implies both the historical past of the Reformation and Francis' own past within his family history: by becoming aware of it and calmly meditating on it, he has achieved a measure of tranquillity. On the other hand, old Norton, bitterly meditating that the rebel forces have agreed to retreat, and already sensing the ruin of his hopes, is led to think of his reluctantly obedient daughter and his defaulting son, and to look back on the time when their mother converted them to the reformed faith:

> Far back – far back my mind must go
> To reach the well-spring of this woe!   887–8

For Norton, awaiting action, memory, reflection on the past, reveals only sorrow, and its slow growth in time.

This same sense of the past within the narrative relates to Emily too: after Francis has left her, and she is awaiting the outcome of events, she wanders uneasily in the ornamental garden at Rylstone; as she approaches a rustic Shed

> Hung with late-flowering woodbine, spread
> Along the walls and overhead,
> The fragrance of the breathing flowers
> Revived a memory of those hours
> When here, in this remote alcove . . .
> A fondly-anxious Mother strove
> To teach her salutary fears
> And mysteries above her years.   1022–32

An image, an actual vision of her mother returns to her, and she is soothed by this memory. But she is too preoccupied with the immediate future for any lasting consolation; she is anxious, impatient, and only the injunction laid upon her by her brother prevents her going after him and her father.

It is this harsh and metaphysical injunction which creates the time-world in which Emily will eventually achieve her spiritual triumph. 'Hope nothing' he has said to her;

> Hope nothing, I repeat; for we
> Are doomed to perish utterly . . .
> Weep, if that aid thee; but depend
> Upon no help of outward friend;
> Espouse thy doom at once, and cleave
> To fortitude without reprieve.

He prophesies a total destruction for Rylstone, for its gardens, for its animals – and for his sister,

doomed to be
The last leaf on a blasted tree . . .

And, although he bids her

> Be strong; be worthy of the grace
> Of God, and fill thy destined place:
> A Soul, by force of sorrows high,
> Uplifted to the purest sky
> Of undisturbed humanity . . . ,   583–7

he has nothing constructive to offer: he can recommend only what
Emily comes to recognize in him,

> . . . that most lamentable snare,
> The self-reliance of despair.   1055–6

It is the function of the Doe to help Emily save herself from this.
Emily knows that she must maintain a 'wise passiveness' – she knows,
as Wordsworth pointed out in his I.F. note to the poem, 'that her duty
is not to interfere with the current of events', but to wait patiently and
'finally secure' her triumph over all affliction. The Doe's part in this
Wordsworth makes quite clear; Emily achieves her triumph 'not
without aid from the communication with the inferior Creature, which
often leads her thoughts to revolve upon the past with a tender and
humanizing influence that exalts rather than depresses her'. Looking
back on what she has endured, 'revolving her thoughts on the past',
Emily gradually becomes free of human time, while the Doe becomes
almost a symbol of this past, of the sense of it and of memory: if the
principal character in the poem is Emily, the prevailing influence is the
Doe. But first of all, Emily has to learn something of human endurance
in Time. She is a creature of human time, subject to its laws: Wordsworth insists on this. When Emily has retired to Norton Tower,
Wordsworth makes the contrast between the gay times it once knew
when all 'the youthful Nortons' met there, and now, when she, the
only one, walks there 'with anguish pale': and he goes on

> 'Tis well that she hath heard the tale,
> Received the bitterness of woe:
> For she *had* hoped, had hoped and feared,
> Such rights did feeble nature claim . . . ,   1190–3

'such rights', in fact, as any human bound to time cannot help claiming. And similarly, much later, after Wordsworth invoked his muse to

> take her anguish and her fears
> Into a deep recess of years! 1566–7

he emphasizes, describing her dress as being one like a 'wandering Pilgrim's', that she could not remain in an utter stillness of suffering:

> And she *hath* wandered, long and far,
> Beneath the light of sun and star . . .: 1611–2

human action was a necessity. She had tried to obey her brother's command of complete passivity, and its implication, almost total despair: and when the old retainer had offered to help her, while the course of events was still in doubt, she had asked him to go to her father – and had added:

> but on my mind
> A passive stillness is enjoined. 1086–7

Yet this was not to be so easily attained: and it is only after, as it were, Emily admits fully her subjection to human time that it could be. And it is with the help of the Doe that Emily finally achieves this peace. The Doe is a thing of mystery: this is made clear from the start. Wordsworth places himself in historical time

> (For 'tis the sunrise now of zeal;
> Of a pure faith the vernal prime –) 40–1

very firmly in company with the Doe, but does not commit himself to the physical reality of the creature – in fact the historical sense adds to the mystery:

> 'Tis a work for sabbath hours
> If I with this bright Creature go:
> Whether she be of forest bowers,
> From the bowers of earth below;
> Or a Spirit for one day given,
> A pledge of grace from purest heaven.

And among the watchers he describes, the mystery is further increased by various irrelevant, and, as is suggested, all-too-human fancies about why the Doe appears. The watching boy (who, mysteriously enough, blushed, 'A shame-faced blush of glowing red!') is unsure:

> Bright was the Creature, as in dreams
> The Boy had seen her, yea, more bright;
> But is she truly what she seems?
> He asks with insecure delight –   192–5

And this doubt, Wordsworth says, extends to all the watchers; and this, he emphasizes, goes on

> spite of sober Truth that sees
> A world of fixed remembrances
> Which to this mystery belong . . .   208–10

And, having outlined some of the fantasies which accumulate around the Doe, he repeats that they persist 'in spite/Of recollections clear and bright' (ll. 316–7) – recollections, these are, as to the real historical circumstances of the case. What Wordsworth has felt he must establish is that, for the watchers, the historical past is obscured by the Doe's mystery: and that it is his, Wordsworth's, duty to remember this factual past clearly the better to illustrate, to illumine the true spiritual mystery. By clearing the ground of the factual past (a narrative and ballad past, that is, rather than an antiquarian past) he is able to concentrate on the mystery and its relation to the time and events of the story.

As far as its influence on the action of the poem is concerned, the Doe only comes into its own after Emily's return from her long, pilgrim-like wanderings: when a troop of deer come sweeping past Emily and the Doe detaches itself from the onward rushing, and greets her softly, as it seems, diffidently:

> So to her feet the Creature came,
> And laid its head upon her knee,
> And looked into the Lady's face,
> A look of pure benignity,
> And fond unclouded memory.   1653–7

The 'memory' here, the 'unclouded' look, is primarily one of recognition: though there is also a suggestion of a purity in time perhaps only to be found in an animal: its natural innocence preserves the past unclouded, keeps it permanently with it. And, in fact, this is one aspect of time which the Doe represents, a narrative continuity, bridging the past action with Emily's present state of comparative calm.

> It is, thought Emily, the same,
> The very Doe of other years!

And it is this recognition which will complete her restoration, induce her to a genuine 'passive stillness'.[1]

Emily has already, by a conscious awareness of time, furthered her restoration and ultimate spiritual triumph. After her wanderings, 'long and far', she has returned to her 'native wilds':

> Hath seen again her Father's roof,
> And put her fortitude to proof;
> The mighty sorrow hath been borne,
> And she is thoroughly forlorn:
> Her soul doth in itself stand fast,
> Sustained by memory of the past
> And strength of Reason . . .   1618–25

The value of memory is that it enables her fully to accept the onwardness of human time – and by fully accepting it, to be 'redeemed' from it, to suffer no regret at

> The memory of what has been,
> And never more will be.[2]

A deep awareness of the past has now created a sense of time which is purely forward-looking.

To complete that progress forward, a state in which even the sense of time will disappear, unheeded, must be achieved. It is to be reached by an awareness and a deep understanding of the past which identifies the past of human time with the past, or rather the timelessness, of immortality, and this is what, with the Doe's help and through her influence, Emily finally does achieve. This help is the Doe's true function, and, at the very end of the poem is revealed her true nature, which enabled her to perform it;

> 'Thou, thou are not a Child of Time,
> But Daughter of the Eternal Prime!'   1909–10

[1] l. 1087: v. supra.   [2] 'Three Years she grew', ll. 41–2.

A thing of Eternity, she yet remains embodied on earth, a thing of nature: and by taking part in human life, in human time, her function is changed, or enlarged.

The Doe, then, here takes on a restorative function; she becomes an influence by which time is transcended: she represents 'the lovely phantom of buried memories'[1] – for Emily she is

> This lovely chronicler of things
> Long past, delights and sorrowings.   1674–5

The Doe's persistence in following Emily, without any positive encouragement, adds force to its symbolic function, its embodiment of memory and the past. Emily shrinks, on one occasion, when seeing the Doe unexpectedly; but yet resolves not to 'shun', but to 'feel' and 'bear' (l. 1699). Eventually, as though time were redeemed, as though Emily were completely reconciled with the past in the achievement of present calm, she looks unflinchingly:

> For she hath ventured now to read
> Of time, and place, and thought, and deed –
> Endless history that lies
> In her silent Follower's eyes . . .   1714–7

Now Emily feels she is able to return to Rylstone for good (after her return from wandering, she had not at first been able to remain there): with the Doe she returns:

> And, ranging through the wasted groves,
> Received the memory of old loves,
> Undisturbed and undistrest,
> Into a soul which now was blest
> With a soft spring-day of holy,
> Mild, and grateful, melancholy . . .   1753–8

So it is that with the Doe's help Emily learns to accept the past, to feel the memory of all that has gone before equably and with calm pleasure: the past is no longer a time of either present suffering, or a sense of inaccessible joy. Time now, and memory, are practically superseded by stillness; and when, at last, Emily's soul 'Rose to the God from whom it came' (l. 1868), she herself was but 'faintly, faintly tied/

[1] Legouis, in *C.H.E.L.*, XI.

To earth'. The Doe it is who remains: this symbol of past time, of continuity, and of perfect innocence,

> Partakes, in her degree, Heaven's grace;
> And bears a memory and a mind
> Raised far above the law of kind . . .   1876–8

Time has become something real to her animal nature: the 'memory' and the 'mind' she bears has at least the virtues of a human sense of time; but if as animal the Doe has gained her 'apotheosis', as Wordsworth said she did,[1] by contact with Emily, by participation in human life, yet as a principle, governing the poem and Emily's spiritual growth, she has also led the action to that eternity outside human life, to that place of light beyond the borders of day-to-day living which, for Wordsworth, was at once the source and striving-point of memory and of poetry.

---

[1] v. *PW* 3, pp. 543, 547 (I.F. note; letter to Wrangham, January 18, 1816).

CHAPTER 4

The Landscape of Memory

IF *The White Doe* represents a triumph of 'passive stillness', of 'wise passiveness' in Time – a state in which action becomes calm endurance, and in which, eventually, the passing of time seems no longer to be felt–it may further be read as a culmination of certain of Wordsworth's native ideas about time – those ideas which reveal themselves throughout the ten or so years of his finest poetry and which are an integral part of his awareness, experience, and poetic use of memory. It will be worth while to examine more closely a few of these ideas, for, in terms both of imagery and of narrative situation, they help to illuminate certain aspects of Wordsworth's poetic thinking – in particular, the deep relationship between memory and landscape, and the contrast, understood by way of memory, between nature's time and man's.

Hart-leap Well, for example, is a poem whose connection with *The White Doe* is not confined to the theme of animal innocence; it is also a poem about the power of nature's time over human activity: just as Emily, with the help of the Doe, is redeemed from human time, so, it is suggested, the desolate spot that Wordsworth comes upon, tainted by 'the hand of man' (l. 112), will eventually be restored to its pure and natural state. The idea is not here worked out in the action, nor is it stated in the implicitly Christian terms of *The White Doe*: but the 'reading' of Time put forward is essentially the same. The first half of the poem describes the hunting and death of the Hart: Wordsworth brings a sense of mystery to the ballad-like scene, if only to prepare for the strange desolation and the reflectively spiritual comfort of the second half.

> – This chase it looks not like an earthly chase;
> Sir Walter and the Hart are left alone.   ll. 27–8

Hunter and animal, man and nature, are opposed. At the spring where the Hart dies the knight builds 'a pleasure-house' and 'a small arbour', and 'a basin for that fountain' framed by 'a cunning artist': and he boasts that

> 'Till the foundations of the mountains fail
> My mansion with its arbour shall endure . . .'   ll. 73–4

Flowers intertwined with trailing plants and trees grow up, dancers and minstrels come, and Sir Walter leads there 'his wondering Paramour'. But, of course, such revelry and such merely human activity are not destined to last:

> The Knight, Sir Walter, died in course of time . . .   l. 93

And with him died his boast; human life had intruded on animal innocence, artificial life had intruded on natural simplicity: a desolation comes, which is the state, the ruined and blighted scene, that Wordsworth encounters, and which, as he says, provides 'matter for a second rhyme'.

The second half of the poem – a pastoral after the ballad – leads up to the moral (ll. 179–80) not only that we should not 'blend our pleasure or our pride' with harm to anything of Nature's ('With sorrow of the meanest thing that feels'), but also that Nature will, in her own way, take 'a deep and reverential care' (l. 167) of any place or creature against which man has acted with presumption. Such care will be made known through time, through the action of time. Wordsworth, finding the spot now both ruined and desolate, deserted as it seemed by Nature (ll. 115–16), yet finds reassurance in a contemplation beyond the present moment.

> 'The pleasure-house is dust: – behind, before,
> This is no common waste, no common gloom;
> But Nature, in due course of time, once more
> Shall here put on her beauty and her bloom . . .'
>   ll. 169–72

Just as Sir Walter had died 'in course of time', so Nature, at some point in the future, will return to the place she only seems to have deserted. 'In due course of time' the spot will revert to its natural state.

Wordsworth, in recognizing that the desolation is 'no common' one, suggests that the continuity of nature's time is maintained, poetically, by the influence (as in *The White Doe*) of the animal, in this case, through the memory of the dead Hart. The shepherd has said

> '. . . we cannot tell
> What cause the Hart might have to love this place,
> And come and make his death-bed near the well . . .',
>
> ll. 146–8

but the implication is that, poetically, there is a very natural cause:

> 'This water was perhaps the first he drank
> When he had wandered from his mother's side . . . ,
>
> . . . he perhaps, for aught we know, was born
> Not half a furlong from that self-same spring.

And so he had returned to this source, almost, of his life, and the symbol of its continuity. When he had died, stretched out on the ground, his nostril, says Wordsworth, had touched this spring,

> And with the last deep groan his breath had fetched
> The waters of the spring were trembling still.   ll. 43–4

Now, says the shepherd, often, at night, this water 'doth send forth a dolorous groan' (l. 136). It was as though, at the end of the Hart's life, no less than near its beginning, his breath had impregnated the water: the natural continuity of the flowing spring is now linked with a definite past and future, instilled with that breath which images the animal life, and represents the unnatural interruption of it.

The ruins still exist to emphasize, for Wordsworth, the moral lesson. Nature, he says,

> . . . leaves these objects to a slow decay,
> That what we are, and have been, may be known;
> But at the coming of the milder day
> These monuments shall all be overgrown.   ll. 173–6

The present human condition, and the historical past, are made evident by this ruined place: but the ultimate reversion to a pure and natural landscape, when everything shall be 'overgrown', is only a matter of time – of a future and certainly metaphysical time, yet a time which is not, Wordsworth seems to have thought, entirely out of reach of the human present.

The Hart, like the White Doe, is a child of 'The Eternal Prime', though in a more subdued and, in so far as it was actually dead, realistic sense. The everlasting Spring, 'the milder day', which the Hart embodies in the poem, this ultimate reward of human life, seemed to Wordsworth, at this period, about the time of his composing *Hart-leap Well*, to have been attainable even on earth – as he was also to suggest in the later lines of his epigraph to *The White Doe*. At least, such an idea is indicated in a passage, occurring in MSS A and B of *The Recluse*, written soon after *Hart-leap Well*, which forms, as de Selincourt points out, 'an interesting commentary on the spirit in which he composed the poem'.[1] It gives, amongst other things, a further indication of how Wordsworth's understanding of natural time in relation to human time worked in close conjunction with his ideas of memory and landscape. He describes a moment when he and Dorothy were on their way to take up residence at Dove Cottage, a moment

> when the trance
> Came to us, as we stood by Hartleap Well,
> The intimation of the milder day
> Which is to be, the fairer world than this . . .[2]

'The milder day', that time when, as it seems, the fretful life of man will have been spiritually taken up, overwhelmed and 'overgrown', by Nature, seemed then to be almost accessible – for Wordsworth and his sister at least: for, having contemplated the sad story of the Hart, and having received an intimation of this better time to come,

> Both in the sadness and the joy we found
> A promise and an earnest that we twain,
> A pair seceding from the common world,
> Might in that hallow'd spot to which our steps
> Were tending, in that individual nook
> Might, even thus early, for ourselves secure,
> And in the midst of these unhappy times,
> A portion of the blessedness which love

---

[1] v. *PW* 2, pp. 514–15.   [2] *PW* 2, p. 515.

And knowledge will, we trust, hereafter give
To all the vales of earth and all mankind.

The idea of redemption from time, 'the coming of the milder day',[1]
is here found in close relationship with the idea of seclusion, of finding
a 'hallow'd spot', an 'individual nook'. In Wordsworth this particular
landscape idea of seclusion seems to be closely related to the idea of
memory – memory (and the tranquillity necessary for its poetic working) imagined as a type of seclusion of the mind. Wordsworth's conceptual landscape has certain steady features, and certain recognizable
places to which he constantly returns, which at least indicate a need for
stability and continuity. He devoted much of his sense of time to the
workings of memory in relation to landscape: here we shall try to
indicate the connection of ideas of seclusion, and of assured place, with
various deeply remembered sources of poetry.

We have noticed 'Picturesque' and 'sensuous' ways of looking helping to associate particular events and occasions with the landscape
observed: but there is another kind of landscape, more ideal, more
inwardly symbolic (best exemplified by Lucy's Heath), with which not
so much event as recurrent spiritual situation is identified. The tranquillity of the Heath was, we suggested, both an image and cradle of
memory – and the retirement of the valley at Grasmere suggests, and
may have suggested to Wordsworth, that seclusion in which the past
could be poetically contemplated and invoked.

The landscape at Hartleap Well, presenting as it did 'no common
waste, no common gloom',[2] had an obvious symbolic quality – a
quality in Wordsworth's poetry remarkably consistent, in which
certain natural objects take on a curious emblematic significance: perhaps the most striking example is the imagery of 'The Thorn'. The
sinister tree, the mossy hillock, the muddy pond, these and other
mounds of turf, admonitory trees, little pools, growths of moss, these
strange emblems seem closely connected with various 'green spots'
and landscape nooks, signs and places which may be further classed
together with a consistent imagery of 'enclosure': a good example of
one of these significant spots is the place where Peter Bell found the
Ass.

[1] *Hart-leap Well*, l. 175. [2] *Hart-leap Well*, l. 170.

Beneath the clear blue sky he saw
A little field of meadow ground;
But field or meadow name it not;
Call it of earth a small green plot,
With rocks encompassed round.

The Swale flowed under the grey rocks,
But he flowed quiet and unseen: –
You need a strong and stormy gale
To bring the noises of the Swale
To that green spot, so calm and green![1]

This 'soft and fertile nook', this 'deep and quiet spot', as he goes on to call it, has all those elements of tranquillity and seclusion which go with the deepest workings of Wordsworth's imagination. An equation of such emblems and spots with the notion of 'spots of time'[2] would be difficult to substantiate; but they form a complex of imagery which suggests some obscure connection with the workings of memory: they seem to stand as focal points of significant experience (such as memory dealt with), they seem to be locations at once of calm atmosphere and heightened emotion.

At all events, the idea of seclusion, protection, is often important in Wordsworth's poetry. The White Doe, for example, at the end of the poem, at Rylstone,

Loves most what Emily loved most –
The enclosure of this church-yard ground;[3]

and this seems but a small change, in terms of symbolic imagery, from

The grassy rock-encircled Pound
In which the Creature first was found.[4]

It was a spot which Emily held 'sacred' partly for this reason; and it seems to indicate something of the Doe's special and enduring significance as a thing set apart. Most of these particular images of enclosure, the sheepfold in *Michael*, for instance, or the churchyard in *The Brothers*, would be fully explained only in terms of close individual

---

[1] *Peter Bell*, ll. 366–75.   [2] *Prel* XI, 258.
[3] *The White Doe*, ll. 1881–2.   [4] ibid., ll. 1803–4.

analysis: but the larger, more overtly landscape idea of seclusion is immediately apparent and worth considering, in fairly general terms, in relation to Wordsworth's sense of time and memory.

For Wordsworth, then, there seems to have existed an ideal landscape, an inward landscape of the mind, in which certain secluded spots, and certain numinous images, together with, as we shall see, certain larger seclusions and certain larger forms, had a permanent validity. It is not only the significance of Lucy's Heath which suggests that they were things of memory and of time. Wordsworth's time-sense is shown working strongly in his two major pastoral poems, *The Brothers* and *Michael* – both of which were written in 1800, during the same period of composition as *The Recluse* fragment and *Hart-leap Well*. The action of both takes place in a landscape-setting 'out of time', outside the main stream of human activity: reflecting the literary significance, while drawing little or nothing from it, of Pastoral and the Arcadian world. *Michael* indicates as much in its opening lines:

> If from the public way you turn your steps . . . ,

then, we are told, you may come upon that 'hidden valley', the 'utter solitude', in which the action of the poem takes place. Similarly, the action of *The Brothers* takes place in a remote mountain churchyard. *The Brothers* is a poem of return, and of remembering – and like *The White Doe*, it shows an awareness of the workings of memory within the action, which contributes towards a total and more absolute feeling of the power of time and memory together. The churchyard, in its mountain setting, is a place of seclusion and of nature's time. Leonard, the returning brother, puts it truly enough to the priest:

> You live, Sir, in these dales, a quiet life:
> Your years make up one peaceful family;
> And who would grieve and fret, if, welcome come
> And welcome gone, they are so like each other,
> They cannot be remembered?   ll. 121–5

The years blend into each other with that continuity which is a gift of nature, and not of any human sense of time. Yet, as the Priest insists, the native time-sense of the dales is strongly aware of human passing, of human life and death – but with no very absolute sense of the past. There are no tombstones in the graveyard not because, as Leonard suggests, the people of the district are 'heedless of the past', but because the memory of those who are gone seems to continue unaided in the present:

> We have no need of names and epitaphs;
> We talk about the dead by our fire-sides.
> And then, for our immortal part! *we* want
> No symbols, Sir, to tell us that plain tale:
> The thought of death sits easy on the man
> Who has been born and dies among the mountains.
>
> ll. 178–83

As Leonard sees it,

> Your Dalesmen, then, do in each other's thoughts
> Possess a kind of second life . . .

It is, then, to such a setting, in which the human past is overcome, cancelled almost, redeemed from time, that Leonard returns. It is a place of continuity and calm – for those who are part of it. So it is that when Leonard eventually discovers that his brother has died, he remembers his past in the valley, and, in becoming strongly aware of his separation from it (in terms of time no less than of space, during his twenty years' absence as a sailor), he feels that the calm is too much for him: he cannot bring himself to reveal his identity and to bear his grief with the understanding of acceptance – a thing he would have learnt within the temporal calm of the mountains – and so he must leave this quiet valley, representing, as it does for him, 'the memory of what has been and never more will be'. It no longer seemed possible to stay: Leonard, when he had heard the full story of his brother's death, continued on his journey; then stopped short for a moment,

> And, sitting down beneath the trees, reviewed
> All that the Priest had said: his early years
> Were with him: – his long absence, cherished hopes,
> And thoughts which had been his an hour before,
> All pressed on him with such a weight, that now,
> This vale, where he had been so happy, seemed
> A place in which he could not bear to live . . .   ll. 420–6

'His early years were with him' – the force of memory, pressing, weighing on him, an almost physical power, the sense of time as he

144

reflects on the distance separating him, by way of 'his long absence', from his mountain childhood, these are too great to be borne passively. He has not yet come to that true 'wise passiveness' in time which will enable Emily, for example – eventually, after many years of wandering – to return and settle at Rylstone.

Leonard is a man who has become too strongly infected by way of memory with a sense of human time. At sea he bore with him many traces of his mountain upbringing: although he was twenty years a sailor, yet

> he had been reared
> Among the mountains, and he in his heart
> Was half a shepherd on the stormy seas.
> Oft in the piping shrouds had Leonard heard
> The tones of waterfalls, and inland sounds
> Of caves and trees . . . ,   ll. 44-9

and, in the grip of fever, of the Calenture, he saw, on the sea-bed, mountains, and sheep on the 'verdant hills', dwellings, 'And shepherds clad in the same country grey/Which he himself had worn'. Yet now that he has actually returned to this 'inland' place, the past evoked in memory is too much, the 'pressure' is too great for him. It is as though, having left his native mountains and the world of natural time, he finds the power of memory doubly intensified – by his becoming aware of the world from which he was separated, he first became aware of human time and memory, and now, bearing the weight of a particular memory (his brother and all that meant to him), he realizes the power anew, and at the source of his whole awareness of it.

Certainly, in the description of Leonard's return, there is an explicit emphasis on his awareness of memory's working. Wondering if his brother had died (so that there would be another grave in the church-yard at that spot where his family were laid), he indeed finds another grave:

> near which a full half-hour
> He had remained; but, as he gazed, there grew
> Such a confusion in his memory,
> That he began to doubt; and even to hope
> That he had seen this heap of turf before, –

> That it was not another grave; but one
> He had forgotten.   ll. 85–91

This thought brings him to a recollection of a more immediate act of forgetfulness.

> He had lost his path,
> As up the vale, that afternoon, he walked
> Through fields which once had been well known to him:
> And oh what joy this recollection now
> Sent to his heart!

This awareness of defects of accuracy within the overwhelming total power of memory at once emphasizes the importance of that power, and of the emotion of returning, to Leonard, and shows further how the past is not a question of accurate recollection, but of the sense of time felt as a continuing presence: while, by this inner play of remembering within the narrative, a feeling is built up for the force of change within a remembered past. Leonard went on to imagine that he saw

> Strange alteration wrought on every side
> Among the woods and fields, and that the rocks,
> And everlasting hills themselves were changed . . .:

which, up to a point, they were. Change, even in landscape, is to be expected, though it will not always be noticeable. Leonard imagines certain changes from what he remembered, changes which the Priest doubts; but one feature, the disappearance of one well-known spring from a pair, is plain to them both.

> Ay, there, indeed, your memory is a friend
> That does not play you false.   ll. 138–9

This change in nature is an admonitory symbol of what Leonard must be prepared to hear, the death of his brother.

The vale, then, is a place where poetic memory – the sense of time past felt as both separation and regret, distance and continuity – is scarcely bearable. Had Leonard remained among the hills, he would have had no experience of time other than that of perfect evenness. Change comes in the valley, but is so naturally recorded that the disturbing power of returning, of remembering in spite of time, does not arise.

As the Priest emphasizes, in reply to Leonard's suggestion about the quiet monotony of life in the dales, there is no lack of 'accidents and changes' – both in the natural world of the mountains and in the domestic world, where 'a child is born or christened', or someone dies or leaves the valley.

> And hence, so far from wanting facts or dates
> To chronicle the time, we all have here
> A pair of diaries, – one serving, Sir,
> For the whole dale, and one for each fire-side –
> Yours was a stranger's judgment: for historians,
> Commend me to these valleys!   ll. 161–6

The passing of time is fully experienced in the valley: but time is there felt to be so natural, that a sense of the past with any feeling of regret or 'poetic memory' is unthinkable. It is after this realization on his own part that the Priest goes on to substantiate that death is hardly to be worried at: it has not occurred to him that anyone should need monuments, gravestones, signposts to mark the route of passing time.[1] Only by the man given over to the power of memory are such things – such as Wordsworth found and made in poetry – truly needed.

It is in the same world of natural time that the story of *Michael* is worked out. It is, in one sense, a poem about failure in continuity. Luke, the long-awaited son, has to leave his native valley, to help Michael maintain possession of his land, and then fails to return: the unfinished sheep-fold remains as a symbol of his defection, and of the destruction of Michael's hopes. Wordsworth, as we noticed, deliberately sets his tale off the public road and in a world of inland seclusion and natural time. And he says,

> I will relate the same
> For the delight of a few natural hearts;
> And, with yet fonder feeling, for the sake
> Of youthful Poets, who among these hills
> Will be my second self when I am gone.   ll. 35–9

[1] In obvious enough contrast to the general Eighteenth-century and Romantic interest in monuments, obelisks, tombs: particularly as landscape objects and architectural symbols. Wordsworth's three essays on Epitaphs indicate his own poetic interest in the matter.

This recalls Leonard's remark in *The Brothers*, about how the Dalesmen

> do in each other's thoughts
> Possess a kind of second life,

and shows again Wordsworth's strong sense of continuity in nature, and the close relation of his own thinking with the time-world of the poem. As in *The Brothers*, the story is instinct with a sense of time in relation to human activity and to nature's.

As Wordsworth pointed out, the story was based on 'two of the most powerful affections of the human heart; the parental affection, and the love of property, *landed* property, including the feeling of inheritance, home, and personal and family independence'.[1] The close relationship of these two affections is implicit in Michael: indeed Wordsworth emphasizes that Michael's son was dear to him

> Less from instinctive tenderness, the same
> Fond spirit that blindly works in the blood of all –
> Than that a child, more than all other gifts
> That earth can offer to declining man,
> Brings hope with it, and forward-looking thoughts . . . ,
>
> ll. 144–8

and Wordsworth knew, in describing this looking to the future, the strong connection it had with the earth, the land. And the same connection applied in the other, backward-looking ways of the time-sense, where land was seen as an image and source of memory. What Wordsworth knew as spiritual property, as landscape, was, he suggested, felt as strongly in Dalesmen, such as Michael, as landed property. He illustrated this understanding in a letter he wrote to Fox (January, 1801);

> Their little tract of land serves as a kind of permanent rallying point for their domestic feelings, as a tablet upon which they are written which makes them objects of memory in a thousand instances when they would otherwise be forgotten. It is a fountain fitted to the nature of social man from which supplies of affection, as pure as his heart was intended for, are daily drawn.[2]

Just as various landscapes are a source of memory for Wordsworth in

---

[1] *EL*, p. 266.   [2] *EL*, p. 262.

his poetry, so the setting in which the story of Michael takes place, and the 'little tract of land', the fountain of pure feeling and memory of the past, round which the story centres, are places which make the deep value of continuity in time, as in possession, doubly clear.

In the poem this continuity is suggested in various ways – in the 'endless industry' of Michael and his wife, in the image of their lamp 'going by from year to year',[1] but the time-sense which Wordsworth had particularly in mind is perhaps best illustrated in a manuscript passage which was not finally incorporated with the poem. He describes how

> Among the hills
> Moreover, shepherds' children, when they play
> In those wild places, seem almost to lose
> The quality of childhood, for their sports
> Are sanctified by such collateral aid
> Of majesty as fits them for the hearts
> Of men made grave by years.[2]

It is, in Wordsworth, a surprising enough notion that children should, as it seems, benefit by 'losing the quality of childhood'; but he goes on to explain what he means, and how this state comes about:

> And thus it is
> That in such regions, by the sovereignty
> Of forms still paramount, to every change
> Which years can bring into the human heart
> Our feelings are indissolubly bound
> Together, and affinities preserved
> Between all stages of the life of man . . .

---

[1] l. 119; Wordsworth's imagery is always so naturally part of the world he is describing that its symbolic power is easily overlooked: or rather, such tasks as carding 'Wool for the Housewife's spindle' (l. 107), or repairing 'sickle, flail, or scythe' (l. 108), are so obviously part of Nature's time-world, that their poetic time-symbolism works as naturally as it has always, popularly, done. Cf. *The Brothers*, ll. 17–28, for how the closed circle of Nature's year is suggested; 'a July evening', the Priest 'employed in winter's work': the 'busy hands and back-and-forward steps' with which his youngest child was turning her spindle, 'her large round wheel': the enclosed air of the Parish Chapel, 'Girt round with a bare ring of mossy wall'.

[2] *PW* 2, p. 481.

Continuity in time, a sense of endless and remembered being, that is the great reward for a true feeling for nature, in this case, for the forms of landscape, of the great hills.

Wordsworth, in this fragment, goes on to describe Michael's pleasure in walking the hills with his son, how (as it is stated in the poem, l. 203) 'the old Man's heart seemed born again';

> Hence with more pleasure far than others feel,
> Led by his son, this shepherd now went back
> Into the years which he himself had lived;
> And natural feelings coming from within
> And from without, he to the present time
> Link'd the dear memory of old histories . . .

Past time among the hills is, for Michael, a deeply experienced continuity; perhaps more than those Dalesmen described in *The Brothers* he knows the force of memory as well. He is, after all, a man of special 'Wordsworthian' stature, and one who has recognized the power of landscape and mountain forms to impress themselves for the benefit of future good thinking and pure feeling. Wordsworth emphasizes that Michael was not indifferent to his native landscape, to the streams, and rocks, and hills

> which had impressed
> So many incidents upon his mind
> Of hardship, skill or courage, joy or fear;
> Which, like a book, preserved the memory
> Of the dumb animals, whom he had saved,
> Had fed or sheltered . . .

The landscape is full of a sense of the past: the setting is seen, in all its seclusion, as a spot (similar to that described in a manuscript passage which, according to de Selincourt, 'may have been intended as part of an Introduction to *Michael* . . .')

> Shut out from man, some region – one of those
> That hold by an inalienable right
> An independent Life, and seem the whole
> Of nature and of unrecorded time;[1]

[1] *PW* 2, pp. 479–80.

in some such a place, Wordsworth goes on to say, especially if he has happened upon 'Some vestiges of human hands . . .',

> I look into past times as prophets look
> Into futurity . . .

The geological and human past holds him: and he implied this further background throughout the whole story of *Michael*, based as it is on the hope that past time will be continued in natural evenness: and as Michael feels a rejuvenation and yet a natural continuity, indeed a forward-looking, as he walks the hills with his son (and his wife, as they decide for their future benefit, as they hope, to send Luke out into the world, is busy in her mind, at a more domestic level, 'looking back into past times'),[1] so the sheepfold is to be an emblem of this continuity and security. Michael tells his son:

> . . . let this sheep-fold be
> Thy anchor and thy shield; amid all fear
> And all temptation, let it be to thee
> An emblem of the life thy Fathers lived.[2]

But it is not to be: Luke fails him, and the old man, denied any future hopes for his land, cannot bring himself to complete the building. And so, eventually, amid many changes in the surrounding landscape, it lies, as Wordsworth described it, in a manuscript passage, a heap of stones

> . . . that seem to keep themselves alive
> In the last dotage of a dying form.[3]

Like the ruins at Hartleap Well, it is destined, as a symbol of human activity and of human time, to decay completely: it is a form which, betrayed by human weakness, cannot be part of nature's continuity. 'The unfinished Sheep-fold' makes a poignant contrast with the ever-flowing water near where it lies, 'Beside the boisterous brook of Greenhead Ghyll'.[4]

If the Sheepfold seen by Wordsworth 'In the last dotage of a dying

---

[1] *Michael*, l. 257.
[2] ibid., ll. 406f.: (in 1800 version only – changed perhaps because of the slight mixing of metaphors).
[3] *PW* 2, p. 482, (a).   [4] *Michael*, ll. 481–2.

form' was felt to be a symbol of human activity in time, there were other 'forms' which expressed a greater permanence, forms which, having impressed themselves on memory and thought, were experienced ultimately as things of the mind. Wordsworth had various notions about 'forms' and it would be a separate task to investigate all of these fully and to establish their relationship to his poetry: but in one or two ways in which he thought of certain landscape ideas in relation to a sense of time it has seemed worth illustrating how they worked for him, and how he used them. Before we deal any further with the relationship of landscape to memory, it will be useful to consider one or two of the characters in Wordsworth's poetry who inhabit the landscape of natural time.

Wordsworth's sense of memory and the past often expressed itself as time embodied – not only in his own remembering self, in that way of sensuous continuity which we have tried to describe – but embodied in other things and creatures. We have noticed how he felt a secluded spot in the mountains to seem 'the whole/Of nature and of unrecorded time': or how, in *The Brothers*, the Priest saw the natural and domestic worlds, the hills and the fireside, as 'A pair of diaries'; or how, in *The White Doe*, the animal is seen by Emily as 'This lovely chronicler of things/Long past'. It was in a similar sense that Wordsworth described the Waggoner, in the poem of that name, written in 1805:

> A living almanack had we;
> We had a speaking diary,
> That in this uneventful place,
> Gave to the days a mark and name
> By which we knew them when they came.
>
> Cto. 4, ll. 220–4

He associates this recognition of the Waggoner's regular time-scheme with the working, in himself, of memory: for, in his conclusion to the poem, in the lines immediately preceding this definition of the Waggoner, after having stated how he had long left the theme 'untouched', on account of 'scruples', seemingly about the worthiness of the subject, he goes on:

> But Nature might not be gainsaid;
> For what I have and what I miss

152

> I sing of these; – it makes my bliss!
> Nor is it I who play the part,
> But a shy spirit in my heart,
> That comes and goes – will sometimes leap
> From hiding-places ten years deep;
> Or haunts me with familiar face,
> Returning, like a ghost unlaid,
> Until the debt I owe be paid.   ll. 206–15

This is a plain recognition on Wordsworth's part of the autonomy of memory – and of the sense of continuity in time it brings: he distinguishes two kinds of autonomous working, the one hidden, and returning with a flash, the other recurring more persistently, both implying an awareness of continuing time, And it is for this reason, as he goes on to make clear, that he has had to write about the Waggoner.

> Forgive me, then; for I had been
> On friendly terms with this Machine:
> In him, while he was wont to trace
> Our roads, through many a long year's space,
> A living almanack had we . . .

And it is perhaps the sense of loss, the fact that the Waggoner is no longer travelling, a living symbol of natural time, which gives the situation an added poignancy for Wordsworth. For while he, and all the people of the district,

> Through all the changes of the year,
> Had seen him through the mountains go,
> In pomp of mist or pomp of snow,
> Majestically huge and slow . . . ,

it was as though, an impressive and slightly mysterious presiding spirit, he had been a living reassurance of natural continuity. Now the loss of his regular journeys had cast doubt on this; and for Wordsworth, perhaps, at this date, sensing (as he did in the *Prelude*, Book XI) something of his own failing continuity with the past, the feeling of something lost was particularly strong; and, most of all on stormy nights, he said, 'Do I regret what we have lost'.[1]

---

[1] *The Waggoner*, Cto. 4, l. 265.

A much earlier example of time embodied (in a poem otherwise very different) was the Old Cumberland Beggar, to whom was closely related the 'Old Man Travelling' – that figure who seemed to be almost completely detached from mere human time, who, 'travelling on', seemed to have no awareness of the human world, 'insensibly subdued', as he was, 'to settled quiet'. The Old Cumberland Beggar's most explicit function is one something similar to that of the Waggoner, in that he represents both continuity and regular recurrence in time: as Wordsworth's note at the beginning tells us, the typical beggar had a 'stated round' and certain 'fixed days' on which he would receive alms.

> While from door to door,
> This old Man creeps, the villagers in him
> Behold a record which together binds
> Past deeds and offices of charity
> Else unremembered . . .   ll. 87–91

From door to door he travelled – and (l. 51) 'from day to day'. It was the old Beggar's quality of embodying a sort of pure continuity, going forward in solitude, in isolation, which, at least in the first third of the poem, was of primary importance to Wordsworth. (His social importance[1] as a member of human life, society, and good action – giving scope for those 'little, nameless, unremembered, acts/Of kindness and of love'[2] – is closely related to Wordsworth's own sense of nature's time.)

> Him from my childhood have I known; and then
> He was so old, he seems not older now;
> He travels on, a solitary Man . . .   22–4

Ordinary considerations of age are irrelevant; he seems to be untouched by human time; yet all the while, he is continuing on his way. This quality of perseverance is repeated and emphasized:

> He travels on, a solitary Man;
> His age has no companion. On the ground
> His eyes are turned, and, as he moves along,

[1] v. H. V. D. Dyson, ' "The Old Cumberland Beggar" and the Wordsworthian Unities', in *Essays . . . presented to D. Nichol Smith*, Oxford, 1945.
[2] 'Tintern Abbey', ll. 34–5.

> *They* move along the ground; and, evermore,
> Instead of common and habitual sight
> Of fields with rural works, of hill and dale,
> And the blue sky, one little span of earth
> Is all his prospect.

This curious 'closed' vision, coupled with his endless motion on-wards (which yet, 'he is so still/In look and motion', is barely apparent), makes him a kind of thing of the earth; he seems almost identified with the earth itself. And for this reason he is someone out of human time; he goes on, inevitably, like the road on which he travels – and on which he sees the marks of wheels, but only moment by moment, always

> in the same line,
> At distance still the same.

He has no sense of past or future: he represents complete passiveness in time.

As a symbol also of calm endurance in time, from whom Words-worth could draw strength, he shares an affinity, in this sense, with the Leech-Gatherer, whose body

> was bent double, feet and head
> Coming together in life's pilgrimage.[1]

The Old Beggar, in much the same posture, metaphysically no less than physically, makes up a kind of circuit in close contact with the larger circling earth: he might be taken to represent a way of seeing which is not concerned with the outer world of human activity or even of natural scenery – he presents a state of 'wise passiveness', of tran-quillity in time and the 'quiet eye' of inward vision, which Words-worth, of the 'sensuous' eye, of the backward-looking in memory, and the forward-looking desire in work, could not hope to achieve.

It was in the circling of the earth that Wordsworth sensed most deeply an ultimate calm, in the endless repetition, the assured circle which is Nature's time. If we entertain a slightly ludicrous picture of the Leech-Gatherer or the Old Beggar rolling along like a kind of hoop, this is one way of seeing what Wordsworth means by them; the closed circuit of their vision and thought images the only sense of time

---

[1] *Resolution and Independence*, ll. 66–7.

they know, and brings them towards that ultimate calm which Lucy, or whatever else is the subject of Wordsworth's 'sublime epitaph', enjoys:

> No motion has she now, no force;
> She neither hears nor sees;
> Rolled round in earth's diurnal course,
> With rocks, and stones, and trees.[1]

This calm is almost like Lucy's Heath – a thing of memory, something of the past, ever-present in Nature, though inaccessible. Here, she is in the earth, as she is in a place of natural time, a place of ultimate stability – permanently located within the permanent reassurance of circling day or circling year.

Natural time, then, Wordsworth feels to be fused with earth, embodied in it, something solid, complete, and continuing. But for Wordsworth, given over to the creation of poetry, the sense of human time was less absolute, embodied as it was in the active eye and the power of memory. Stability of place could also remind him strongly of the passing of time. We are often aware, in reading Wordsworth, of a complex of ideas relating place with time: the ideas of tranquillity, landscape seclusion, and the workings of memory, date, as we have seen, from his earliest poetic thinking. The mountains and valleys of his native region contained all the elements of his conceptual landscapes.

We have seen, in the 'Immortality' *Ode*, his fullest expression of human time as a sense of distance, of travelling 'daily farther from the east'; and, as we noticed, this travelling is experienced, celebrated, and in part overcome, or cancelled, by the workings of memory. The 'shadowy recollections' of immortality counter human time: yet human memory can create a sense of tranquillity and seclusion which persists in human time:

> Hence in a season of calm weather
> Though inland far we be,
> Our Souls have sight of that immortal sea
> Which brought us hither,
> Can in a moment travel thither,

---

[1] 'A slumber did my spirit seal', ll. 5–8.

And see the Children sport upon the shore,
And hear the mighty waters rolling evermore.

ll. 162–8

'Inland' he must be, the man bound to human time; the 'immortal sea' is beyond the course of everyday life. Elsewhere the idea of 'calm weather' and of 'inland' seclusion is closely related to the true working of memory. Wordsworth's description, in the *Prelude*, of his childhood visit to Furness Abbey, seems to foreshadow this whole feeling, and shows how it impressed him. It was, he says,

> A holy Scene! along the smooth green turf
> Our Horses grazed: to more than inland peace
> Left by the sea wind passing overhead
> (Though wind of roughest temper) trees and towers
> May in that Valley oftentimes be seen,
> Both silent and both motionless alike;
> Such is the shelter that is there, and such
> The safeguard for repose and quietness.   *Prel* II, 114–21

The calm, the seclusion, is the important feature; man seems almost out of time, and memory of such a spot will at least be a reassurance in human time. In 'Tintern Abbey', the river Wye, rolling with a 'soft inland murmur,'[1] suggests the same feeling: the ever-rolling water is coupled with a very absolute concept of 'inland', although, as Wordsworth indicates in his note, he is standing at a point only a few miles from where the river does become tidal. The actual sea did not, for him, mirror the immortal sea: as for Leonard in *The Brothers* (l. 48), so for Wordsworth it is 'inland sounds' which are important, which seem to hold a mystery, something of the larger past of nature's time – and for the man born into human time, the landscape of seclusion is an immediate image of his own remembered past, and for the more immediate sources of human life.

We have seen how Wordsworth thought of Michael's son feeling continuity in time (while 'losing the quality of childhood')

> by the sovereignty
> Of forms still paramount . . .

[1] l. 4: and v. Wordsworth's note.

It is these 'forms', the great outlines and solid mass of his native hills, with which Wordsworth identified his best feelings; and it is these forms which impressed on him the workings of memory and the sense of time – impressed them on him, that is, unconsciously when he was a child, these impressions being continually repeated and intensified by later reflection and creation in poetry.

The connection of landscape with particular events and occasions was a strong factor in the growing power of Wordsworth's memory: this, coupled with a strongly sensuous eye, and perhaps a trace of Picturesque 'discipline', impressed on his mind features as well as emotions. But, as well as these landscapes of event, and in addition to those landscapes of seclusion, and of natural time, Wordsworth also understood, in the forming of his mind, a more absolute, more ideal landscape which *shaped* his feelings, a conceptual landscape which was constantly and implicitly remembered in the brooding presence of his native mountains. Of the Wanderer, in *The Excursion*, Wordsworth wrote that

> Early had he learned
> To reverence the volume that displays
> The mystery, the life which cannot die . . .[1]

(i.e. the Bible); yet this was not the same as truly experiencing such immortality, and the sense of time which goes with it, as a thing both of mind and body:

> But in the mountains did he *feel* his faith.
> All things, responsive to the writing, there
> Breathed immortality, revolving life,
> And greatness still revolving; infinite . . .

Wordsworth knew the 'impressive' power of such landscape when taken up into the mind, as clearly as he also knew its embodiment of nature's time, endless and 'revolving': here, the gaining of such power was still a thing of the eye – the sensuous eye working with a larger inwardly-receptive vision.

> There littleness was not; the least of things
> Seemed infinite; and there his spirit shaped
> Her prospects, nor did he believe, – he *saw*.

[1] *Excursion* I, 223–5 (*Ruined Cottage*, ll. 146–8).

Such visual contemplation, pure seeing opening on memory, was how best to store the mind with poetic influences for good: and,

> by contemplating these Forms
> In the relations which they bear to man,
> He shall discern, how, through the various means
> Which silently they yield, are multiplied
> The spiritual presences of absent things.[1]

This was the great joy in memory described, experienced, and further intensified by Wordsworth at Tintern – the enduring presence of remembered beauty. In London too he had felt, as he described it in Book VII of the *Prelude*, the reward and benefit of his earlier looking:

> Attention comes,
> And comprehensiveness and memory,
> From early converse with the works of God
> Among all regions; chiefly where appear
> Most obviously simplicity and power.
> By influence habitual to the mind
> The mountain's outline and its steady form
> Gives a pure grandeur, and its presence shapes
> The measure and the prospect of the soul
> To majesty . . .   716–25

Wordsworth fully understood his debt to 'the forms/Perennial of the ancient hills' – as also to 'The changeful language of their countenances . . .'; his native regions were a permanent image of the past, and they became a true symbol and a true location of the workings of memory – of memory, not only as a steadying influence, but in all its modes.

Phantoms of lost power, sudden intuitions, and shadowy restorations of forgotten feelings, sometimes dim and perplexing, sometimes by bright but furtive glimpses, sometimes by a full and steady revelation, overcharged with light – throw us back in a moment upon scenes and remembrances that we have left full thirty years behind us. In solitude, and chiefly in the solitudes of nature; and, above all, amongst the great and *enduring* features of nature, such as

---

[1] *Excursion* IV, ll. 1230–4.

159

mountains, and quiet dells, and the lawny recesses of forests, and the silent shores of lakes, features with which (as being themselves less liable to change) our feelings have a more abiding association – under these circumstances it is that such evanescent hauntings of our past and forgotten selves are most apt to startle and to waylay us.

So de Quincey:[1] a subjective and inclusive development of that old landscape idea expressed, for example, by James Beattie, of how the 'durable things' of nature 'take faster hold of the memory'.[2] For Wordsworth, both the idea and the involuntary emotions described by de Quincey played important parts. But his poetry emerged by way of memory most powerfully and most valuably through those deeply impressed feelings which Nature 'Thrusts forth upon the senses',[3] through his native landscape being continuously experienced both in actuality and in memory as an enduring presence.

In Book VIII of the *Prelude*, 'Retrospect', Wordsworth, in tracing his development, and recounting his growing awareness of 'human passions', recalled the strength he drew from such memories of his native district. He congratulates himself (and goes on to contrast his luck with that of Coleridge, city-bred) that

> in the mid st
> Of these vagaries, with an eye so rich
> As mine was, through the chance, on me not wasted
> Of having been brought up in such a grand
> And lovely region, I had forms distinct
> To steady me; these thoughts did oft revolve
> About some centre palpable, which at once
> Incited them to motion, and control'd . . .   ll. 594–601

Wordsworth felt secure in that he still, as he put it,

> At all times had a real solid world
> Of images about me . . .

And so his natural feeling for landscape, for 'forms distinct', preserved, in several ways, his sense of the past; not least, in the almost physical sense of having a 'centre palpable' around which memories of the past

---

[1] *Works*, vol. 2, p. 118.   [2] *Dissertations* . . . (1783), vol. I, p. 106.
[3] *Prel* XIII, 86.

became active. Wordsworth's feeling for place worked at all times in the closest conjunction with memory.

There is one other aspect of this feeling for place which we may consider briefly; it is in this same Book (VIII) of the *Prelude* that Wordsworth describes something of his growing awareness of man, both within his own native regions and during his first coming to London—and in so doing he intimates two fairly general aspects of his sense of time which he yet closely relates to his own feelings and memories. He brings forward a sense of a kind of pastoral time, and of historical time.

The movement of the Book is interesting in the way it blends these two ideas of the past into each other. The book opens with a description of a country fair, held in the shadow of Helvellyn. It proposes, in a secluded setting, a rustic scene and a rustic people:

> Immense
> Is the Recess, the circumambient World
> Magnificent, by which they are embraced.   ll. 46–8

This pastoral seclusion, the world of *Michael* and *The Brothers*, is remembered with gratitude by Wordsworth; and it was here, as he goes on to say, that he felt, in the figures of various shepherds, or rather in the ideal form of 'the Shepherd', his first awareness of Man's importance as well as Nature's. He describes a childhood incident:

> I remember, far from home
> Once having stray'd, while yet a very Child,
> I saw a sight, and with what joy and love!   ll. 81–3

This was a shepherd and his dog, seen suddenly, from below, emerging from a gentle, swirling mist: and he goes on to describe another shepherd and his dog, who also make an appearance in *An Evening Walk*. These are scenes to which Wordsworth, as he now gratefully recalls, was led by Nature: in retrospect, scenes in which Man and Nature seem perfectly fused.

Wordsworth goes on to describe his native regions as a 'Paradise' – a paradise, and yet also a place where nature formed a sense of man's working life, a place, in fact, where man and nature work together. Of 'these two principles of joy', he says,

> I have singled out
> Some moments, the earliest that I could, in which
> Their several currents blended into one . . .   ll. 173–6

Such memories lead to a further contemplation of the pastoral life: he considers various poetic aspects, Arcadian, Shakespearian, Spenserian, and regrets the disappearance of practically every rural custom connected with it, of dancing and singing, of Maypoles and garlands. Then, having recounted an actual tale, a wintry contrast to such 'lighter graces', of a local shepherd, his son, and a lost sheep, he returns to the historical-pastoral again.

> Smooth life had Flock and Shepherd in old time . . .   l. 312

The purpose of introducing this poetic rural past is half to contrast, half to supplement the story of Wordsworth's own actual past in relation to those shepherds who were, as he said (l. 182), 'the men who pleas'd me first', and further to give a complete sense of the past, of Arcadian no less than childhood innocence now irrevocably gone. And finally, when Wordsworth has established both the strange sense of mystery and power attaching to the figure of the Shepherd among the hills (felt and seen as a 'Lord and Master', as a 'giant', as 'an aerial Cross') and his feeling that the Shepherd was the first representative of Man and of human work, he can go on to describe his first feelings of poetry, of his own work, the growing powers of his poetic imagination and its development through periods of 'Gothic' and sentimental embroidery (with 'all the long Etcetera of such thought'), and finally to touch again briefly on his time at Cambridge. There, he insists, he was 'An Idler among academic Bowers' –

> yet here the vulgar light
> Of present actual superficial life,
> Gleaming through colouring of other times,
> Old usages and local privilege,
> Thereby was soften'd, almost solemnized,
> And render'd apt and pleasing to the view . . .   ll. 649–56

In fact, he says, an inkling of an historical sense gave meaning to an otherwise fairly profitless period.

But London was quite another matter: and it was a sense of history which, working on his own memory, gave significance to the great city and helped him to understand or at least to accept it. He returns 'willingly' in Book VIII to this theme of London; he has not yet treated it with the seriousness it requires, having regarded it only (in Book VII) with 'a simple look/Of child-like inquisition . . .'. But he saw, and understood, more deeply.

> Never shall I forget the hour
> The moment rather say when having thridded
> The labyrinth of suburban Villages,
> At length I did unto myself first seem
> To enter the great City.   689–93

He sat on the roof of the carriage bearing him in, and the teeming life about him, men and houses, seemed truly enough 'vulgar forms', 'mean shapes':

> but, at the time,
> When to myself it fairly might be said,
> The very moment that I seem'd to know
> The threshold now is overpass'd, Great God!
> That aught *external* to the living mind
> Should have such mighty sway! yet so it was
> A weight of Ages did at once descend
> Upon my heart; no thought embodied, no
> Distinct remembrances; but weight and power,
> Power growing with the weight . . .   695–706

The experience was primarily one of history: no doubt Wordsworth had prepared himself for it – and was fortunate enough not to be disappointed in his expectations. It was an experience difficult to describe clearly in poetry – indeed, even poetry broke down in trying to do so: 'alas!' he goes on, 'I feel /That I am trifling . . .'. Yet, it was something to be remembered, as an intimation of the historical past, and as an intimation of further knowledge and experience to come – one of those moments of which the soul remembers 'how' she felt, though not 'what' she felt:[1]

> 'twas a moment's pause.
> All that took place within me, came and went

---

[1] cf. *Prel* II, 334f.

As in a moment, and I only now
Remember that it was a thing divine.   707–10

It was also a moment *in* which the soul took on the character of memory, though without being able to tell 'what' it was remembering: a sense of time and weight descended, though without 'distinct remembrances'. This particular remembered incident was both created by a sense of history and in itself furthered the sense of history.

Wordsworth responded fully to London, 'teeming as it did/Of past and present'. He goes on to make a disclaimer that English history has ever meant much to him.

'Tis true the History of my native Land,
With those of Greece compar'd and popular Rome . . .
Had never much delighted me.

And, he goes on to say, perhaps deliberately dissociating himself from any sort of Eighteenth-century 'sentimental' or romanticized view of history, that he, 'less than other minds', found in place or thing little pleasure which was owed merely

To extrinsic transitory accidents,
To records or traditions . . .

Yet, in London,

a sense
Of what had been here done, and suffer'd here
Through ages, and was doing, suffering, still
Weigh'd with me . . .   781–4

and he concludes (implying that in place of the 'vulgar forms', 'mean shapes', it was a powerful sense of the past, both immediate and historical, which, here in London, went to the forming of poetic memory),

not seldom
Even individual remembrances,
By working on the Shapes before my eyes,
Became like vital functions of the soul;
And out of what had been, what was, the place
Was throng'd with impregnations, like those wilds
In which my early feelings had been nurs'd . . .

Memory, it seems, already trained by his native regions

> (. . . naked valleys, full of caverns, rocks,
> And audible seclusions, dashing lakes,
> Echoes and Waterfalls, and pointed crags
> That into music touch the passing wind),

is now felt to be working outwardly, helped by the sense of an historical past, on the incidents he observes. Wordsworth closes the book with an 'individual remembrance', the description of a man sitting in the sun with his 'sickly babe', and eyeing it 'with unutterable love'.

It has seemed worth while to emphasize the importance of a sense of historical past to Wordsworth, if only to show how closely it was related to the workings of his own memory. Wordsworth was not averse to history, though as a poet, he was, and considered himself to be, a trafficker primarily in the ideal. His vision on Salisbury Plain, described in Book XII of the *Prelude* –

> I had a reverie and saw the past,
> Saw multitudes of men, and here and there,
> A single Briton in his wolf-skin vest –   ll. 320–2

was for him a true sign of the restoration of his imagination: while in such a poem as *The White Doe*, though no antiquarian (he reproached Scott for his 'industrious Antiquarianism' in sending him some authentic details about the Norton family), the historical feeling is strong. The historical sense in Wordsworth was closely related to personal memory: and as a concluding illustration of this, we may consider Wordsworth during that historical experience which affected him, for better or worse, most deeply.

When he returned to Paris from Orleans, the time was still 'enflam'd with hope': lying in his hotel bedroom, Wordsworth senses the killings of a few weeks back:

> With unextinguish'd taper I kept watch,
> Reading at intervals; the fear gone by
> Press'd on me almost like a fear to come;
> I thought of those September Massacres,
> Divided from me by a little month,
> And felt and touch'd them, a substantial dread . . .
>
> Prel X, 61–6

This is a vivid example of that 'sensuous' and palpable way of feeling which in Wordsworth is always closely related to the workings of memory; and the sense of poetry, and his deepest sense of time, works together with it:

> The rest was conjured up from tragic fictions,
> And mournful Calendars of true history,
> Remembrances and dim admonishments.
> 'The horse is taught his manage, and the wind
> Of heaven wheels round and treads in his own steps,
> Year follows year, the tide returns again,
> Day follows day, all things have second birth;
> The earthquake is not satisfied at once.'

So Wordsworth thought then – sensing the immediate historical past, and turning it to poetry which had already known that world of memory and time in which he had been born, and which he would feel yet in his finest work. 'Remembrances and dim admonishments', whether in history, or in Wordsworth's own past, brought with them that knowledge of a greater, more permanent time, which gave the calm and the continuity not to be found in human life.

CHAPTER 5

Wordsworth's Originality:
Comparisons and Conclusion

TIME, then, and memory are forces with which Wordsworth and his poetry are deeply involved. We have tried to show something of Wordsworth's awareness of these forces, something of their interaction in his work, and their relationship to the general development – and eventual decline – of his poetic thinking. We have traced the idea of memory from his earliest writing onwards: it first appeared mainly in terms of anticipation, of the conscious feeling that present experience would eventually be felt as memory, the fusion of present landscape (his 'dear native regions') and the acknowledged probability of a later desire to cast on it 'the longing look', 'the backward view' – the prospect, as it were, of a retrospect. We have also noticed Wordsworth's conscious dedication to poetry, through his resolving to observe 'natural appearances', and how, in thus imprinting images on his memory, they became associated with moments of heightened emotion. As this discipline developed, he became strongly aware of the sensuous nature of 'the eye' – and later, by a kind of diffusion of the senses, he became strongly, poetically, aware of his whole conscious being (what he seems to have meant by 'the bodily sense'). This particular kind of sensuous awareness was closely related to the formation, working, and further activity of memory: situations and emotions, no less than images, seemed almost literally 'impressed' within the memory, and, in the act of remembering, the whole self was experienced sensuously in relation to the passing of time – memory was felt as a kind of bodily continuity.

Yet, in contrast to this 'sensuous' achievement – unity of self, a unity of present feeling extended also into the past – Wordsworth had formed an ideal of 'wise passiveness':[1] first, in connection with his response to immediate landscape (the attaining of a 'quiet eye'),[2] and then in relation to the whole self within passing time. Memory – the emotion either of excitement (the re-creation of some former feeling) or of regret – is stilled in favour of an understanding and acceptance of the passage of time. Memory's powers of 'restoration'[3] – of spiritual reinforcement – are still working; but they grow more mystically inclined, as in the 'Immortality' *Ode*, and become less and less needed – at least in the writing of poetry. The past comes, for Wordsworth, to be calmly contemplated, and he reaches a state in which memory – the 'inward eye' and his whole being – works 'quietly', a state in which the past can be drawn on for comfort and restoration in almost complete detachment. Eventually, he seems to achieve – what he expresses in *The White Doe* – a kind of mystical release from time, the ultimate reward of 'a passive stillness'[4] in human life.

This release from time was a state Wordsworth had already observed and understood in, for example, the Old Cumberland Beggar or his close relation, the Old Man Travelling; it may be that Wordsworth achieved this particular kind of peace, – that

> peace so perfect that the young behold
> With envy, what the Old Man hardly feels – [5]

largely through the writing of the *Prelude*. Having, from one side, observed the release from time objectively – and denoted it with a sense of longing, for the Old Man's 'settled quiet' seems a peculiarly Wordsworthian object of 'envy' – he emerges on the other side of the time-ridden ebb and flow of the *Prelude*, of the tugging and pulling of its remembered emotions and its own progress forward, to observe and feel objectively the release from time even in himself. In fact, much of Wordsworth's poetry expresses either the wisdom of 'passiveness' in regard to time (as in the 'Matthew' poems, or in *The Old Cumberland Beggar*) or the delight, and value, in the evocation of his own former experience (as in 'Tintern Abbey' or in most of the *Prelude*). It is through this tension between the desire for peace (in Nature's time) and the joyful struggle with remembered emotions (in human time) that some

---

[1] 'Expostulation and Reply', l. 24.
[2] 'A Poet's Epitaph', l. 51.
[3] *Prel* XI, 343.
[4] *The White Doe*, l. 1087.
[5] 'Animal Tranquillity and Decay', ll. 13–14.

of his best poetry is worked out. All Wordsworth's feelings for time and memory may be found, in one form or another, from his earliest work onwards; but their relative importance at any given moment varies considerably, so that a development in these feelings can be traced. This is why we have not attempted to categorize, to draw up 'types' of Wordsworthian memory: each remembered experience and each reflection on it is unique, evoking and creating its own particular circumstances – but a consideration of various important moments or statements helps us to undestand Wordsworth's poetic development and his own progress in time.

In conclusion, then, and towards a general summing-up of Wordsworth's use of memory in poetry, we will try, by a few, necessarily highly selective, glances at one or two writers of similar ways of thought, to emphasize both Wordsworth's great originality and his representative character: and in the process, to consider further some points about Wordsworth's sense of time, its relation to his work and to the age he lived in.

The two main and most obvious features of Wordsworth's originality are, as we have already noticed, that he wrote, in poetry, so much about himself, and that the sense of time, of the relationship between present and past, is so marked – that much of his finest work is autobiographic and consciously retrospective. In the sense that Wordsworth's great poetry is personal, autobiographic and centred on self, anything which he writes about is bound to be an affair of memory, of past experience recalled in poetry: but there is a great difference between mere recollection and that emotion which is felt strongly and particularly as a working of memory – an emotion which emphasizes both time present and past, and which grows from memory working constantly and with accumulating intensity. It is in terms of this emotion that Wordsworth may be said to have been given over organically to the power of memory. To remember was, for Wordsworth, to be a poet. Yet his presentation of the self in time was, to some of his younger contemporaries, notably de Quincey and Hazlitt, something to which (without any real knowledge of the *Prelude*) they responded with the deepest intuition.

As a first general concluding point, we can suggest that Wordsworth, by about 1808, had arrived at a sense of time in which the past was more purely observed, less sensuously or emotionally felt. In other words, the power of memory (by which the sense of time had grown and with which it had been all along interfused) became, in poetry, almost completely inactive. However, he had already done enough to make quite clear the importance of the remembering self – to establish the poetic rather than the psychological, or even philosophical, importance of the man bound to human time and his own past. Wordsworth had shown an awareness of memory – of how it formed, of how it worked, and of how it was a reassurance of continuity in time, of what de Quincey called 'the grandeur of human unity'[1] – an awareness which gave the first complete poetic statement of a new and growing sense of time. Much of de Quincey's writing, for example, gives a full recognition of the complexity of memory's working, of time passing, of the endless relationships between past and present experience – and in a general furthering of the awareness of self and time, he elaborates (with, of course, the help of opium) on a number of poetic truths first made plain by Wordsworth. He knew how time was felt, cumulatively, and how recollections might leap from 'hiding-places' of not, in his own case, merely ten years' depth, but of forty or more.[2] He knew the complex ways in which memory worked and shaped emotion, how – as he put it in his *Autobiographic Sketches* –

> far more of our deepest thoughts and feelings pass to us through perplexed combinations of *concrete* objects, pass to us as *involutes* (if I may coin that word) in compound experiences incapable of being disentangled, than ever reach us *directly*, and in their own abstract shapes.[3]

In Wordsworth's case, the repeated sight of known landscape, together with the repeated emotion of pleasure in it and memories of former pleasure, 'feeling coming in aid of feeling',[4] produced many of these '*involutes* of human sensibility; combinations in which the materials of future thought or feeling are carried as imperceptibly into the mind as vegetable seeds are carried variously combined through the atmosphere, or by means of rivers, by birds, by winds, by waters, into remote

---

[1] *Works*, vol. 16, p. 18.
[2] *Works*, vol. 16, p. 116: and cf. *The Waggoner*, Cto. 4, 212.
[3] *Works*, vol. 14, p. 13 (de Quincey's italics).
[4] cf. *Prel* XI, 326–7.

countries.'[1] And de Quincey knew, as Wordsworth knew, how human emotion, at its most valuable, is formed by memory in time without any exact sense of origin – how the soul, and the origin of memory itself, 'in the words of reason deeply weigh'd/Hath no beginning':[2] and how memory, 'the deep memorial palimpsest of the brain', was a poetic power capable of infinite organization, dealing with every available permutation of experience.

What else than a natural and mighty palimpsest is the human brain? Such a palimpsest is my brain; such a palimpsest, oh reader! is yours. Everlasting layers of ideas, images, feelings, have fallen upon your brain softly as light. Each succession has seemed to bury all that went before. And yet, in reality, not one has been extinguished. And if, in the vellum palimpsest, lying amongst the other *diplomata* of human archives or libraries, there is anything fantastic or which moves to laughter, as oftentimes there is in the grotesque collisions of those successive themes, having no natural connection, which by pure accident have consecutively occupied the roll, yet, in our own heaven-created palimpsest, the deep memorial palimpsest of the brain, there are not and cannot be such incoherencies. The fleeting accidents of a man's life, and its external shows, may indeed be irrelate and incongruous; but the organising principles which fuse into harmony, and gather about fixed predetermined centres, whatever heterogeneous elements life may have accumulated from without, will not permit the grandeur of human unity greatly to be violated, or its ultimate repose to be troubled, in the retrospect from dying moments, or from other great convulsions.[3]

This, from the *Suspiria de Profundis*, expresses, in its own elaborate way, that essential unity of self and continuity in time which Wordsworth understood and expressed by way of poetic memory: and Wordsworth, in his last 'retrospect', must surely have recognized a unity in that poetry of his which was written deeply out of memory, which gave more value to his life than the rather arbitrary unity which he claimed for the Gothic-cathedral bulk of all his collected work.[4] We may also imagine that Wordsworth was, in some final 'retrospect', true to his youthful vow and feeling that he would cast 'the backward

[1] *Works*, vol. 14, p. 121.   [2] *Prel* II, 236–7.
[3] *Works*, vol. 16, pp. 18–19.   [4] v. Preface to *Excursion* (1814).

view' on his native regions: though by then, it may be, he had tamed memory to the extent that he had no need to say, with de Quincey, that 'Martyrdom it is and no less, to revivify by effect of your own, or passively to see revivified, in defiance of your own fierce resistance, the gorgeous spectacles of your visionary morning life, or of your too rapturous noon-tide, relieved upon a background of funeral darkness'.[1] Wordsworth refused, in his poetry at least, to become a 'martyr' to memory: though it is possible that he became one in his own life, and that this had an inhibiting influence on his later years. Whatever, in his later years, Wordsworth felt about his most deeply remembered past, the poetry of his finest years preserved it: in letting de Quincey speak for some of these points about Wordsworth's use and awareness of memory – its essential unity, its cumulative power, its continuous presence – we have tried to suggest how far the poetic idea of memory had come since the Eighteenth century; and Wordsworth's whole feeling for time, as for childhood in particular, was, in its poetic application, equally original.

It could be said that in the growth of Eighteenth-century sensibility, the feeling for time had been more indulged than the awareness of memory: that is to say, melancholy and the nostalgia of retrospection (together, perhaps, with a feeling for history, or at least for antiquity and ruins) had been induced by a very general sense of past time rather than by powerful individual feeling: there was a sense, perhaps merely of flux, of passing time, with only a few examples of a sense of particular points or locations; there were certainly no 'fixed predetermined centres' (no more in landscape than in the mind) around which memory might accumulate and work. The sense of time can exist without any autonomous working of memory: though the strong working of poetic memory cannot help creating a sense of time. Today when our literature and whole conduct of life is unthinkable without a sense of time and the past, when practically no emotion can be felt without some reference of it to earlier experience or to childhood, and when no public action can be taken without reference, before and after, to historical analogy, it is worth considering very seriously those periods in which such ideas were arising and beginning to develop. The ways of experiencing time are some of the deepest modes of human feeling and of human progress.

[1] *Works*, vol. 16, pp. 116–17: *Portrait Gallery* ('Sir William Hamilton').

In England, Wordsworth was the first writer to give radically new meaning to the growing Eighteenth-century sense of time. That particular, as it were, empirical consciousness of self which, stemming most obviously from Locke, had grown throughout the Eighteenth century, had remained primarily a matter of psychology and aesthetics. In literature, personal memory remained a minor aspect of that time-melancholy made of landscape nostalgia and varying notions of Augustan, Arcadian, Gothic, and primitive pasts. Wordsworth furthered Romantic sensibility – Romantic, that is, in its broadest, European sense – by emphasizing the poetic memory and the poetic self in time.

If, in England, this consciousness of self was first given clear and powerful expression, and turned to poetry, by Wordsworth, it is perhaps only fair to emphasize the representative nature of this achievement in the broadest terms by insisting on the developments which preceded it: we may further demonstrate something of Wordsworth's achievement by a few comparisons with, for example, a predecessor of similar stature, and far greater influence, in the understanding of both self and Nature – namely, Rousseau. No complete comparison (even on an extended scale) would be possible – any more than it would be with, say, de Quincey or Hazlitt: for immediately we consider the time-sense of any writer at all closely, we realize the infinite variability and complexity of his attitudes, and how each experience of time he may express modifies every other experience of time within that temporal unity which is his whole work. Time is a shifting element, mocking any claims to certainty of definition or permanence of belief. The gathering force with which men began to think and feel in terms of time owed much, perhaps, to Rousseau's impulse. 'Rousseau's great discovery was revery', as Irving Babbitt observes:[1] 'this imaginative melting of man into outer nature' was frequently, as we shall see, a result of that extreme self-consciousness which included a sense of personal time: while that other of Rousseau's great enlargements of Romantic sensibility, the feeling for a kind of primitive innocence, which, though lost, was still to be understood in Nature, and was therefore closely related to self and society, to the present, became the important part of that more general sense of time (conveniently identified with Shaftesbury) which included a sort of primal idealism

[1] *Rousseau and Romanticism*, Boston and New York, 1919: p. 269.

and a worship of classical antiquity. Once the Eighteenth-century time-sense had gone beyond the stage of mere classical or historical nostalgia, or of primitivism, it turned itself forward as well: development, evolution, the shaping of the future, these made up a strong current in thought and feeling. Goethe's idea of morphology,[1] the study of organic forms, in motion, endlessly changing, is one poetic expression of this time-sense; and the feeling with which Wordsworth struggled – that poetry was a shaping of his emotions and experiences understood as a continuous process, the feeling that self-observation in time was continuous and always changing, that ideas of flux and of permanence were inseparable – is another. The sense of moving forward was ever-present: though for Wordsworth, the feeling for the past, the importance of the past, was much greater than it was for Goethe, within this sense of change, of flowing onward.[2] Goethe lived more in the present; but his sense of continuous shaping within time recognized how past experience continued to develop. 'Meine Reise nimmt eine Gestalt', he wrote from Italy:[3] the more he moved on, the more it took on form and meaning. Wordsworth's travelling, his sense of development, had, while it lasted, the same shaping force; at the end of his Duddon journey, it was backwards that he looked to find that reassurance of permanence embodied in the onward-flowing river:

> I thought of Thee, my partner and my guide,
> As being past away. – Vain sympathies!
> For, backward, Duddon! as I cast my eyes,
> I see what was, and is, and will abide;
> Still glides the Stream, and shall for ever glide;
> The Form remains, the Function never dies . . .[4]

It was the backward look that gave him both understanding and a poetic faith; it was from his sense of the past that he was both able and impelled to trace the 'Growth of a Poet's Mind': perhaps, after *The White Doe*, that Growth, its *Gestalt* and Wordsworth's understanding of

---

[1] For the relation of this to his poetry, v. L. A. Willoughby, *Unity and Continuity in Goethe*, Oxford, 1947.

[2] For an interesting comparison, showing the poetic importance of the past for Wordsworth, of the present for Goethe, v. Barker Fairley, 'Goethe and Wordsworth', *Publications of the English Goethe Society*, New Series, vol. X, 1934.

[3] Quoted Willoughby, loc. cit. p. 30.

[4] *The River Duddon*, XXXIV, 1–6.

it, was as complete as it would ever be – in recognition of which the final Duddon Sonnet was a later, isolated and elegiac, expression. As the sense of onward movement died, so the past, the source of poetry, lost its value. Eventually, Wordsworth's time-sense led him to with-draw almost entirely from his own past, and even from that present which was made more rich in meaning by bearing the past continu-ously with it. An 'Animal Tranquillity' of his poetic mind had been achieved – and with it, some decay: animal calm, if it was part of 'Nature's social union',[1] also provided the idea of a refuge from any too intense human life in time; for all its passivity and lowliness, it could be envied.

> Still thou art blest compar'd wi' me!
> The present only toucheth thee:
> But oh! I backward cast my e'e
>   On prospects drear!
> An' forward though I canna see,
>   I guess an' fear![2]

Yet, if Wordsworth no longer made use of his personal past, a recog-nition of the value of passiveness within a strongly experienced time-sense was not his alone: a glance at Rousseau in particular may help us finally to illuminate this important aspect of Wordsworth's poetry, the idea of 'passive stillness' or the escape from time.

Hazlitt recognized a very direct similarity between the two writers: his criticism of Wordsworth is always perceptive – and it is worth remembering that he did not have the *Prelude* to work on. In his essay 'On the Character of Rousseau' he comes to the conclusion that 'The writer who most nearly resembles him in our own times is the author of the *Lyrical Ballads*'.[3] Rousseau is, of course, one of the extreme ex-amples of literary self-consciousness. Indeed, according to Hazlitt,

> The only quality which he possessed in an eminent degree, which alone raised him above ordinary men, and which gave to his writings and opinions an influence greater, perhaps, than has been exerted by any individual in modern times, was extreme sensibility, or an acute and even morbid feeling of all that related to his own impressions, to

---

[1] Burns, 'To a Mouse', l. 8.   [2] ibid., ll. 43–8.
[3] *Works*, vol. 8, p. 92.

the objects and events of his life. He had the most intense consciousness of his own existence.

This is the same quality which in Wordsworth was turned to poetry.
Hazlitt, continuing his comparison, says: 'We see no other difference
between them, than that the one wrote in prose and the other in poetry;
and that prose is perhaps better adapted to express those local and
personal feelings, which are inveterate habits in the mind, than poetry,
which embodies its imaginary creations.' Hazlitt goes on to expand
this distinction by suggesting that Wordsworth introduces too much
comment – something of the 'palpable design' on us – when he should
rather let the situation speak for itself.

Yet Wordsworth, as we saw in Chapter I, had achieved his own unique
kind of what Johnson called 'local poetry', in which place and meditation were closely bound up in the reflective memory. Hazlitt (having
said that he 'will confidently match the Citizen of Geneva's adventures
on the Lake of Bienne against the Cumberland Poet's floating dreams
on the Lake of Grasmere') goes on to say:

> Both create an interest out of nothing, or rather out of their own
> feelings; both weave numberless recollections into one sentiment;
> both wind their own being round whatever object occurs to them.
> But Rousseau, as a prose-writer, gives only the habitual and per-
> sonal impression.

Wordsworth, he complains in a Johnsonian cadence, 'tries to paint
what is only to be felt'. Yet, although Hazlitt seems to think that because Wordsworth turns his consciousness of self to poetry he is forced
to idealise, to impose moral significance (and this was anyway part of
Wordsworth's character), it is in this idealizing tendency that poetry
working through memory has perhaps the final advantage.

For it is in the process of synthesizing 'numberless recollections',
of reading over 'the deep memorial palimpsest of the brain', that the
true poetic power of the sense of the past is shown. Hazlitt certainly
understood this process in Wordsworth, for he repeated the idea in his
essay on *The Excursion*. Wordsworth's 'descriptions of natural scenery',
he said, 'are not brought home distinctly to the naked eye by forms and
circumstances, but every object is seen through the medium of in-
numerable recollections, is clothed with the haze of imagination like

a glittering vapour, is obscured with the excess of glory, has the shadowy brightness of a waking dream'.[1] This, then, is a recognition of the comprehensive and cumulative nature of Wordsworth's memory – and it is true with regard to emotions no less than to landscape forms – as one of the fundamental characteristics of his poetry. Hazlitt's own term, in *The Spirit of the Age*, for Wordsworth's imagination – 'synthetic'[2] – is perhaps the best single label to apply to it: unity of self in time was the goal of Wordsworth's poetry and memory helped him to attain it.

There are, of course, a great many dissimilarities between Wordsworth and Rousseau – certainly today these would seem to present themselves more immediately, and it is significant of 'the spirit of the age'[3] that Hazlitt, who was fully aware that Rousseau's 'authority would perhaps have little weight with Mr. Wordsworth',[4] should have been so straightforwardly insistent on the resemblance. Yet the differences, as far as they relate to autobiography and to the sense of self in time, are of degree rather than of kind. There is, of course, nothing in Wordsworth of Rousseau's minute and inclusive sensuousness, nothing of that slightly exhibitionist honesty about actions and feelings; yet both writers were impelled by a basic desire to tell the truth about themselves as they thought it should be told. Wordsworth's was a poetic honesty, more in relation to his craft and art than to himself; whatever he fused, or whatever he may have omitted, was for an ideal purpose. Rousseau's honesty is much more directly related to himself, to his actions and character as they further, not poetry, but self-presentation. 'There is', said Carlyle, 'a sensuality in Rousseau. Combined with such an intellectual gift as his, it makes pictures of a certain gorgeous attractiveness: but they are not genuinely poetical. Not white sunlight: something *operatic*; a kind of rosepink, artificial bedizenment.'[5] Wordsworth's sincerity emerged more firmly if only by way of the moral seriousness of work by which he makes poetry

[1] *Works*, vol. 4, p. 112.

[2] *Works*, vol. 11, p. 91; 'Mr. Wordsworth's mind is obtuse, except as it is the organ and the receptacle of accumulated feelings; it is not analytic, but synthetic; it is reflecting, rather than theoretical.'

[3] *O.E.D.* gives first record of the phrase (v. 'Spirit', 10b, in the sense of 'The prevailing tone or tendency *of* a particular period of time') in 1820, used by Shelley. Hazlitt's *The Spirit of the Age* was first published in 1825.

[4] *Works*, vol. 4, pp. 116–17.

[5] *Heroes and Hero-Worship; Works*, vol. 5, p. 187.

from his remembered past; and poetry, his work, if not always illumined by 'white sunlight' was never artificially lit: the gleams and
flashes spoke always of some distantly remembered but absolute truth.

However, the area of experience in which comparison can most
usefully be made is in the sense of duration, of time passing. Rousseau's
whole attitude to self and memory may be examined through this
sense, and the question has been admirably treated by Georges Poulet
in his chapter on Rousseau in *Studies in Human Time*. Here we should
look briefly at the idea of 'passiveness' in time. A useful distinction
between Wordsworth and Rousseau is found in the simple fact that,
as Poulet observes, memory came to Rousseau as a powerful force
most strongly in his later years. It came to him when the 'anticipatory
imagination' had died; but whereas in Rousseau the 'anticipatory
imagination' had always been directed at life, at living itself, in Wordsworth this looking-forward had, more or less from the start, always
been thought of in close connection with work, with poetry; so that
when the direction of looking was reversed, and poetry written out of
memory, there was, after a time, little work left towards which he
might look forward – Wordsworth's deepest memories were simply
perhaps 'used up'. Both men, however, came, by way of memory,
to desire, and in part to achieve, what can only be called an escape, a
release from time.

It is, then, their respective attitudes to this escape, and the relative
periods of their life at which they approached it, which supply, for
our purposes, the most illuminating comparison and contrast between
Rousseau and Wordsworth. For Rousseau, the escape from time became one of the leading ideas of his existence; it became identified with an escape from that existence of, as it seemed to
him, continuous persecution. For Wordsworth, in the character of
responsible poet, no such escape was permitted. Rousseau gives a full
expression to this particular feeling about time in *The Reveries of the
Solitary Walker*.[1] He writes these meditative autobiographic accounts,
he says, for himself only; they are written within an acceptance of
human time: it is one of their chief purposes to maintain the function
of memory and the value of past experience. 'If in my oldest age, at the
approach of my departure, I remain, as I hope, in the same disposition

[1] Quotations from *The Confessions of J. J. Rousseau: with the Reveries of the
Solitary Walker*, London, 1783 (2 vols.).

as at present, reading them over may recall the charms I feel whilst writing them, and thus renewing time past, will, in a manner double my existence.'[1] Like Wordsworth, though at a relatively much later date, he wants 'to enshrine the spirit of the past for future restoration':[2] and relying, as Wordsworth does, on 'feeling coming in aid of feeling', he hopes by the working of memory to intensify future emotion, to 'double' his existence – by 'remembrances' and 'the power they leave behind',[3] he will be able to bear the passing of time.

But, in *The Reveries*, Rousseau describes certain experiences which to him had a special virtue in overcoming the passing, the insistence of time. The Fifth Walk, in particular, deals very lucidly with the consciousness and position of self in Time. Rousseau describes the intense happiness of his life for three months on the island at Lake Bienne, and then tries to define 'what was there so attracting as to cause in my heart that regret so violent, so tender, and so lasting, that, at the end of fifteen years, it is impossible to think on this lovely habitation without each time being transported by rapturous desire.'[4] It emerges that the essential quality of this life was a kind of evenness of delight, a state in which feeling was confined to an ideal continuous present. But first of all Rousseau has this to say about the forming of memory and its continuing power.

> I have observed, that, in the vicissitudes of a long life, the periods of the sweetest enjoyments, and the liveliest pleasures, are not, however, those whose remembrance most wins or touches me. These short moments of delirium and passion, however lively they may be, are no more, and that from their vivacity even, than very distant points pricked on the line of life. They are too rare and too rapid to constitute a state; and the happiness my heart regrets is not composed of fugitive instants, but a simple and permanent state, which has nothing violent in itself, but whose duration tempers the charm to a degree of reaching, at last, supreme felicity.

Rousseau, then, regrets most strongly the feeling of a calm continuing present. Those memories which emphasize the passing of time, the linear sense of human life, pricked out by 'very distant points', are not those of the greatest value. It is the 'state' which is important – some-

---

[1] op. cit., vol. 2, p. 154.   [2] v. *Prel.* XI, 342–3.
[3] *Prel* XI, 325–6.   [4] *Confessions*, vol. 2, p. 219.

thing which seems very like the 'settled quiet' of Wordsworth's Old Man Travelling or that same state of 'passive stillness' which Emily in *The White Doe* seems at last to have attained. For Rousseau, the sense of time and the power of memory are seen here working closely: and it is the remembering of such a 'timeless' state which is matter of the greatest regret. 'Short moments of delirium and passion' are not so powerfully, nor so valuably, remembered: this is in direct contrast to the Wordsworthian moment, those 'fleeting moods of shadowy exultation' and the 'spots of time',[1] which are the chief inspiration and object of poetic memory. For Wordsworth, the moment of autonomous experience was the most deeply felt and was taken most deeply into his mind. The calm, which he saw in others, and towards which he and his poetry in its greatest years worked, was only made valid, given meaning, by these moments of excitement.

As we have suggested, the history of Wordsworth's memory in time might be read as the ultimate resolution of a conflict between such moments of intensity, poetic 'gleams', and the desire for a mystic 'settled quiet'. Wordsworth knew, at least in human life, what Rousseau goes on to describe, how 'every thing on earth is in a continual ebb'[2] – a recognition Wordsworth could never entirely balance by perceptions of eternity or of that which was seemingly permanent in nature.

Nothing can keep a fixed and constant form; and our affections, attached to external things, necessarily change with them. Always before or behind us, they recall the past, which is no more, or anticipate the future, which perhaps will never be: in all that there is nothing solid to which the heart can cleave. Neither have we here below scarcely any other than passing pleasure; as to continued happiness, I doubt if it is known. There is hardly a single instant of our liveliest enjoyments of which the heart can truly say, *I wish this instant would last for ever*. And how then can we call a fugitive state happy, which leaves uneasiness and void in the heart, which leaves regret for something preceding, and hope for something after it?

The spirit of this paragraph is in complete antithesis to Wordsworth: he would never have admitted so personal a discontent. Except in occasional very general remarks, Wordsworth never admits a total

---

[1] *Prel* II, 331–2; *Prel* XI, 258.　　　　[2] *Confessions*, vol. 2, p. 219.

regret. He insists always on the value of the past, on its moral value, and he tries always to draw strength from even the deepest sense of loss: he does not admit the luxury of absolute regret or of absolute pessimism within the knowledge of passing time. Wordsworth knew too well that the instants of his greatest understanding, and of his greatest happiness, would not 'last for ever'. But what remained of them in memory was, he hoped, a 'perpetual benediction'.[1] Joy, a permanent feeling, rather than mere 'pleasure', or 'happiness', was the greatest reward of life; yet if joy came through nature (though only as a thing of gleams and flashes), and if nature herself did also supply something solid (if only 'a real solid world of images')[2] on which memory might centre its recollection of joy, Wordsworth also knew the value of the calm, the tranquillity, where nature seemed to take him 'out' of time, or where he was in that close contact with nature where human time seemed irrelevant. And this calm Rousseau too, at least in the natural world of Lake Bienne, seemed in part to attain, despite his discontent, his piercing sense of time and flux.

But if there is a state in which the soul finds a seat solid enough entirely to repose and collect there its whole being, without being obliged to have recourse to the past, or stretch towards the future; where time is to her a void; where the present continually lasts, without, however, denoting its duration, and without the least sign of succession, without any other sense of privation or enjoyment, of pleasure or pain, hope or fear, than solely that of our existence, and that this sentiment alone is able wholly to occupy it; as long as this state lasts, he who finds himself in it may call himself happy, not from a poor, imperfect, relative happiness, like that we feel in the pleasures of life, but from a full, perfect, and sufficient happiness, which does not leave the least void in the soul it would be glad to fill.[3]

For Rousseau, this state, in which, on St. Peter's Island, he often found himself, was something quite closely related to his own observation, his sensuousness and his empirical self-consciousness: for Wordsworth, perhaps, the nearest state to this was that simultaneous annihilation of time and place in which his soul 'had sight of the im-

[1] 'Immortality' *Ode* l. 135. [2] *Prel* VIII, 604–5.
[3] *Confessions*, vol. 2, p. 220.

mortal sea', when, in 'a season of calm weather', and in 'a moment', it travelled thither.[1] This half-mystical present, far 'inland', was one of a sort of spiritual seclusion, half out of time. And Rousseau, in his own kind of seclusion, has described much the same tranquillity which, in human time, Wordsworth strove towards as the greatest good. We emphasize this insistence of Rousseau's on the feeling of duration if only to illuminate a time-sense which continually informed Wordsworth's poetry – a time-sense which certainly he never made fully explicit. Wordsworth, because he was in no way a 'psychologist', never elaborated any kind of systematic statement or theory about time and memory; it was no part of his character to have that continuously probing awareness that someone like Rousseau might have been expected to have: rather, he let these forces work in and through him. But that he was continually working by way of memory towards a deep understanding of time is implicit in his poetry – an understanding which included that state which Rousseau, in having recalled his 'retired meditations' at the Lake and on the island, must now go on to define. 'In what,' he asks, 'consists the enjoyment of a like situation?'

In nothing external, nothing but one's self, and our own existence; as long as this state lasts, we are sufficient to ourselves, like God. The sense of existence, stripped of every other affection, is of itself a precious sense of contentment and peace, which alone would suffice to render this existence lovely and sweet, to him who knows to remove from his mind all those terrestrial and sensual impressions which incessantly arise to distract and to trouble our comfort here below. But the greatest part of mankind, agitated by continual passions, are little acquainted with this state, and, having imperfectly tasted it a few moments, preserve an obscure and confused idea of it only, which does not enable them to feel its charms.

The ideal state of the continuing present is, then, equivalent to a feeling of pure, 'stripped' existence; not so much that sort of existence which Wordsworth described in the child, as that state of 'wise passiveness' (with which most people would be 'little acquainted'), that state of calm, in which the being seems free of all 'terrestrial and sensual impressions'. To escape from the feeling of everyday life, to feel oneself beyond 'sense', the 'bodily sense', is a state we have noticed Words-

[1] 'Immortality' *Ode*, ll. 162–8.

worth trying deeply to achieve and describe. The union of a feeling for time, duration, with the 'sense', however, with that feeling of bodily existence and continuity, which in Wordsworth is an aspect, an embodiment of memory, is also hinted at here by Rousseau. It is as though such a feeling of sheer existence can only be attained after both experiencing and ridding oneself of that strongly sensuous awareness of which memory takes part and to which it contributes.

Rousseau proceeds to say that 'it would not be proper, even in the present constitution of the world, that, fond of these gentle extasies, they should take a disgust for their active life, whose continual growing wants have prescribed it a duty'. For Wordsworth, the 'active life' was the writing of poetry: and this qualification of Rousseau's (who, rather in the manner of Wordsworth and Dorothy 'seceding from the common world',[1] thought that for the moment the state only applied really to him, its expounder) suggests a further general distinction between his attitude and Wordsworth's to the escape from time. What Rousseau stated and worked towards (in writing, at least, systematically) – the retirement from life and the escape from time – Wordsworth, as a public figure, as an acknowledged poet, could not, despite all his Recluse qualities, and retired situation, bring himself to attempt. A 'settled quiet' (what the Old Cumberland Beggar, what Emily achieved) Wordsworth could not and, in the eyes of the world, was not expected to achieve. His vocation as poet kept him working. Yet in the *Ode to Duty*, written in 1804, he had already sensed a change in his poetic thinking, and had expressed, 'in the quietness of thought', a desire for a peace which was even and consistent: 'I long for a repose that ever is the same' (l. 40). There is no one reason for the decline of his powers – but that he had, by the time he completed *The White Doe*, worked through, by way of memory, to an attitude of passiveness in time, after which memory had no real function, and so poetry no real aim, is one very possible interpretation of his development. There is, of course, no point in criticizing Wordsworth for not attaining a system in which the awareness of memory, and its poetic use, might have been extended: nor, for that matter, since memory was primarily an autonomous power, for his becoming increasingly unresponsive to the idea of self in time. But it might be suggested that Wordsworth's sense of responsibility (embodied perhaps in the task of having to produce *The*

[1] *PW* 2, p. 515: v. supra, Ch. 4.

Recluse – the poem, not the man) prevented him from attaining a further poetic power in the direction it was most likely to be found, by
plunging more deeply into his own sense of self and the past. Perhaps,
in himself, he reached that state which Rousseau said was essential to
the achievement of this calm. 'It is necessary the heart should be at
peace, and that no passion arises to trouble the calm . . . It does not
demand an absolute repose, or too great an agitation, but an uniform
and moderate movement, without fits or intervals. Without motion,
life is a lethargy. If the moment is unequal or too violent, it awakens;
in shewing us surrounding objects, it destroys the charms of thought,
and tears us from ourselves . . .'[1] Motion with evenness ('an uniform
and moderate movement'), such as the Old Beggar's, was perhaps
Wordsworth's intent in life, if it was not his conscious aim in poetry.

If, for Rousseau, the escape from time, the tranquillity of the continuous present, was even more important than it was for Wordsworth,
and more worked out, it was achieved by the same way of thinking,
by turning inwards, by looking 'within' and concentrating on the self.[2]
More consciously, but not more intensely, related to self than Wordsworth's, Rousseau's conception of tranquillity in time is further illuminated by an experience described in the Second Walk, his account
of an accident he suffered in being bowled over by 'a large Danish dog'.
Rousseau describes himself walking and botanizing near Ménil-
montant on the outskirts of Paris:[3] it is autumn, just past the vintage,
the countryside beginning to turn to winter; he sees in this state 'a
mixed impression of sweetness and melancholy, too analogous to my
age and fate for its application to be passed over'. He reflects on his life,
his achievements and disappointments: 'I called over the movements of
my soul from my youth', he runs over the emotions he has experienced
since he has been 'sequestered from human society'; and he was, he
continues, 'preparing to recall them sufficiently to describe them with a
pleasure nearly equal to that I had felt in giving in to them'. Here he is,
then, to all intents and purposes 'recollecting emotion in tranquillity',
in order to recreate it. This was a recognition of the true poetic, or
literary, value of memory: but in the height of these 'studies', he goes
on, 'I was taken from them by an event which remains to be told'. And
this event is worth quoting here, as it affords an interesting example of

[1] *Confessions*, vol. 2, pp. 221–2.   [2] v. *Confessions*, vol. 2, pp. 156–7.
[3] ibid., pp. 158–60.

how extreme consciousness of self can sustain a tension between the value of remembered experience and the desire to escape from it, and shows a not entirely arbitrary connection between the use of memory and an ultimate release from time.

So it is that, having pursued his meditations with a view to writing them down later, his thoughts are suddenly interrupted by the accident of being knocked down by the Great Dane. Rousseau, after trying, unsuccessfully, to jump over the rushing animal, hits his head severely on the ground, and loses consciousness. When he comes to, 'the situation', he says, 'in which I found myself at that instant is too singular for its description to be passed over.'

Night was advancing. I perceived the heavens, some stars, and a little verdure. This first sensation was a delicious moment. I felt nothing farther. I was returning at this instant to life, and it seemed to me I filled, with my frail existence, every object I perceived. In this state I recollected, at that instant, nothing; I had not the least distinct notion of my individual, not the least idea of that which had just happened; I knew not who or where I was; I felt neither pain, nor fear, nor uneasiness. I saw my blood run, as I had seen a stream run, without, in the least, dreaming that this blood belonged to me in any sort. I felt all over my frame a ravishing calm, to which, each time I recall it to my remembrance, I never felt any thing comparable in the greatest activity of known pleasures.

The most notable feature of this calm is that it is at once outside passing time, and outside sensation. For Rousseau, it is similar to that enduring, self-sufficient present he felt at Lake Bienne. And yet this calm, so deeply remembered and regretted, must, by the very depth of the impression thus made, have been, in part, sensuously felt. If it expresses that pure sense of existence which is the stage beyond sensuous memory, it can yet only be reached, in retrospect no less than in looking forward, by way of that memory. Rousseau finds himself beyond memory: he 'recollected, at that instant, nothing'. But the 'ravishing calm', felt all over his frame, is a last trace of that diffused sense which preserves the feeling of bodily continuity (as well as that feeling of 'pantheistic' diffusion, of unity, filling with his existence every object that he sees), and it does, in fact, take this moment up into memory, so that it can be later recalled and regretted, though never re-created. It is a moment of heightened experience similar, in its way of working, to those Wordsworth tried to express: and perhaps also an equivalent of that regret Wordsworth knew – 'the memory of what has been and never more will be'.[1]

For the whole incident expresses a need for tranquillity; and following, as it does, a period in which emotions were being deliberately recollected in tranquillity for the purpose of re-creating them, it suggests the need for a more permanent tranquillity, one without memory, a calm and enduring present out of time. But of course this is not possible; even this calm is in time, is remembered, if only because Rousseau is there to recall it: it has, in this manner, an affinity with that calm Wordsworth knew as a deception.

> A slumber did my spirit seal;
>   I had no human fears:
> She seemed a thing that could not feel
>   The touch of earthly years.

Wordsworth seems here to recall and imply a state of calm outside time and sense: he feels, like Rousseau, no fear, no uneasiness; his slumber is a state of pure existence. (This is one way in which his spirit was 'sealed' – it was neither fully involved in human life – and so imprisoned, workless – nor was it in a fully asleep body and so able to 'migrate', out of time, to its own immortal regions). Wordsworth's slumber is a kind of half-consciousness of the pure present: for his calm and that of the 'she' (of Lucy, of his spirit?) are closely connected – they are almost two parts of the one tranquillity. But Wordsworth has not finally escaped from time in the way that Lucy is to escape: while he imagined she was free of human time, of 'the touch of earthly years', his spirit was sealed, he himself has no feeling of human time; but –

> No motion has she now, no force;
>   She neither hears nor sees;
> Rolled round in earth's diurnal course,
>   With rocks, and stones, and trees.

By the ballad transition, the change of situation, she is removed from her enduring, but human, present, and returned to Nature's time

[1] 'Three Years she grew', ll. 41–2.

('Rolled round in earth's diurnal course'); Wordsworth is left with only the memory of a calm not likely to be attained again.

It is in such a feeling for natural time that Wordsworth implies the release from human time. Like Rousseau, he understands the value of a calm, a continuing present, which is gained by self-awareness, by turning inwards and by looking back. But for Wordsworth, in achieving a state of pure existence by way of extreme consciousness of self, the workings of memory for their own sake, or for the sake of poetry, were, while they lasted, the most valuable emotion he knew. Wordsworth, in his acceptance of the irrevocability of the past, is at once more elegiac and more positively grateful than Rousseau: and the difference Hazlitt noted between them – not merely the difference between writing in prose or poetry (nor yet the merely relative questions of the value of 'heightened moments' and of permanent 'state') – but the implied difference in Wordsworth's finding, in a devotion, through poetry, to his own remembered past, a restorative, moral value, this difference is what marks the entirely original nature of Wordsworth's contribution to a time-sense and feeling for memory belonging very much to the spirit of the age.

Hazlitt recognized Wordsworth's achievement in the literature of self no less than Rousseau's; and if we go on to reconsider one or two aspects of Wordsworth's time-sense by way of reading Hazlitt, this is not because Hazlitt was, in much of his writing, an obvious literary disciple of Rousseau, but because he so clearly demonstrates that feeling for time and self, which, in English literature, Wordsworth was the first to express – although certainly much of Hazlitt's best writing owed its flavour to Rousseau and much of his feeling for time and the past seems to grow directly from his reading of the *Confessions* (with which would have been included *The Reveries of the Solitary Walker*) and the *New Eloise*. Indeed these two books enter into one of his typically nostalgic cries, informing it no less than impelling it: 'We spent', he says, 'two whole years in reading these two works . . . They were the happiest years of our life. We may well say of them, sweet is the dew of their memory, and pleasant the balm of their recollection! There are, indeed, impressions which neither time nor circumstances can efface.'[1]

Hazlitt's sense of the past – of his own, most often regretted, past, that is – breaks out on many occasions in his essays, lamenting child-

---

[1] *Works*, vol. 4, p. 91.

hood, or some particular period of his life, some far-off love or lost sensation – or, for that matter, the younger Coleridge:[1] it is sometimes rhetorical or mock-heroic; but also it is sincerely felt, the underlying attitude is real. Hazlitt gives a full and personal expression to the enigma of time, that particularly Romantic form of enigma, which in Wordsworth is so deeply fused with his poetry that the poetry is literally the enigma itself; it becomes a matter of pure mysticism, a problem between Wordsworth and Nature. It is worth emphasizing how clearly, how naturally, Hazlitt recognizes the sense of time, how consciously he implies it or refers to it: what is a deeply personal mystery for Wordsworth, something he had to worry at and work out for himself through poetry, has become fully acclimatized. The enigmatic nature of time in relation to the thinking and reflective self is now fully understood as a problem. Hazlitt's first and, in many ways, his most ambitious work – by which he hoped to make his reputation as a philosopher– *The Principles of Human Action*, which appeared in 1805, turned basically on an interpretation of time, namely, the difference between past (and present) time and future time, the difference between memory (and sensation) and freely-directed will. He tries to show that, in the conduct of human life, the mind is disinterested in regard to future action; that, in fact, there is a *moral* difference between past and future. The future is an area of infinite possibility, the past is fixed within our own being. The mind, he suggests, 'is naturally interested in its own welfare in a peculiar mechanical manner, only so far as it relates to its past, or present impressions'.[2] The past is in imagination a purely *personal* matter. 'As an affair of sensation, or memory, I can feel no interest in anything but what relates to myself in the strictest sense': or as he puts it later, 'I do not *remember* the feelings of any one but myself'. This amounts to saying that sensation and remembered sensation, or emotion, are incommunicable: the workings of memory, and this particular awareness of it, may well be thought to contribute to a sense of Romantic isolation – as, by the demands they made on introversion, no less than by their inwardly felt restorative powers, they certainly intensified Wordsworth's solitude. But, in part, this isolation is what literature tries to overcome, and Hazlitt in fact mentions in a note how Rousseau is able, through his writings, to produce 'the same kind of interest in the mind, that is excited by the events and recollections of our

---

[1] cf. *Works*, vol. 5, p. 167.   [2] *Works*, vol. 1, p. 1.

own lives'. This emphasis on how the past is so much the property of the self is coupled by Hazlitt with a recognition of how strongly the sense of self combines with the sense of time – but only in the direction of memory, that is backwards. The being is aware of himself, of 'a community of feelings' which are definitely his own; 'so that' says Hazlitt, 'whatever interests me at one time must interest me, or be capable of interesting me, at other times. Now', he insists, 'this continued consciousness only serves to connect my past with my present impressions. It only acts retrospectively . . .'

The importance of these points for our purpose is, then, that Hazlitt is found emphasizing the sense of time, its relation to the past, and to the sense of self, the sense, in particular, of a continuing feeling self. He has, in putting a personal sense of time to philosophical use, adumbrated one or two poetic attitudes which will reappear in his later writing, and which Wordsworth had in his poetry already illuminated. The giving of a philosophical character to the sense of time is shown in Hazlitt's best personal style in his essay 'On the Past and Future'. In the course of the essay, Hazlitt opposes the two in the terms of the Principles of Human Action – but he begins by maintaining a distinct personal allegiance to the past and he decides very firmly in its favour. The future, he says, has always been considered the valuable time, the past of no account: but he is anxious to deny this: 'the past is as real and substantial a part of our being . . . as the future can possibly be'.[1] It is the future which is airy and insubstantial (as for the present, Hazlitt makes a commonsense dismissal of any notion of its being extended beyond the future moment where it is not, or the moment in which it has turned into the past).

Hazlitt confesses to seeing little value in the future, in hoping, in concerning oneself with something which does not yet exist. Even if the past has now no 'real existence', 'it *has had* a real existence, and we can still call up a vivid recollection of it as having once been . . .' And so, rhetorically enough, but with poetic truth, he cries, 'Let us not rashly quit our hold upon the past, when perhaps there may be little else left to bind us to existence.' The feeling is real: he goes on, showing his close involvement with the whole idea, 'to use the language of a fine poet (who is himself among my earliest and not least painful recollections)', by quoting from the 'Immortality' *Ode*, asking if

---

[1] *Works*, vol. 8, p. 22.

nothing 'can bring back the hour of glory in the grass', and demanding: 'yet am I mocked with a lie, when I venture to think of it? . . . It is the past', he continues, 'that gives me most delight and most assurance of reality.' And, he adds, 'What to me constitutes the great charm of the Confessions of Rousseau is their turning so much upon this feeling.' He quotes the opening sentence of the last of the Reveries (about Mme. Warens) and suggests what a 'long, dim, faded retrospect of years' it opened for Rousseau – and yet also what value it had for him, so that he could 'once more be all that he then was'. Hazlitt goes on to an apostrophe of an earlier and better day of his own, a season of love which he associates with the 'woods of Tuderley'; 'wave on . . .' he cries '. . . lift your high tops in the air; my sighs and vows uttered by your mystic voice breathe into me my former being and enable me to bear the thing I am!' As he says, 'The objects that we have known in better days are the main props that sustain the weight of our affections, and give us strength to await our future lot.' This is likewise the main support Wordsworth derived from memory – although in Wordsworth the 'better' or 'happier' days have a more mystical seriousness; there is a greater feeling of their relevance to the present, of their continuing presence. (Hazlitt's apostrophes to such times are equally genuine – they have no merely 'sentimental' luxuriance – but they are expressed in a more rhapsodic style, as though with a kind of energetic recognition or even welcoming of transitoriness). In Wordsworth the feeling of restoration, or the sense of regret, of what 'never more will be', is in either case more absolute.

An essay of Hazlitt's in which he incorporates a number of deeply felt personal memories to great advantage is No. XXVI of *Table Talk*, 'Why Distant Objects Please'. A brief glance at this may help further to illuminate several aspects of memory and the sense of time which we have observed in Wordsworth. Perhaps the most interesting point is that contained, though not explicitly suggested, in the title – the correlation of distance and time. One might expect something about landscape, perhaps, a real one or a painting: but in fact only the opening paragraph deals with distance in space. There are, however, a number of evocative passages about the distant past, about Hazlitt himself – his remembering and remembered self, in time – together with some 'plain reasoning' about the nature of the various senses and their relation to memory, culminating in some long quotations from

'Mr. Fearn's Essay on Consciousness',[1] and, as a sort of coda, a few observations on the fact 'that a nearer and more familiar acquaintance with persons has a different and more favourable effect than that with places or things'.[2]

In this essay, then, another example of Hazlitt's best 'personal' style, he shows a strong interest in the workings of memory – an awareness of their power and a desire to examine them. The following passage is quoted, if as an example of Hazlitt's sense of self and his evocative regret for childhood, then also for the pleasure of its Keatsian richness:

> When I was quite a boy, my father used to take me to the Mont-pelier Tea-Gardens at Walworth. Do I go there now? No; the place is deserted, and its borders and its beds o'erturned. Is there, then, nothing that can
>
> > 'Bring back the hour
> > Of glory in the grass, of splendour in the flower?'
>
> Oh! yes. I unlock the casket of memory, and draw back the warders of the brain; and there this scene of my infant wanderings still lives unfaded, or with fresher dyes. A new sense comes upon me, as in a dream; a richer perfume, brighter colours start out; my eyes dazzle; my heart heaves with its new load of bliss, and I am a child again. My sensations are all glossy, spruce, voluptuous, and fine: they wear a candied coat, and are in holiday trim. I see the beds of larkspur with purple eyes: tall holyoaks, red and yellow; the broad sunflowers, caked in gold, with bees buzzing round them; wildernesses of pinks, and hot-glowing pionies; poppies run to seed; the sugared lily, the faint mignionette, all ranged in order, and as thick as they can grow; the boxtree borders; the gravel-walks, the painted alcove, the con-fectionary, the clotted cream: – I think I see them now with sparkling looks; or have they vanished while I have been writing this des-cription of them? No matter; they will return again when I least think of them.

This is a fine memory-complex, a cluster of sensations, an extended dis-

---

[1] An eccentric work; 'a comely, capacious quarto on the most abstruse meta-physics', 'an original and most ingenious work, nearly as incomprehensible as it is original, and as quaint as it is ingenious'; so Hazlitt described it in his essay 'On People with One Idea': v. *Works*, vol. 8, pp. 63–5.

[2] *Works*, vol. 8, p. 262.

play of Romantic synaesthesia – and in fact, the richness of the whole essay, together with Hazlitt's discussion or 'reasoning' about the senses, makes a good example of that close connection between the poetic workings of memory and the continuity inherent in sensuous feeling. At the same time, its richness is fairly completely opposed to that austere, though also sensuous, remembering (all gleaming light and massive form) in Wordsworth's poetry. Hazlitt here also understands the way memory comes and goes – how writing it down will exhaust the emotion, yet not permanently: by its autonomous power of re-appearance (leaping from its 'hiding-places'), as by the cumulative power of its hidden and continuous working, 'the sparkling looks' are securely kept, and the emotion of remembering accumulates and intensifies them. Hazlitt goes on:

> All that I have observed since, of flowers and plants, and grass-plots, and of suburb delights, seems, to me, borrowed from 'that first garden of my innocence' – to be slips and scions stolen from that bed of memory.

Like Wordsworth, particularly in the early books of the *Prelude*, Hazlitt evokes and recovers his childhood memory of place. This evocation of the garden, of this particular 'bed of memory', grows from an initial deeply-felt childhood experience; 'a new sense' comes upon him, and, by way of memory, he says, the 'splendour in the flower' can be brought back, and he can feel 'I am a child again'. The whole passage is a good example of that excellence of 'personal and local description' which Hazlitt appreciated in Rousseau: and this garden bed of childhood memory is one of those permanent places from which restoration is continually drawn.

In this function it is the equivalent of those 'spots of time' (proposed in Book XI of the *Prelude*) from which Wordsworth drew his strongest sense of restoration: these were primarily particular events (such as he was there describing) but there emotional power was closely connected with place, and their importance was in that quality of retaining a 'vivifying Virtue', of 'nourishing' and 'invisibly repairing' the mind, of, in fact, continuing to exist in memory with their original, and with increasing power. They can be thought of, perhaps, as places in memory: the local-temporal correlation in the phrase is no accident, especially when we consider the emblematic significance that certain landscape 'spots' (the word no less than the notion) had for Wordsworth. By existing as a source, a definite location, they make a distance and a space of memory; but their real value is to make a continuity: for although they are 'spots' – certain heightened moments, definitely located – they are not felt to be emphasizing any discontinuity, but rather they bring a kind of grace, working subsequently, though 'invisibly', all the time, affecting, changing, restoring. They are more rewarding than Rousseau's 'short moments of delirium and passion', those 'very distant points pricked on the line of life'. For it might be said that, if they lay out a sense of distance in memory, they also annihilate that distance, they make a kind of *instantaneous* space of the memory; at least while they are being consciously recalled, they create a pure present, an immediate place, which does not denote duration or locality. To put it another way, the emotion of the past is recreated, the present is displaced, while yet continuing to exist as though suspended; while the memories work their true power of restoration by, in unifying past and present, also unifying the self, the whole being which experienced them in, literally, the first place.

As perhaps Wordsworth's most deliberate notion of how memory worked for him is to be found in a space-time correlation, it may help to make it clearer by looking at that part of Hazlitt's essay which shows a close connection between the ideas of distance and memory. Hazlitt opens the essay with a general statement about distance; he goes on: 'Passion is lord of infinite space, and distant objects please because they border on its confines and are moulded by its touch.' And he continues: 'When I was a boy, I lived within sight of a range of lofty hills, whose blue tops blending with the setting sun had often tempted my longing eyes and wandering feet.' When he eventually approached them he was disillusioned to find them not 'glimmering air woven into fantastic shapes' but 'huge lumpish heaps of discoloured earth'. There is something very much of the Eighteenth century here in Hazlitt's attitude and in the picture he makes. It is almost like a painting, in which the summer haze and far horizons of a Claude play over and inform, create and recall an Arcadia of the distant past (or the seemingly endless summer of childhood) – prospect and retrospect in one. What the paintings of Claude and Poussin and the subsequent Eighteenth-century landscape tradition meant to Hazlitt and his contemporaries is demonstrated very poetically in his essay 'On a Landscape of Nicholas Poussin'. The sense of past time, of both classical antiquity and primitive innocence, is summed up in the inscription on a tomb which a group of shepherds are contemplating – 'et ego in Arcadia vixi' ;[1] while for Hazlitt the shepherds, the wind blowing through the branches and valleys, these and 'the distant, uninterrupted, sunny prospect . . . speak (and for ever will speak on) of ages past to ages yet to come'.[2] Landscape, for Wordsworth, existed in time both as idea and as fact: it represented both ideal desires and human emotions. 'Nature' in Wordsworth often, at its most inclusive, suggests an ideal landscape, a surrounding place of health and innocence, informed by the presence of a diffused spirit, half genius loci, half Almighty Father, and Wordsworth perhaps rarely thought of Nature without some landscape immediately forming in his mind: the landscape of memory was the ideal location of his poetry.

As he is bringing the *Prelude* to a close, he asks Coleridge to remember its beginnings:

> Call back to mind
> The mood in which this Poem was begun,
> O Friend! the termination of my course
> Is nearer now, much nearer; yet even then
> In that distraction and intense desire
> I said unto the life which I had lived,
> Where art thou?   *Prel* XIII, 370–6

It was that past made of landscape, of childhood, and of an ideal innocence, which he remembered and knew was gone. It was an ideal country, in which were gathered up his own life, and the life and desire of his native century; and his poetry was the cry of an ideal nostalgia. 'Where art thou?' 'Schöne Welt, wo bist du?'[3] Poetry looked to the

[1] v. Panofsky's *Meaning in the Visual Arts* for a fascinating account of how this Renaissance phrase came, initially by way of Poussin, to take on the 'pathos of distance' in place of its original 'memento mori' significance. Hazlitt uses the phrase several times – and echoes it in all his evocations of his past.

[2] *Works*, vol. 8, pp. 172–3.

[3] *Die Götter Griechenlands*, st. 12. Wordsworth's question might have been a submerged reminiscence of Schiller's poem; he seems to have had some interest in it – at least, this may be inferred (as by Professor Coburn) from one of Coleridge's more hectic notes, where, amongst a great many other jottings, he has (October 1799) ' – Send for Schiller's Götter des Greekenlandes – & remember W's remark – ' v. *Notebooks of S. T. Coleridge* (ed. Coburn), London, 1957, vol. I, paras. 494, 494n.

horizon of classical antiquity, and to a more subjective horizon of an ideal longing: it was from the sense of this past, ideal, irrevocable, yet of continuing nature and of present landscape, that poetry drew some of its greatest power; yet it was work, moral energy, which justified an ideal existence in the past, even if it did not, could not recreate it in the present. Wordsworth goes on:

> Hear I not a voice from thee
> Which 'tis reproach to hear? Anon I rose
> As if on wings, and saw beneath me stretch'd
> Vast prospect of the world which I had been
> And was; and hence this Song, which like a lark
> I have protracted, in the unwearied Heavens
> Singing . . .   ll. 376–82

His work gives him his hold on the present; the poetic life is seen as a 'course': yet in poetry itself he comes to 'the unwearied heavens', he can see the 'vast prospect', almost all at once, of the landscape with which he so closely identifies himself, 'the world which I had been/ And was . . .' Poetry spread out before him the prospect of the unified past.

Hazlitt's feeling about the mountains is not quite what Wordsworth felt about his native, much closer and more surrounding, regions in the Vale of Esthwaite: yet something of the same longing created by distance is there, that same longing which Wordsworth consciously stored up for himself – stored up, that is, by taking them into memory and into time. And, as the whole Eighteenth-century tradition of landscape is related to time, no less than to place and space, so for Wordsworth his native regions and his distant childhood form an inward landscape in which present and past seem to be unified.

What Wordsworth sensed in his earliest poetry, and later felt in a more mystically diffused way, Hazlitt states here quite explicitly:

Distance of time has much the same effect as distance of place.

The true dimension of memory is suggested in this conception; it provides a text for trying to establish the nature of that extension-which is physical being and remembered existence in time. Memory, the remembering self, works in time, and, in feeling the distance between the original event and the emotion it implants, creates its own kind of space.

The idea, commonplace enough, of life as a 'voyage', a 'journey', is naturally at the centre of Hazlitt's notion of memory and 'distance in time'; and he gives it a realistic meaning, such as it had, perhaps more implicitly, for Wordsworth: the river (like the 'public road') were, to him, constant symbols of time, of both human and natural time. Hazlitt, having enlarged on the idealizing tendency of distance, and memory, goes on:

> Seen in the distance, in the long perspective of waning years, the meanest incidents, enlarged and enriched by countless recollections, become interesting; the most painful, broken and softened by time, soothe. How any object, that unexpectedly brings back to us old scenes and associations, startles the mind! What a yearning it creates within us; what a longing to leap the intermediate space! How fondly we cling to, and try to revive the impression of all that we then were!

'The long perspective of waning years' – the 'long perspective', an image from landscape, perhaps, rather than from painting (it appears more than once in Romantic contexts, e.g. Keats's 'Sleep and Poetry')[1] – for past or future, here the gradual diminishing within a sense of still-recoverable distance – that is what memory (aided by the accumulation of 'countless recollections') at once lays out and looks along.

And Wordsworth might often have failed to 'leap the intermediate space' if he had not had 'a real solid world of images',[2] a native landscape and a remembered place, where he might seem to return. Wordsworth knew this sense of the gap, 'the vacancy between me and those days',[3] between present and past – and how memory would overcome it; and he knew the real, constant motive of this striving too, as Hazlitt does: not merely the bridging of a gap, but the re-creation of a total, as it were, instantaneous continuity. It is not, says Hazlitt, merely a question of trying 'to revive the impression of all that we then were!' 'In truth,' he goes on, 'we impose upon ourselves, and know not what we wish.'

[1] l. 100: and cf. *Descriptive Sketches* (1793), ll. 340–1.
[2] *Prel* VIII, 604–5.   [3] *Prel* II, 29.

196

It is a cunning artifice, a quaint delusion, by which, in pretending to be what we were at a particular moment of time, we would fain be all that we have since been, and have our lives to come over again. It is not the little, glimmering, almost annihilated speck in the distance, that rivets our attention and 'hangs upon the beatings of our hearts': it is the interval that separates us from it, and of which it is the trembling boundary, that excites all this coil and mighty pudder in the breast. Into that great gap in our being 'come thronging soft desires' and infinite regrets.

This, then, is the true continuity of memory: the unity for which it aims is a sense of complete existence, of being 'all that we have since been'. Yet, however continuity is maintained, by whatever sort of sensuous or mystical memory, the unity is never completely achieved; or, rather, common-sensically, if it is, for a moment, wholly instantaneous, the moment cannot last. The 'great gap in our being' is felt too strongly: it cannot be completely filled.

The 'glimmering speck' in the distance ('glimmering', a 'trembling boundary', as though on the edge of a horizon) is the initial location, is, in Hazlitt's phrase, a 'bed of memory', or in Wordsworth's, a 'spot of time'. And, says Hazlitt, 'In contemplating its utmost verge, we overlook the map of our existence, and retread, in apprehension, the journey of life.' In diagrammatic form we might say the sighting of a 'spot' together with an awareness of the 'gap', the separation, produces the real worth of memory, makes a map of existence.

For, initially, such 'spots of time' may have been points of reference, map-making points by whose help the past might be not so much ordered as invoked. But Wordsworth's 'map of existence' was never in his poetry a matter of chronology; the opening lines of *The Recluse* provide, if one is needed, an obvious example, where he describes how once 'a roving Schoolboy' – who, as he goes on to say, is himself – came 'to the verge of yon steep barrier':

> what the Adventurer's age
> Hath now escaped his memory – but the hour,
> One of a golden summer holiday,
> He well remembers, though the year be gone.

Wordsworth's memory was based on moments, and on brief hours of heightened experience: the 'spots of time' were its constant source, and at any later given moment, the value of memory spread out from them in all directions. Memory was liable to overcome the mere notion of chronology. Its autonomous power – and Wordsworth's essentially temporal, rather than chronological, way of thinking – is illustrated, for example, in Book VI of the *Prelude*, in his 'playing', as he puts it, with time. Addressing Coleridge, he says:

> Through this retrospect
> Of my own College life I still have had
> Thy after sojourn in the self-same place
> Present before my eyes; I have play'd with times . . .
>
> ll. 296–9

And he had already said, speaking of walks he had taken – on which he said (in a line which reappeared in Book XI) had fallen 'A spirit of pleasure and youth's golden gleam' –

> O Friend! we had not seen thee at that time;
> And yet a power is on me and a strong
> Confusion, and I seem to plant Thee there.   ll. 246–8

These heightened experiences of memory, then, the 'spots of time', come, eventually, to seem almost outside time: they are not subject to the common laws of decay, but rather to a kind of spiritual growth – a strengthening in which mind and image react on each other. This is certainly, as we have seen, their prime meaning for Wordsworth as he outlines it in Book XI of the *Prelude*. Wordsworth's whole conception, and use, of memory is based, not so much on the idea of return to these 'places', as on the idea that they are sources continually present (in place as in time) within him. For memory is not only a simple continuity, the mind in control of the past: in the mind, the past becomes both distance, which is separation, and that space which is an instantaneous unity.

In 'overlooking the map of our existence' (Hazlitt) we become aware both of the point at which memory was initiated and of the journey traversed between it and the present moment. In moments of deepest emotion, the whole distance covered is gathered into the present 'spot of time', the present working of memory. Space and distance together are the two elements in which memory moves. Space, which can perhaps be thought of as distance in all directions, is something out of time, something permanent and infinitely encircling: it is the element of diffusion, communion, and that memory which grows from the mystical sense of pre-existence. It is the element in which the idea of action, of motion, is irrelevant, the idea of self (pure, unmoving, taking no part in or of time except the fact of consciousness) is all. Distance is *in* time, the sense of travelling and of having travelled (and of being able if not to return then at least to look back): it is the element of work, of the writing of poetry, and of human remembering – the memory of emotion and the emotion of memory.

In these two elements, then, memory exists and takes its own particular dimension. Much of Wordsworth's most poetic thinking is achieved within a space-time correlation – and that diffusion of spirit he sensed might eventually lead him out of human time was part of it: it was something he sensed not only in

> the one
> Surpassing Life, which out of space and time,
> Nor touch'd by welterings of passion, is
> And hath the name of God . . .; *Prel* VI 154–7

it was not only what, in a different form, he knew in London: that

> The Human nature unto which I felt
> That I belong'd, and which I lov'd and reverenc'd,
> Was not a punctual Presence, but a Spirit
> Living in time and space, and far diffus'd . . .;
> *Prel* VIII, 761–4

but a kind of extension he knew in himself; shown in one of the Poems on the Naming of Places, where he speaks of his sister as

> . . . She who dwells with me, whom I have loved
> With such communion, that no place on earth
> Can ever be a solitude to me . . . III, ll 14–16

'Such communion' was not subject to human time: it was part of that continuously rewarding return in memory to the source of experience – a return inherent in, for example, those 'spots of time' he actually described: how not only in human life he returned to the place to 'drink,/As at a fountain', but how in certain later times he imagines 'the workings of my spirit thence are brought'.[1] This diffusion of spirit (and, as it seemed, true unity of self) was also partly a matter of Nature's time, where human distance was not valid; and partly it belonged to that mystical time where space was an instantaneous continuity, where

> . . . in a season of calm weather
> Though inland far we be,
> Our Souls have sight of that immortal sea
> Which brought us hither,
> Can in a moment travel thither,
> And see the Children sport upon the shore,
> And hear the mighty waters rolling evermore,[2]

Time was, most humanly, in Wordsworth's poetry, a course to be traced (not chronologically, but still in terms of general development) –

> . . . we have traced the stream
> From darkness, and the very place of birth
> In its blind cavern, whence is faintly heard
> The sound of waters;   *Prel* XIII, 172–5

but in following it, it became also a gap to be bridged, and, if possible fused. The actual 'cavern' of birth and childhood, the 'stream' of human life, were more insistent, more palpable, than the 'immortal sea' of ideal memory, of pre-existence. Yet even in human life, Time, in memory, was at least ideally unified in the present; it became a matter of pure space, of the remembering mind itself. Memory was, at its most concentrated, a local unity in self. At its most intense, Wordsworth's memory dissolved all boundaries of time and place, of past and present, so that emotion – seemingly lost emotion, emotion remembered, and emotion made new – is one, and the poetry, the present moment, is all.

To sum up, then: memory is the great force in Wordsworth's poetry. He uses it to 'fetch invigorating thoughts from former years':[3] it is, for him, a force of restoration, of 'perpetual benediction'.[4] Yet, as though the past years of childhood were merely the type of a far greater tranquillity and good, the workings of memory, while making him aware of time, also lead him out of time – out of the linear flux of human life into the continuous repetitions of Nature, or, more absolutely, into

---

[1] *Prel* XI, 389.
[2] 'Immortality' *Ode*, ll. 162–8.
[3] v. *Prel* I, 648–9.
[4] 'Immortality' *Ode*, l. 135.

a mystical calm. Memory, at least in its power to make poetry, seems, in Wordsworth, to have become exhausted: perhaps, having achieved the *Prelude* as a sort of confessional, Wordsworth had no further need for his past; and, certainly, the power of memory inherent in the 'bodily sense' declined – naturally, as it does in the course of human life, and anyway, as part of a definite desire and moral aim. The release from time, from human flux and striving, was a more constant aim, and promised a more constant state of good, than the continuing evocation, influence, and presence of the past: memory, for Wordsworth, leads, through poetry, to a 'passive stillness' in Time.

Bibliography

WORDSWORTH
The Poetical Works (ed. de Selincourt and Darbishire), 5 vols.
The Prelude, or Growth of a Poet's Mind (ed. de Selincourt and Darbishire).
The Early Letters, Oxford, 1935.
Letters, The Middle Years, Oxford, 1937.
(For the above, see list of Abbreviations.)

COMPILATIONS
Cooper, L., *A Concordance to the Poems of William Wordsworth*, London, 1911.
Logan, J. V., *Wordsworthian Criticism: A Guide and Bibliography*, Columbus, Ohio, 1947.
Peacock, M. L., *The Critical Opinions of William Wordsworth*, Baltimore, 1950.

CONTEMPORARIES AND PREDECESSOR
Coleridge, *Biographia Literaria*, ed. Shawcross, Oxford, 1907.
Hazlitt, *The Complete Works*, ed. Howe, London, 1930-4: (referred to as *Works*).
de Quincey, *Works*, Edinburgh, 1862-3 (vol. 16, 1871).
Rousseau, *The Confessions of J. J. Rousseau: with the Reveries of the Solitary Walker*, London, 1783 (2 vols.): (referred to as *Confessions*).

WORDSWORTH CRITICISM
Bateson, F. W., *Wordsworth: A Re-interpretation*, London, 1956 (rev. edn.).
Beatty, A., *William Wordsworth. His doctrine and art in their historical relations*, Madison, Wisconsin, 1922.
Burra, P., *Wordsworth*, London, 1936.
Comparetti, A. P. (ed.), *The White Doe of Rylstone*, Ithaca, N.Y., 1940.

Crofts, J., *Wordsworth and the Seventeenth Century* (Warton Lecture), London, 1940.

Garrod, H. W., *Wordsworth: Lectures and Essays*, Oxford, 1927 (rev. edn.).

Harper, G. M., *William Wordsworth, his life, works, and influence*, 2 vols., London, 1916.

Havens, R. D., *The Mind of a Poet*, Baltimore, 1941.

Jones, J., *The Egotistical Sublime*, London, 1954.

Knight, W. (ed.), *Wordsworthiana: a selection from papers read to the Wordsworth Society*, London, 1889.

Leavis, F. R., *Revaluation*, London, 1936.

Legouis, E., *The Early Life of William Wordsworth*, London, 1921 (rev. edn.). (Translated from *La Jeunesse de William Wordsworth*, Paris, 1896.)

Margoliouth, H. M., *Wordsworth and Coleridge, 1795–1834*, Oxford, 1953.

Moorman, M., *William Wordsworth: A Biography. The Early Years 1770–1803*, Oxford, 1957.

Rader, M. M., *Presiding Ideas in Wordsworth's Poetry*, Seattle, 1931.

Read, H., *Wordsworth*, London, 1949 (rev. edn.).

Schneider, B. R., *Wordsworth's Cambridge Education*, London, 1957.

Smith, J. C., *A Study of Wordsworth*, Edinburgh, 1944.

Willey, B., *The Seventeenth Century Background*, London, 1934. *The Eighteenth Century Background*, London, 1940.

GENERAL CRITICISM

Abrams, M. H., *The Mirror and the Lamp:* Romantic Theory and the Critical Tradition, Oxford, 1953.

Bullough, G., *Changing Views of the Mind in English Poetry* (Warton Lecture), London, 1955.

McKenzie, G., *Critical Responsiveness.* A study of the psychological current in later eighteenth-century criticism, Berkeley, 1949.

Other works to which reference is made are given in the text and footnotes. I have not attempted a full Bibliography of works read and consulted: in a study of this sort, one draws widely, but subjectively, and a complete list of works which were helpful or gave inspiration would seem merely pretentious, without expressing any particular debts, and without being of much use to other readers.

Index